CANONS
— AND —
WISDOMS

CANONS
AND
WISDOMS

ALBERT COOK

University of Pennsylvania Press
Philadelphia

Jacket illustration: *Time, Truth and History* (sketch for *Allegory on the Spanish Constitution,* Nationalmuseum, Stockholm),
by Francisco José de Goya y Lucientes.
Gift of Mrs. Horatio Greenough Curtis in Memory of Horatio Greenough Curtis.
Courtesy, Museum of Fine Arts, Boston © 1992.

Copyright © 1993 by the University of Pennsylvania Press
All rights reserved
Printed in the United States of America

Library of Congress Cataloging-in-Publication Data
Cook, Albert Spaulding.
    Canons and wisdoms / Albert Cook.
        p.   cm.
    Includes bibliographical references and index.
    ISBN 0-8122-3204-6
    1. Canon (Literature) 2. Poetry—History and criticism.
3. Wisdom in literature. 4. Literature—Aesthetics. I. Title.
PN81.C75 1993
809.1—dc20   93-16781
                                                  CIP

To the Memory of John Clarke

Contents

Acknowledgments	ix
Preface	xi
1. The Canon of Poetry and the Wisdom of Poetry	1
2. "Most Take All": The Good and the Beautiful in Herbert's *Temple*	27
3. Heidegger and the Wisdom of Poetry	55
4. Finalities of Utterance and Modalities of Expression	81
5. Sound, Sense, and Religion in the Dialogized Context of Donne's Poetry	101
6. Wisdom and Ethics	131
Notes	163
Works Cited	201
Index	209

Acknowledgments

Among those who have responded to all or part of this book, I should like to thank Peter Baker, Clint Goodson, Marshall Brown, Robert Scholes, Gerald Bruns, Michel-André Bossy, and Alfredo Rizzardi, who sponsored my delivery of an earlier version of the first chapter as part of the celebrations around the nine hundredth anniversary of the University of Bologna.

I should also like to thank the journals that have published somewhat modified versions of my first chapter (*The Journal of Aesthetics and Art Criticism*), my third (*The Centennial Review*), and my last (*Modern Language Quarterly*).

All translations, unless they are otherwise attributed, are my own.

Preface

This book aims to help provide justification for the abiding conviction that a profound wisdom inheres in poetry. It addresses what can be claimed for poetry, and for literature generally, after all due allowance has been made for the relativity of canons, the subjectivity of the literary experience, and the large, subtle, and in some ways comprehensive effects of received expectations, idea-systems, impressions, mechanisms, and socialization-deferences that have gone under the name of *mentalités*.

So, to touch at the outset on the climate in which I conceive myself to be writing, I intend this book in no way to dissent from the widely held and anthropologically informed position that we are inescapably conditioned in all our activities, including literary ones, by the social and historical circumstances of our specific situations. But at the same time I am emphasizing the seemingly contradictory position that the most achieved and perduring literary works have ultimately those qualities because they communicate wisdom, from sources fully within their situation but in some ways going beyond it. Since a sense of the implications of our social conditioning has dominated recent discussion, and for reasons that reflect my own conditioning in ways that would take a very long autobiographical discourse to lay out, I am concentrating here on the perdurable wisdom in literary works and what accepting its existence implies. At the same time I would not want my emphasis to give any aid and comfort to those who through anthropological naiveté and social imperialism would assign a special priority to the most enduring works in the Western tradition. To be sure, I have been discussing the Western tradition for most of my career, and it provides the central reference here. However, as the assumptions behind my books *Myth and Language* and *Soundings* imply, the wisdom coded into literary works exists in societies of all sorts all over the world. Even in so restricted a form as the haiku, a Westerner like myself, who has no Japanese, can glimpse the presence of a variety and profundity that would call for a careful ponderation. Doubtless the haiku has gotten this attention in works I cannot read. This would be all the more so for the longer and more elaborate works within that millennial literary tradition. The same must be the case for Chinese, and for Arabic, and for some African traditions. And even where circumstances have allowed me to have some experience of a literary tradition in many respects deeply alien, that in Sanskrit, I am too far outside the hymn-poems of the Vedas or the protracted epic of the *Mahabharata* to be able to assess their wisdom in ways that I am convinced the less alien works of Homer and Sophocles permit me. The assimilative appropriation that allows T. S. Eliot to expand "The Dry Salvages" by touching on the book-length speech of Krishna to Arjuna in the *Bhagavad Gita*, or his use of the Upanishads at the end of *The Waste Land*, while Eliot's own poems are themselves laden with wisdom, do not necessarily imply, let alone constitute, a perspicuous assessment of those alien works. It is a Western-oriented conception, powerful but culture-specific, that energizes the *Satyagraha* of Philip Glass, in which the *Mahabharata* is made to converge with Gandhi. Sanskrit culture developed fairly early a range of notions to assess its literary productions with respect to both rhetorical ornamentation and final effect.[1]

These are not fully available to any Westerner other than one immersed for years in that other culture. We think with what is before us. We can take heart that Kant was able to probe acts of judgment that would include the structure and function of art out of a quite deprived and impoverished acquaintance with the range of works even within his own tradition. But we do not have to jettison our deep sense of literary value in order to preserve our anthropological flexibility and what we can manage of a social egalitarianism.

In this enterprise of probing the basis for a valid canon there is a sense in which, as Christopher Ricks urges, even referring to canonicity amounts to "melodramatizing" the question of wisdom in poetry.[2] And what I regard as the best of my attention to poetry, like the excellence of his attention, under the best circumstances may do well to eschew such gross, prolonged, and ultimately evasive analyses as attention to this essentially social process entails. Yet the process is there. Its meshes are too large, indeed, to discriminate finely just what it means for a work to be "in" or "out" of the canon. Or rather, ideally to be in or out; the very rediscovery of wise works demonstrates that the canon has passed them over, or partially passed them over. Here Ricks's own highly alert reading of Gower recuperates for that poet what amounts to a kind of wisdom, as well as incidentally demonstrating by contrast the moderate inertness of most if not all critical readings of the *Confessio Amantis* since the fifteenth century.³ Such readjustments indicate that other works are dropped once their emptiness is perceived. So in a sense the category "canon" is superfluous. We can make do with the category of "wisdom," allowing for the entailed feature of "beauty." But "canon" will nevertheless hang over our assessments, and the very communicative nature of all human utterance argues for its being aimed at such a social inclusion, one that remains ideal, much like the Platonic state or the heavenly Jerusalem—except that the reach of writers and the alertness of readers, as they experience and account for beauty, is perpetually moving toward an approximation of that ideal, of transmitting and receiving wisdom.

Canons and Wisdoms is organized to claim, and in some ways to reclaim, a territory for the sense in poetry, its wisdom, that finally must constitute the major justification for its highly valued and probably ineradicable position in the discourse of society. The reader may find himself uncomfortable in the face of my failure to define the key term "wisdom." But in following the same strategy I use in *Myth and Language*, where I eschew defining "myth," I am guided by my sense of how large would be such a "preliminary" task. The fact is, on the one hand, that an adequate account of wisdom would require nothing less than the production of an entire philosophical system. And anything less would lay itself open to objections that would also in any case be preliminary, such as providing a full answer to the claim that the very integers of language, diction, and even syntax, are "always already" locked into their foregone codes and the implicit contradictions that arise from trying to produce combinations out of them. Instead, caught as we must be in the hermeneutic circle, I will simply use the term "wisdom," bracket the claims of logocentrism, and proceed to my discussion.

The reader may further find the six probes I am here offering as less satisfactory than a lockstep presentation would be, and I hope he or she will be open to seeing that each of these chapters relates to the others in ways that I feel deepen the question more than an explicit linking of their theses would. Yet they are linked. The Heidegger chapter, for example, was originally a much briefer discussion included within the first chapter. And even after I had written it, I had placed it immediately after the first chapter, until I became convinced that logically the discussion of Herbert's poetry preceded it. The first chapter sets out an argument to "bracket" all the recent relativistic discussion of literary merit by applying, and fleshing out, Kant's antinomy between the subjective and the universal, an antinomy that he argues, as I do, must inescapably accompany any act of aesthetic judgment. George Herbert enlists the subjective and the universal arrestingly by organizing his poems as a devotional project, and the second chapter addresses at some length the procedures by which he resolutely, and with a presumption of directness, sets himself the task of uniting the good and the beautiful in such a way that, I am arguing, one must go along with his project, and not just with his beliefs, properly to understand his work. The implications of our response to Herbert's poetic project, and the project itself, involve going along with that project more fully than a mere suspension of disbelief would allow, and more fully than can be accounted for by the various astute but partial readings that have been offered in the intense interpretive activity around Herbert's poetry of the past two decades. I am convinced that to show this involves a considerable and detailed discussion of what goes on in this poetry. Demonstrating this leads to questions about what the nature of the wisdom in poetry may be. I am asserting that the most profound discussion of this question so far is to be found in the work of Heidegger. I then give an exposition of his views about poetry, assessing the reach of those views while trying to extend them somewhat beyond their limitations by pressing his readings of particular poems of Trakl, Goethe, Rilke, and Hölderlin further than he does himself. Implied in Heidegger's views, and in mine, is an inescapable modality that must accompany a successful poetic act through overcoming the inherent contradiction between its fictiveness and its correspondence to actuality. There are elements, however, especially in modern poetry but probably in all poetry—including that of Herbert—that oblige it in some way to assimilate, incorporate, balance, and master the contingencies of its own fictions in order for it to mount a commanding utterance. This is the subject of the fourth chapter, along with the challenging corollary that the poem when successful has an air of completeness not wholly to be derived from its formal finish. I amplify this discussion by taking a long look at the different sets of implications enlisted by Donne and some of his contemporaries.

As many recent critics have urged, there is also an inescapable ethical dimension to the literary work, and my last chapter concerns itself with test cases of works that in one way or another present ethical difficulties, chiefly those of Pound and Beckett, but also those of Twain, Mailer, and Kleist. In the ongoing argument of this chapter, as of others, I am urging the inadequacy of accounts of this ethical situation on the deconstructive side on the one hand (in the work of J. Hillis Miller) and on the other hand the side of those who argue for too tidy a correspondence of the work to our prior ethical values (in the case of Wayne Booth). The relation between ethics and wisdom, and of literature to both, has exercised thinkers since Plato, as it should, and I offer this book as a contribution to that millennial discussion.

1. The Canon of Poetry and the Wisdom of Poetry

I

Dante assumes a permanence to poetry, or to philosophy, or to both, when he declares that Brunetto Latini taught him *come l'uom s'etterna*, "how a man eternalizes himself." This conception of permanence, of inclusion in a canon to which Dante belongs, has had its emphasis modified in recent critical discussion, when the question of canonicity and all its large philosophical issues of epistemology, the sociology of knowledge, psycho-social orientations, and the construction of verbal artifacts—rhetoric, in one sense—are made to converge in such a way as to relativize the series of judgments that contribute to the formation of a canon.

What does one do in the face of this relativizing, or pluralizing, situation, with the strong conviction that a given poem or other literary work has conveyed to the reader some sense of achieved wisdom? There is a wisdom in the best poetry that makes it universal, rather than just subjective; and indeed, such wisdom derives from the engagement of a subjectivity[1] into language in ways that interpreters keep drawing attention to. An account cannot be given of the connection between the power of poetry and the wisdom of poetry other than by some such construct as Heidegger offers, which is circular in the way that demonstrations of various social constraints on poetic expression and reception should not be, but accounts of deep experience cannot escape being.[2] Power and force in poetry and in art generally present a central experiential fact which persists in the face of various relativizations and skeptical questions raised while accounting for the attendant epistemological and social processes.

However oversimplified the term "presence" may be as a name for this power and force, through the qualifications of such accounts, we need not discard it into disreputability. The joy of red or blue in the eye does not disappear as what can be called a presence just because our perception of the color is radically contingent upon experiences, some serial and some simultaneous, in the physiology of the eye. On this principle, however complex the constituents of an experience may be, and however disjunct from each other, they do not prevent it from being ultimately unitary. And our very attention to the best poetry depends on its presentation of the power of this wisdom, for which there are many names—the "immediacy" of several critics, the "transcendent meaning" of Thomas McFarland,[3] the "imagination" of Coleridge, the "feeling" of T. S. Eliot.[4] Wisdom comes about in poetry through a strategic combination of features, the phanopoeia, logopoeia, and melopoeia of Pound, or in my formulation (leaving out rhythm), thought, image, and story.[5] For of image in its honorific form and in its use as symbol, Yeats says evocatively, "When sound, and colour, and form are in a musical relation, a beautiful relation to one another, they become, as it were, one sound, one colour, one form, and evoke an emotion that is made out of their distinct evocations and yet is one emotion."[6] Yet in this evocative account Yeats goes on to distinguish these "emotional symbols" (which are not exclusively emotional, since they carry cognitive force) from "intellectual symbols." The distinction is easy to understand in a preliminary way but hard to make stand, much like Pound's phanopoeia, logopoeia, and melopoeia.

All these accounts cannot avoid either simply naming that which is apprehended in an overriding conviction, like music or like myth, or providing a taxonomy that fatally lacks the principle of fusion.

As Hans Blumenberg says, "As humans our frontal optics make us creatures with a lot of 'back,' who have to live under the condition that a large part of reality lies behind us and is something that we have to leave behind us."[7] In the paradox of poetry, we feel its impact as it brings forward what remains behind us—to stay with Blumenberg's metaphor. We thus accord poetry the status of wisdom, while at the same time it remains elusively behind us. We cannot more than approximately formulate that wisdom, though if we become convinced that the poetry's possession of wisdom is an illusion, if we come to classify it as trite, then it loses its power, whatever other features it may have. The rejection of a poetry recognized as trite is a kind of counter-demonstration, since it bases itself on a rejection, often, not of any formal features in the poem, but of idea, and hence of a perceived lack of wisdom. In that rejection what had seemed to be beautiful will also disappear.

Just the imaged symbols in artistic presentation, whether couched as metaphors or not, resist translation into predicative statements, however contributory such statements may be in a preliminary way. Questions of power and force remain, and of the wisdom which seems on the face of it to hinge on what amounts to predicative statement, but which transcends it, after all the dissections of metaphor along predicative lines from Aristotle to the present day.[8] As Robert Greer Cohn well says,—and the symbol is just one constituent or angle of a poem—

> An artistic symbol is a highly convergent image. It is *synthetic* (ambitiously trascendent, whole-seeking); *vibrant* with the rich reality it stands for and is *suggestive* of (overtones); it is a monad, a link in the mystic or Neoplatonic "chain of being," representative of the whole. Hence the feeling of *universal analogy* (correspondences), of harmony in a firm yet fluid (organic) cosmos.[9]

All of this has cognitive bearing while it resists cognitive translation.

If Dante's permanence is construed as entailing and deriving from Dante's wisdom, then Dante's notion of "how a man eternalizes himself" relates to the superlatives he applies to Aristotle, the master of those who know, "il maestro di color che sanno" (*Inf.* IV.131) as well as to the poet Vergil, sea of all sense, "mar di tutto 'l senno" (*Inf.* VIII.7).[10] But in any case Dante's assertion takes us well beyond his corollary observation that meter adds "stability" (*stabilità*; *Convivio II*) to poetry.

The elaborate and self-flanking dialectic of our time could be realigned to the posited experience of an implicitly universalizing wisdom, by insisting that the socially relative or subjective on the one hand and the experiential universal or assumed universal on the other, are central aspects to discussion about an art (though these are unresolvable, if not irreconcilable). The subjective and the universal are halves of an antinomy already phrased by Kant in the *Critique of Judgement*, where he declares aesthetic judgments to be both subjective and universal:

> Cognitions and judgments must, together with their attendant conviction, admit of being universally communicated; for otherwise a correspondence with the Object would not be due to them. They would be a conglomerate constituting a mere subjective play of the powers of representation, just as scepticism would have it. But if cognitions are to admit of communication, then our mental state, i.e. the way the cognitive powers are attuned for cognition generally, and, in fact, the relative proportion suitable for a representation (by which an object is given to us) from which cognition is to result, must also admit of being universally communicated, as, without this, which is the subjective condition of the act of knowing, knowledge, as an effect, would not arise.[11]

Kant's application is a general one, and it would require much argument to apply it to specific acts of assessing poems. But his point, that our consciousness when making aesthetic judgments is necessarily caught in the antinomy between subjective and universal, has a validity beyond his specific system.[12] This validity could apply, beyond all relativizing and not wholly in subjection to social conditioning, when, for example, someone like Derrida reveals comparative literary values, and a judgment about what amounts to wisdom, when he chooses to write about Ponge rather than Béranger; or when someone like Hillis Miller reveals values in choosing to write about Mrs. Gaskell rather than about Mrs. Oliphant. The value of implied wisdom intrinsic to an achieved poem is shared, even by relativists, who will show the value by a persistent recursion to honorific examples, or even by partially eschewing them, the way Roland Barthes had the habit of dragging in James Bond for illustration, lest anyone get the idea he was confined to the high cultural productions that, on the evidence, did in fact educe his most prolonged and painstaking attention.

We cannot escape Kant's antinomy. The effect of a description or even a deep analysis of the social constituents of canon formation is implicitly (or even explicitly) to downplay the felt universality of the experience of "taste"—and thereby to discount our giving it the cognitive extension that in some instances even Kant would withhold from it.

Cary Nelson frames the issues well, coming at the question in the now usual way, from the vantage of the social constituents and constraints on utterance: "Thus whatever qualities are attributed to poetry so that it is admired, idealized, or hierarchically elevated in the culture's value system are necessarily differentially related to, and dependent on, all the other cultural domains that have acquired comparable attributes."[13] But how comparable these other attributes are, and in what way, is exactly the question. Is a poem comparable to a rite? If a rite encodes wisdom, and in a sense it must, then the wisdom "encoded" by the rite must be decoded by another form of discourse, by mythography or a theology. But a poem, whatever its bearing, simultaneously encodes and decodes its wisdom. If it is included in a rite, then to that degree its wisdom is submerged in an act, as happens when a poem of Blake is set to music for a hymn. It thereby becomes "phatic" in Barbara Herrnstein Smith's sense, submerged in the act of worship. "And did those feet in ancient time / Walk upon Englands mountains green"—when the poem that begins thus is detached from the illuminated, prophetic *Milton*, it loses dimensions of its signification. When it is set to music, away from the visual context of Blake's illuminations, and when it is made public and communal from a communicative set that is intrinsically (though complexly) private, then it is altered. The nationalistic component of the poem is unwarrantedly amplified, and it is put at the service of a state church that Blake rejected, an action that is justifiable devotionally, perhaps, but not hermeneutically. Is a poem comparable to political speech? Much of Blake's poetry is comparable to a political speech, but differing in its wisdom by transcending the specificity of its occasion.[14] Most of the poems discussed by Nelson do not do so; with or without a modernist veneer, they are not just comparable to political speeches, they *are* political speeches, completely bound to the specificity of their occasion. They are advice or protest, but they do not attain to wisdom, as Blake's poems do, or as do the works of poets like Louis Zukofsky and Charles Reznikoff, contemporaries of those he discusses, who draw on the same material of protest but also transmute it.[15]

Nelson, as he goes on, wishes the relation of poetic statement to the social constituents to be controlled by them:

> Considered as a field of discourses displaying an intelligible (though shifting and contested) range of aesthetic variations, poetry's generic, internal characteristics nonetheless remain relational. Its internal characteristics are defined by their similarities to and differences from other discourses, both literary and nonliterary. Only these external relations—affirmative, negative, competitive, indifferent—enable poetry to be a genre with socially accepted internal boundaries and a degree of independent cultural meaning. Thus we cannot choose *whether* poetry will be articulated to such areas as common sense, human relations, politics, religion, education, cultural myth, philosophy, sexual difference, and a whole range of idealized and debased cultural domains.

All this is well put. It is unexceptionable so far as it goes—which is not far enough to join at all with the critical issue of aesthetic merit. Crucially, these relations which it summarizes must be modalized inside the poetry to constitute it as such. Thus, to be sure:

> A denial of poetry's relation to politics and cultural struggle is thus itself a constitutive, structural definition of poetry; the denial in a sense establishes a version of the very relation it would deny, turning poetry into the fixed "other" of the political, the everyday, the contingent.

But it is not a question of denying globally a relation to politics and cultural struggle of poetry, but rather of assessing that relation in its function as a constituent of expressed wisdom, as with Blake.

It is true that "poetry is always a function of such articulations," but it equivocates to say that:

> When we speak of "poetry," it is to this discursive formation that we refer. It is a formation constituted not only by the subject matter and style of poetry, by statements about poetics, and by the struggle over the changing social functions poetry serves, but also by all alternative efforts to define and co-opt the other social domains poetry addresses.

Attempts like those Nelson describes to define and co-opt social domains can enter into poetry—but the mode, power, and depth of that address determine the wisdom and beauty of the poem. Poetry is not just the cry of its occasion, and to call it that is a statement itself modulated crucially by many others in the obliquities of the long poem of Stevens where it occurs.

A properly dialectical view of this complex situation can be held in balance by keeping somewhat in step with Theodor Adorno, the theoretician who is perhaps best known for his keen delineation of the social constituents in art, literary and other, but who insists with equal force throughout his work on the interaction of those constituents with what he does not hesitate to call a truth content germane to the art work itself. As Adorno has consistently maintained, any art work must mediate its relation to society in order to be successful: "Art is the social antithesis to society, and not to be deduced from it without mediation."[16] The process of mediation is an elaborate one, just because of the connection: "Works of art are after-images of the empirical living element, insofar as they permit an approach to it which is denied them from the outside, and thereby are freed from it, to which their thing-laden memorized experience directs them."[17] Thus a reflexivity which is removed from direct social commentary resides in the very conception of an art work, "The truth content of art works is fused with their critical content."[18] And further, "The spirit [mind] of works can be non-truth. For the truth content postulates something real as its substance, and no spirit is unmediately something real."[19]

The function of a truth content, a core of wisdom, is complex in an art work, as Adorno keeps insisting:

> The relation of epistemology and art can be seen in reversal. The former is able to destroy the solipsistic territory through critical self-reflection while the subjective point of relation for art, real before and after, is that which

solipsism invents in reality directly. Art is the philosophical-historical truth of a solipsism that in itself is untrue. In art the position cannot intentionally be transgressed which philosophy has hypostasized into incorrectness. Aesthetic appearance is that which, outside aesthetics, solipsism exchanges with truth.[20]

And from a different angle:

> The aesthetic manner of control is the capacity to verify more in things than they are; it is the look under which that which is transforms itself into image. While the manner of control effortlessly can be contradicted as inadequate by the existent, it is still uniquely open to experience.[21]

In the light of such complicated and transcendent processes, it is consistent that "the aesthetic control is neither unmediately mimesis nor the repressed but the process by which it disengages and in which it modifies and sustains itself."[22] The limited version of artistic success, then, in Adorno's eyes (one might qualify the assessment) is the topicality, however purified, of Brecht. "The work of art that believes it possesses its content by itself is through rationalism naive in a pejorative sense: that would be the historically visible limit of Brecht."[23] But the social constituents must also be held in dialectical balance with the artistic act that transforms them: "Taking art extra-aesthetically or pre-aesthetically, in a connection non-prejudicial until now with a formation that is, to be sure, misconceived, is not only a barbaric backwardness or a need for a regression in consciousness. Something in art opposes that. If it is taken strictly aesthetically, is it not correctly taken aesthetically."[24] In Adorno's dialectic, truth and history merge with special intensity, rather than illustratively, in the art work, through processes that bear the impress of Hegel as well as of Nietzsche: "Axiomatic for a reoriented aesthetic is the realization developed by the late Nietzsche against traditional philosophy that what has come to pass, too, can be true. The traditional viewpoint he demolished should be stood on its head: Truth is uniquely that which has come to pass."[25]

As Kant goes on in his own discussion:

> The necessity of the universal assent that is thought in a judgment of taste, is a subjective necessity which, under the presupposition of a common sense, is represented as objective.
>
> . . . Hence common sense is a mere ideal norm. With this as presupposition, a judgment that accords with it, as well as the delight in an Object

expressed in that judgment, is rightly converted into a rule for every one. For the principle, while it is only subjective, being yet assumed as subjectively universal (a necessary idea for every one), could, in what concerns the consensus of different judging Subjects, demand universal assent like an objective principle, provided we were assured of our subsumption under it being correct.[26]

Kant's insistence is directed not at literary judgments, but at judgments in general. *The Critique of Judgment* is the third critique, as in Kant's scheme it must be, since it of necessity derives from the whole of his perceptual and conceptual apparatus. It is this necessity that complicates the question of what we are doing when we make aesthetic judgments, not only in Kant's terms but in any, whether systematic or ad hoc. To be sure, our sense of the social circumstances, and of the flexibility of a reader's consciousness in them, gets fleshed out if we give our attention to these questions on the "subjective" side of the antinomy. There is, however, a gain in essential perception about poetry if we come down once more on the "universal" side. In terms of a canon this means bracketing—or otherwise suppressing and therefore, to be sure, dissolving any antinomy— the questions about the subjectivity and relativity of canon formation that are so astutely, but of course incompletely, discussed by Jauss, Iser, and their followers over the past decades in Europe, and in America by Stanley Fish[27] and Barbara Herrnstein Smith,[28] among others, as well as by those whose attention to the "reader" goes along the lines of psychoanalytic query. Psychological structures represented in writing may well evoke comparable ones in the reader—or different ones, since the inescapable flaw of such approaches is to turn attention away from the message to the conjectural interaction through which the message, with all its hermeneutic problems on its head, may be conveyed. Even if the interaction between text and reader is part of the message, as well as integral to it, that interaction is clear as part of the message only if the overall message remains the primary ideal focus of hermeneutic attention.[29] Again, Gadamer offers mediated combinations and caveats against simple relativizing: "Is the phenomenon of understanding suitably defined when I say, understanding means avoiding misunderstanding? Does something like a 'carrying agreement' not underlie all misunderstanding?"[30]

Now to try to recuperate a communicative act in its fullness calls on all the resources of philosophy. Not just Gadamer but earlier Dilthey, following Kant's lead, retreated to the ground of constructive epistemology in order to account for the hermeneutic process. We can, however, make some observations without either constructing a complete epistemology or relativizing our sense of what makes a work worthy of canonization. We begin with the experience, simple as a fact though its structure, to say nothing of its justification, is extremely complex: the fact that as a person experiences a work he is convinced that his experience has a yield in perception, that it constitutes beauty or sublimity—to combine the Kantian terms—and that this experience has a cognitive content, a wisdom, not subsumable otherwise. All this, put so, is quite commonplace, but that is no reason to pass over it in favor of sociologizing or psychologizing the constituents of the experience, which do not displace it as they orient it and contribute to it.

No account, however lengthy or reticulated, resolves, or could resolve, Kant's antinomy between subjective and universal because such an account would have to be circular. It would have to keep returning to its vocabulary of descriptive characterization, which would not make it either inconsistent or trivial. But in directing critical attention, ultimately one must move out of the antinomy between subjective and universal. Astute critics of our time have come down on the "subjective" side, leaving, as they must, unresolved, or bracketed, questions arising from the "universal" side, and particularly the important questions about the wisdom that is communicated in poetry.

Bracketing the questions about wisdom, the relativists must also bracket, or at least partially suspend, the question of a possible common domain to which poetry and philosophy, though clearly distinguishable, are sometimes associable approaches. Not only the language of Dante, Blake, and Wallace Stevens or T. S. Eliot, but that of any poet, is a special, ordered version of Jürgen Habermas's assertion that "every natural language is its own metalanguage."[31] The consideration, itself ideal, of an ideal transmission of wisdom would carry Habermas's "metalanguage" all the way to the high language, the "Sagen" of Heidegger's assertion that poetry is a supreme human speech. And we need not—in a sense we cannot—fully attain the ideal of fully grounding such considerations, which is all the more reason for keeping them steadily in view.

II

Attention to the *process* of canonization immediately sets us into historical relation to the way texts of many sorts were scrutinized by ecclesiastical committees in the early centuries of our era, and to analogous processes right up to the role of the modern university in establishing or challenging the literary values that crucially contribute to canonization.[32] But attention to the *result* of canonization rather than to the process will help to bracket these analyses in favor of a text, in the present instance, a poem or body of poems in view. Nor does committing oneself to a text entail the old unwarranted (and impossible) suspension of the text from its contributory social conditions in space and time and from its communicative matrix.

Like love, the transmission of the wisdom in poetry takes place between two subjectivities in an initially social setting. And as with love, considerable prior structurings and considerable mechanisms of communication are involved (including those we bring to bear on explaining love). This transmission from individual writer to individual reader is single and intersubjective, though there can be some theoretical gain for some questions in dispensing with the term "subject," as Heidegger and others have urged. And allowing for intersubjectivity, "practically" in confronting a poem, as well as "theoretically" in accounting philosophically for it, we must continue to have recourse to the unexamined and circular analogy, as in Husserl's thinking, between one person and another at the nodal point of the communicative act. We must also, moreover, idealize the communicative act, and assume that the perfect assessment of the wisdom in a poem will itself be exactly just rather than approximate. And it will be, finally, instantaneous when the whole poem is apprehended, rather than gradual, as it must be while the poem is being read and reread. This is an idealization, but an idealization formed in the trust offered to the work, and to our experience of the work, in assessed, integral, dynamic, "unclinical" response to it.[33]

This second set of assumptions would put the reader in the position (which I believe he or she occupies, or at least I believe I occupy when I read) of moving, by a desire of intellect, toward an ideal he or she will actualize more or less completely. That is, the fallibility of human judgment in general, or in a particular case, while it is a constraint of more or less force according to cases, does not set a limit against moving toward the actualization of the ideal apprehension and assessment of the wisdom in a poem. This essential personal act is prior to, and constitutive of, the longer social process of community adjustment that takes place in canon formation, even in view of the necessary circumstance that the individual experience is built of social constituents, the first of which is the common language. All the social conditions in space and time that obtain for this intersubjective experience are preliminary—the special codes of language groupings, including class (or those that suspend class), the macro-codings of the rhetorical matrices we give the names of genres, the horizon-fusions from one time to another, and so on. The relativistic strategies, in fact, would come specially into play for works to which we deny the response of universal aesthetic value. That is, a disappointment on the universal half of Kant's antinomy would call the other half into play. However, for those works we do accord such universal value, while the social constraints do come no less into play, our account of the universalizing wisdom coded into them is obliged to go beyond as well as to survey all these social-linguistic conditions. This is what I am in effect doing, to take my cases from the domain of American poetry, when I site a poem historically, briefly or at great length, through its social-linguistic conditions, and then when briefly or at great length I accord it a value that proximately or ultimately is intricated in my sense of its wisdom.

Some of our historical (as well as critical) definition of a kitsch national pseudo-epic like *Hiawatha*—were we to undertake such a definition—would involve setting up terms that would analyze the poem's similarities to its original, the *Kalevala*, in order to discriminate the differences residing in and resulting from the likelihood of superior wisdom in the latter. The surface notation of thematic echoes in *Hiawatha*, or even of skillful writing and minor graces in it as a sort of desperate recuperative gesture,[34] would run the risk of diverting attention from, or more likely overlooking the irreducibly subjective and seemingly vague, but equally inescapable, question of the absence of wisdom in this work.[35]

The lyric poet rises to a sort of stability, to a wisdom of saying that persists, though of course this cannot be proved conclusively, since the art of saying constitutes an expression, and revelation, of a true state of affairs. The kitsch evocation of self-satisfaction can only temporarily seem to stand in for the true poetic revelation. So have quickly faded recent poems of the "kitchen Auschwitz" variety, where some set of images, like chickens roasting on a spit behind a glass window, was supposed to illustrate a deep, ineradicable vein of unconscious sadism in the whole social process. These have been largely discarded, though this particular vein of what Hans Egon Holthusen has called "sour kitsch" continues to be worked by some poets of inflated reputation.[36] More common is self-congratulatory political poetry, where the congruence with our own opinions seems for a while to substitute for poetic perception, especially if the verse is reinforced by skillful rhetoric.

A poem that encodes wisdom is not just a rhythmed repetition of received opinion, like Longfellow's "The Building of the Ship," though that poem, at a length comparable to that of Whitman's "By Blue Ontario's Shore," touches on a Whitmanian public optimism and even attempts a version of Whitman's sweep across the geography of the country—raising the question of where the difference is in aesthetic value, and concurrently of cognitive weight, between the two poems.

> Thou, too, sail on, O Ship of State!
> Sail on, O UNION, strong and great!
> Humanity with all its fears,
> With all the hopes of future years,
> Is hanging breathless on thy fate!
> We know what Master laid thy keel;
> What Workman wrought thy ribs of steel,
> Who made each mast, and sail, and rope,
> What anvils rang, what hammers beat,
> In what a forge and what a heat
> Were shaped the anchors of thy hope!

Such lines, climactic ones in "The Building of the Ship," would today embarrass even a patriot. The trite and tangled metaphors here are not by themselves enough to sink this poem, nor is the rhetorical control enough to raise it into the sort of Parnassian it might be taken for. In a negative sense, we would simply assert, and perceive, that there is no wisdom at work here at all; that is its capital sin of omission. The sin of commission resides in the interwoven pieties and lies, not least the lie that all of humanity is breathlessly watching the United States and hanging on its fate. If this might have been true in some sense in 1776, it is certainly not true in the middle of the nineteenth century. So banal is this poem that one feels foolish even making these obvious points, but it is important to distinguish these features from the competent formal ones of the poem. And if today the rejection of such a poem would command assent from relativists, it should be asked on what ground other than the (disappointed) expectation of a universal wisdom in poetry such relativists would be withdrawing their approval. The faint pastiche of Blake's "Tyger" in the last three lines quoted could have issued in a more passable, normal verse. Yet if we lack a criterion of wisdom to hold against canons, this poem and many like it would have to be admitted, because it was de facto a part of our canon for at least a century. Any assertion of the primacy of social constraints on canon formation must also be circular in the sense that it cannot ask about or deal with such questions of intrinsic or universal value. Even in a poem like "By Blue Ontario's Shore," not one of Whitman's best, one can perceive the obscure but distinct transmutation of banalities into poetic perception:

> I listened to the Phantom by Ontario's shore,
> I heard the voice arising demanding bards,
> By them all native and grand, by them alone can these States be fused into the compact organism of a Nation.
>
> To hold men together by paper and seal or by compulsion is no account,
> That only holds men together which aggregates all in a living principle, as the hold of the limbs of the body or the fibres of plants.
>
> Of all races and eras these States with veins full of poetical stuff most need poets, and are to have the greatest, and use them the greatest,
> Their Presidents shall not be their common referee so much as their poets shall.
>
> (Soul of love and tongue of fire!
> Eye to pierce the deepest deeps and sweep the world!
> Ah Mother, prolific and full in all besides, yet how long barren, barren?)

The "Phantom" of this first line, which itself verges on "pure poetry," richly modalizes Whitman's assertions and provides a semantic correlative to the openings broached by his varied, free rhythms. The Phantom is Ghost and anti-self and will-o'-the-wisp and persona and illusion, all in one. The act of "listening" locates itself at the juncture of private and public, validating the possibility that the expressed sense of "the voice . . . demanding bards" can carry a force beyond the pale and questionable echo of Shelley's "unacknowledged legislators" in "Their Presidents shall not be their common referee so much as their poets shall." The play of association upon "compact organism" evokes the principles of *Gemeinschaft* over *Gesellschaft*. The parenthesis with which this passage concludes carries forward its simple juxtapositions, its ellipses, and its randomizing afflatus of sound into a sense that sets past, present, and future into an illumined relation, like so many others in Whitman's repertory of verbal gestures.

The traces of this poetic energy and wisdom, for a while obscured and undervalued in Whitman, gradually asserted themselves, whereas this is little likely to happen with most if not all of Longfellow. Now, and very likely forever, "The Building of the Ship" has faded, like such once forceful nineteenth-century evocations of public sentiment as Tennyson's "Charge of the Light Brigade" and Scott's "Lay of the Last Minstrel," or like such modern evocations as the graphic calls to social justice by versifiers of unimpeachably good intentions. Such poems may indeed clearly demonstrate their effectiveness at focusing strong feeling. Yet, in the absence of a created wisdom, that feeling is not enough. Left to itself, it fades fairly quickly. The term "sentimental" would be misleading here, and the term "kitsch" would be finally obfuscating. There would be little to choose between the sentiment of such poets and the sentiment of Whitman or Dickinson, were it not that the poets who abide have fused their sentiment with what finally amounts to a cognitive freight of a wisdom become inseparable from it. It is not just the conventional allegorical structure and the lack of true rhythmic invention that keep Longfellow's expression from permanence. One could loosely parallel either attribute in some fine poems by Melville, or even by Frost. Longfellow's allegorical conceit, of bringing building materials for the "ship of state" from various places in the nation, lacks force and depth.

Longfellow's metaphor lacks a resonance, which in effect it attempts to borrow from the rhetoric of national self-congratulation. "The Building of the Ship" resembles all bad poems, and only superficially is the sentiment the same as the positive affirmation of the Union in Whitman, who has risen to the expression of encoded wisdom in ways we would of course have to expound further to explain, in the necessary absence of full definition.[37] A wisdom can be found, too, in the most famous, and one of the most successful, of Frost's excursions into patriotic utterance, "The land was ours before we were the land's." "I Hear America Singing," while not one of Whitman's best efforts, still carries through, taken with other poems in *Leaves of Grass*, while his rhymed poem based on a version of Longfellow's metaphor, "O Captain, my Captain," has now faded to triviality. The wisdom of Whitman at his successful best is far more complex than Longfellow's. It is "original," and to place what it transmits, even if only virtually and only ideally, would involve the long hermeneutic task of connecting the rhythms of *Leaves of Grass* and all its procedures, including its base in proprioceptive particularization, to the burden of that wisdom. That such a hermeneutic task is endless makes it no different from any other philosophical enterprise.

Nor is the *ideal* of a wisdom that leads to canonization modified essentially by the obvious situation that the best social assimilation of that wisdom is itself gradual, and constantly changing. Forty years ago a shadow lay across both Frost and Whitman, a shadow that a poet, Randall Jarrell—not all of whose own poems command our admiration—did much to dispel. "The Ship of State," all nine pages of it, was included in an anthology of American poetry about a decade earlier, as it would not likely be included today, an anthology edited by another professor-poet, Mark Van Doren.[38] Even if we do not yield to an endless relativism, we would be inclined to characterize Van Doren's judgment as here benighted by a historical sense, and one insufficiently supple, though he had been the author of a judicious book on Dryden, as well as of some good poems and a number of less good ones, including the now happily forgotten book-length narrative, *Jonathan Gentry*. Yet in his pedagogic role Van Doren over a long time sponsored a number of commanding poets, among them John Berryman, John Hollander, Louis Simpson, and Allen Ginsberg, in addition to poets arguably lesser but of great flair, like Thomas Merton.

In the ideal situation which we must be envisaging when we undertake to judge poems at all, they are finally conceived of as partaking in and communicating a wisdom encoded through the "beauty" of the work. This wisdom abides, in such a way that it has a sort of stability, "Was bleibet aber / stiften die Dichter" ("What abides, though, do poets establish"), as Heidegger stresses when he quotes these lines from Hölderlin. These constituents, called into play by the poem, also contribute to its expression of a cognitive yield, wisdom. The "abiding" of wisdom suggests a permanence that relates it to a situation in time, and to call it "the wisdom of the past" would underplay the "founding" or "establishing" act of the poet. Yet to overemphasize the discontinuity of the poet's utterance with the past would obscure the crucial element in his "originality" of calling the past into play. Originality does not just superadd a twist to given constituents. It deeply wakens them and somehow transposes them.

Some analogue to the poet's integrated evocations are offered by what Homer says of Calchas the seer—not a poet, since in that already elaborate society the function of poet had already been split off from that of seer:

Calchas, "who knew what is and what is to be and what was" *(Iliad* 1.70). The gathered past and the luminous present and an opening on the future converge in the wisdom of the poem. Nor would an exposition of subtlety and richness in an utterance by itself establish the presence of wisdom. Ordinary language is in itself, and characteristically, extraordinarily rich and subtle, capable of the sort of analysis that William Labov and David Fanshel have accorded, at the length of hundreds of pages, to just a few sentences from one psychoanalytic interview.[39] Moreover, the cues for a poetic utterance are "stiffer" and narrower in poetry than Erving Goffman has shown them to be for ordinary discourse,[40] though we would expect and even assume the contrary to be the case. The two-tiered analysis assumed even by Heidegger, between ordinary language and poetic utterance, runs the risk of obscuring the strength that poetry draws from its rootedness in a common tongue. Mallarmé understood this in speaking of the poet's aim to "donner un sens plus pur aux mots de la tribu," where the perfect equivocation, and mystery, between "donner un sens plus pur" and "les mots de la tribu" itself rises to poetry. To stray from this base makes it impossible for the poet to find his best expression, as I would assume such a sterile effort as Petrarch's *Africa* would demonstrate. Eliot's deliberate slanting of his translation-assimilation of this line, "To purify the dialect of the tribe," emphasizes the temporal and spatial specificity of the language, as "dialect," rather than its generic character as "words" or "language."

Instead of further assessment of the arguments of current relativists, we might continue to take cues from Theodor Adorno, who operates equivocally across the line of Kant's antinomy, constructing concrete extrapolations about what amounts to the subjective and socially dialecticized conditions of artistic expression, while writing from a fundament of universal assumption about the masters of music and poetry. "From the beginning I experienced . . . the art work," Adorno says, "not as a simple theory of knowledge, as the analysis of the condition for intellectually valid judgments, but as a sort of coded writing, out of which was to be read the historical condition of the spirit, with the vague expectation that thus something of truth itself might be found in it."[41] There is no reason one cannot allow both the social circumstances of the work and its truth, buttressing this "vague expectation" with some version of Heidegger's hermeneutics. Here, indeed, as by anticipation, there are strands in Adorno's position that can be related to Heidegger's "Sagen" on the one hand while connected with the hermeneutics of Gadamer and the historicism of Jauss on the other. Or, as Adorno says further, "Even presumably extreme individual modes of reaction are modified by the objective situation to which they respond and must be aware of this mediation for the sake of their own truth content."[42]

Now of course Adorno would not have subscribed to Heidegger's definition of truth as a laying-bare of a whole human situation, an uncealedness or *Unverborgenheit*. But his underlying assertion is reconcilable with Heidegger's, and it is based on an assumption virtually identical insofar as it bears on the work of art. In favoring the "universal" side of the antinomy between subjective and universal, this assumption, which I believe the responsive reader cannot help sharing with Adorno and Heidegger in practice (whatever the theory), will simply not dissolve under relativizing or subjectivizing arguments.

It is necessary to perform an act of bracketing to make any philosophical point whatever. That we thus abrogate various questions of epistemological, ontological, and sociological relativizing when we accord a stability, or a permanence, or a canonical status to a work of art should not disturb us, any more than we should be disturbed by the circularity that is a necessary condition of explaining the human situation, in Heideggerian or other terms.[43] Indeed, a poem arguably begins by itself assuming such circularity; in other terms, it begins by communicating that it is, in the ancient words of Hesiod, "lies similar to truth." Once we have made this point, we could cease to be surprised that in its circularity the poem may not get through to us with instantaneous directness.

Heidegger, for example, draws on Hölderlin, Rilke, Trakl, and George as virtual equals, but these four poets came through into his culture at different rates. In an overall look at these rates of assimilation, there are two different phenomena that are connected with the variability of canonicity, "fading" or discarding, and "brightening" or consolidation. Fading is easily understood, and, to stay with American poetry, it is not likely that the once canonical Longfellow and Holmes and James Russell Lowell, or even Whittier, will be re-brightened and reinstalled in a canon of live works, though an inertial process of social transmission will continue to have them read in universities, if only for "historical" reasons. But the "brightening" of their contemporaries Whitman and Emily Dickinson is a much more complicated affair. Just as it took over a century for Blake to be understood as more than a writer of some lovely lyrics, and just as it took almost two and a half millennia for the poet-philosopher Heraclitus to be understood as more than just the author of a couple of aphorisms and some blurred, outdated philosophical positions, so the power of Emily Dickinson, the conceptual depth of her wisdom, has taken much of a century to establish itself, well after the discovery of her poems and even well after the establishment of what we may call canonical texts. The abrupt assimilation in 1939 of the late-seventeenth-/early-eighteenth-century poet Edward Taylor after his rediscovery was simple by comparison, largely due to the accident that his work was lost for a much longer time. It was easier with Whitman, but understanding him has been attended by a number of complications, beyond just the usual hermeneutic constraints. These poets have now been brought up close to a full magnitude of brightness; it seems as little likely to me that they will fade as that Vergil and Dante, Chaucer and Shakespeare, will fade. But fading or brightening, once they have run a usually short-term course, rarely reverse themselves inside one language area, though variations occasionally occur across language barriers—Dante was a faded poet for Goethe, as Shakespeare was for Voltaire.

Fading and brightening are perhaps the main phenomena in canonization, and ultimately the social factors in the process yield to the immediacy of a cognitive content, a wisdom, aura and all, in the poetic work. Fading and brightening are not inversions of the same process, but results of very different processes. Fading practically always happens the same way. A work once registered as having an impact that comprises wisdom is revealed as lacking wisdom, and concurrently it loses its impact.[44] Consolidation or brightening in the first place is a complex social process that operates in a range of combinatory interrelations between the works in question and the changing society. Here interpretive communities do come into play, synchronically and diachronically, but as instrumentalities, not as final values. Frost, for easily perceptible reasons, was consolidated quickly, if not without adjustments of focusing, more rapidly than the Pound who aided that process for Frost. The very radiance of Pound's major work and its complexity delayed the process for him, as did the various kinds of notoriety and justified disrepute to which Pound subjected himself. The bracing complexity that Charles Olson built behind the surface flatness of *The Maximus Poems* has comparably delayed his full assimilation.

Part of the complexity in Pound's wisdom derives from the interweaving of the personal and the public, as with Whitman. This complexity can be traced at many angles in Pound's work, as, say, in his relation to Venice, where the proper angle of Pound's view of his youth to his view of Malatesta requires much plotting, and would issue in the attestation of a composed wisdom.

Memories of Venice begin in Canto 3, and in some senses even earlier. Venice gave Pound "a run for his money," to apply to him the phrase he applied to his globetrotting aunt who took him on a first European trip in the latency of his boyhood, a trip that included Venice. He would visit it with the woman who was to become his wife, and then after he married her, and then many times thereafter, settling there for his old age with another companion of long standing and finally dying there. It was in Venice that he had brought out his first book of poems, "A Lume Spento," that title drawn from Dante's account of the death of Manfred, another contumelious wanderer in Italy.

Of ten central cantos in the first thirty, Hugh Kenner notes that "Venice is perhaps the central preoccupation of the sequence . . . a splendid mortuary place entoiled for centuries with the history of fanciful practices."[45] Between the medieval time on which Pound's academic formation centered and the nascent modernism of his literary foundations, the actual city of Venice rose to its peak and declined. The evidences of that history impressed him as he settled there, but it was not until he had got into the *Cantos* nearly twenty years later that he was able to incorporate the renaissance career of the city. By that time, the Spain which had been his first goal, where he intended to write a doctoral thesis on Lope de Vega, had receded somewhat to the margins. It took the whole doctrine of the *Cantos* to gravitate his constructive imagination back around Venice, as the Lombards come into prominence toward the end. He has managed to shed various light on the thematic reverberations of the city in what might seem the mere poignancy of nostalgia in Canto 83 and in the Pisan Cantos generally. Take this run from Canto 83:

San Gregorio, San Trovaso
Old Ziovan raced at seventy after his glories
    and came in long last
and the family eyes stayed the same Adriatic
    for three generations (San Vio)
and was, I suppose, last month the Redentore as usual

Will I ever see the Giudecca again?
    or the lights against it, Ca' Foscari, Ca'Giustinian
or the Ca', as they say, of Desdemona
or the two towers where are the cypress no more
    or the boats moored off le Zattere
or the north quai of the Sensaria   DAKRUŌN   ΔΑΚΡΥΩΝ[46]

That the Sensaria is a brokerage house, and the last named in this list, connects it to the complex role of money factoring through history in the *Cantos*. How does this, and the other historical relations, connect to Pound's personal ruminations here, caught as he dramatizes himself speaking in another historical situation? Between what might be called the lyricism of this passage and the epic note of "a poem that includes history" there are connections we have not fully settled in our hermeneutic assessment, even assuming that we ever could do so. But the surfacing of the question contributes to, and validates, the "brightening" of Pound, the wisdom of achieved utterance that justifies our considering him canonical.

To stay with American poetry as an exemplary case: since World War II many poets of deeply divergent practice have come through the stages of orderly consolidation that we call a career. To name just three of those who are still living, Richard Wilbur, John Ashbery, and Robert Creeley have come through comparable consolidations at every stage, for all the vast differences among them, and for all the partialities of the influential groups that would want to stress one to the exclusion of one or both of the others.

But irregularities of all sorts play across the process of consolidation. In the case of Charles Reznikoff, obscurity, followed by a moment of attention, followed by long obscurity, moved him toward attention in his eighties. While consolidation has been taking place steadily over the past decade, we have still not come to what one could call a plateau of hermeneutic adequacy for Reznikoff, as we have fairly done with Louis Zukofsky, another poet who went through more modified times of obscurity. Lorine Niedecker, once she was singled out from the throng of her contemporaries after her death, has been consolidated fairly easily; her work is personal, and this involves only a sharpening of the hermeneutic assessment of her means in order for her brightening to come up to something approaching its proper magnitude. Ashbery at first was widely regarded as a coterie poet, but his wisdom told through the difficult modality of his language, which is also the bright center of his poetry. William Stafford's slippage of inference and construction was at first too quiet to be given its due weight, and Robert Bly had seemed too programmatic, but the delays in their cases were only relative.

I am far from asserting that wisdom is to be found only in connection with complexity. In Villon or Burns or Landor, and also in Frost and at times in Wordsworth, it may reside in a radiant simplicity, where the hermeneutic justification of the attribution of wisdom must address not the far-reaching conceptual coherences of the poem, subserved by its rhythms, but the particular arrangement of language that brings about so penetrating an utterance. It may be found, indeed—as we have been asked to acknowledge and celebrate since Percy, if not since the Spanish romances that Sidney praised—in ballad and song. And, in a reasonably short time, the songs of Bob Dylan would seem to have been brightening their way into the canon, in a normal course to be accompanied by those of others, as many songs of his most popular contemporaries quickly fade.[47]

There is also a third theoretical case, if the social circumstances of canonization are viewed in the light of the wisdom inherent in achieved poetry—the case of poetry heavily obscured or even lost. Poems may fall away from social attention for a complex of other reasons than the "fading" attendant upon work that is essentially trite. Wisdom, to inhere in the poem, does not have to continue to get a social hearing. The Byzantine theocracy put the poems we have of Sappho in the shade. In the extreme case of the lost groups of poems of Sappho, there is every likelihood that they would compare well with the few we have. It is quite easy to imagine the circumstance that the poems of Emily Dickinson would still be buried in an attic, or forever thrown away. But that would not affect the achievement of wisdom and beauty in them, only the communication of what they had achieved. The communication is potential; culture is enriched if the communication is actualized, but the value of achievement in the utterance does not change. Dickinson herself was even more severe on this point, "Publication—is the Auction / Of the Mind of Man—." And in this poem at least she sees the communication as a kind of sullying: "We—would rather / From Our Garret go / White—Unto the White Creator—/ Than invest—Our Snow—" (Poem 709). The slight but distinct force of Trumbull Stickney's work has not diminished because he is little read, and the same situation may obtain for poets of this generation who have already died. L. E. Sissman and John Logan, for example, poets again very different, left behind statements of a richness that is independent of how often they continue to be read: the wisdom is achieved in any case.

It is almost the entire task of interpretation, as it rests on critical judgment, to carry out the ascertainment and assessment of what such wisdom is and how it works in its intimate association with beauty, or with sublimity. And we can combine these two terms, beauty and sublimity, though Kant follows his contemporary tradition in dividing them, because we are not obliged to rest with the definitions within his systematic presentation to adopt points from it. "We are agreed about the affirmative answer," Habermas says, "but not agreed about how to determine the preliminary consensus."[48] And we can function well under such a supposition, especially since, as Habermas reminds us, "Gadamer . . . sees no opposition between authority and reason. The authority of an utterance is not achieved blindly, but through reflexive recognition by those who, standing within a tradition, understand it and develop it by application."[49] Our approach to constructing an account of what is communicated in the combination of statements and effects in a poem will range from the very words of the poem, taken individually, to the elaborate complex of the poet's communicative utterance in a social context. As for the words, Emerson's "language is fossil poetry," or even Vico's heightened and broadened use of the term "poetic" is only a beginning, since these terms will not carry us into the uses that are specific to poetry, as against the uses in ordinary language.

In the passage from Pound quoted above, something is going on that frames and highlights the names of locations in Venice, lining the names up in a way most mysterious with the seventy-year-old native running a slow race, as well as with the towers, the boats, and the cypress. The iconic character and the rhythmic emphasis on these three nouns slur them into a rhythmic nostalgia and make this whole run quite different from its distant parent, the catalogue of Whitman. All Pound's evolved theories of image and ideograph in between have been brought to bear, and can be shown to be incorporated in the *Cantos* generally, and specifically here, through the evocations in these bare words and their conjunction.

In this passage, the "tears," the "DAKRUŌN," are elusive. Surely they are something like Vergil's *lacrimae rerum*, first given in the Greek word, capitalized for ideographic echo, and then transliterated into actual Greek letters, ΔΑΚΡΥΩΝ. These words are impossible to say, since the capitals would urge a shout and the Greek—all the more for the break between Roman and Greek letters—would recommend an undertone. The break between these two anapests both of orthography and rhythmic pause keeps them from speeding up and thus holds a continuous rhythmic veil over the words. The slowing for ideogram-like emphasis on the repeated "DAKRUŌN" is further highlighted by Pound's typographic practice of double-spacing before each of its two occurrences.

Are towers and boats and cypress metaphors in this passage? Are other locutions also? These are profound questions, raised by the depth of Pound's practice. But certainly they are not metaphors in the ordinary, schematic sense. The water, of which the tears must be accounted an example, works thematically, and paleosymbolically, through this canto. Venice is a city of water, and Canto 83 begins with water, repeated again in both Greek and Roman forms: "ὕδωρ / HUDOR et Pax / Gemisto stemmed all from Neptune / hence the Rimini bas reliefs." This takes a Renaissance metaphysician for whom water was of crucial explanatory significance, and it couples him with both paleosymbolic and political thought, with the Greek god, and with bas reliefs in the orbit of Malatesta. Some forty lines later Pound will quote Heraclitus, *panta rei*, "All flows." The tears enter into these intricacies, evoking the profound symbolic extensibilities of water.[50] And as Samuel Levin reminds us, taking any poetic metaphor seriously as wisdom rather than as a turn of phrase characterized by deviance, will call into play the categories of many of the most sophisticated philosophers in our entire tradition, Kant, Husserl, and Aquinas among them.[51]

Further, as Neil Hertz makes clear, Longinus points to the psychological process, here crucial, that the figurative substructure of metaphoric statements tends to disappear in the directness of a poetic apprehension: "Sublimity and emotion are a defense and a wonderful aid against the suspicion which the use of figures engenders. The artifice of the trick is lost to sight in the surrounding brilliance of beauty and grandeur."[52] Something like this happens, for example, in Whitman's "When Lilacs Last in the Dooryard Bloomed," where the poet's very clumsiness in providing a match of figurative substructures is lost in the uptake into sublimity brought about through the resonance, both semantic and rhythmic, of the terms he has conjoined.

Towers and boats and cypress have much resonance in Pound's lines. So does Desdemona and all the action she stands for and evokes. But to call such words "paleosymbols" with Habermas, while it will throw into relief their rootedness in the deepest levels of culture, will tend to obscure the intricacies of how those levels operate. Yet we must begin by realizing, as he says, that "we are dealing with relationally directive symbols and not just with signs, for the symbols have a genuine function of reference: they represent experiences of interaction. Besides, all the properties of normal speech are absent from this level of paleosymbols."[53] As Habermas goes on, registering some important constraints: "Paleosymbols are not arranged into a system of grammatical rules. They are not ordered elements and do not appear in connections that are subject to grammatical transformation. For this reason the functions of these pre-linguistic symbols have been compared to those of analog, as distinct from digital, computers."[54] And without going further into the comparison, we can see that, once they enter the language of a poem, the "paleosymbols" harmonize the other words of the poem into a new paleosymbolic system, having what could be called the attributes both of a digital computer, insofar as it sets up, as in Pound, one-for-one correspondences through its separate references; and also, as Habermas says, something like the analog computer, insofar as the text obscurely, and even rhythmically, maps its perceptions by points of correspondence to something only recognized in its fullness when heard and read.

As Adorno says, "What history is in [art] works is not ready-made, and history first freed it from mere positing or confection: the truth content is not outside of history but its crystallization in works."[55] What Adorno means by crystallization, perhaps borrowing the term from Stendhal's characterization of falling in love, has at least a triple projection: in addition to indicating the relations, themselves manifold, of a work both to its own historical situation and implicitly to that of the reader or experiencer, it points at the structure of the art work, but also at the effect on the reader. "Aura" is another name for this crystallization, and to experience the work the aura must be perceived, which means that not just the attention but the whole complex of communicative awareness in the reader must be engaged, "affectively." There is no neutral or objective apprehension of the poem, correctly read, partly because a poem cannot be truly neutral, even if, as in some modern works, it includes a surface of neutrality in its structure. The metalinguistic posture of some modern poems is strong enough for them to stand as "pulverized poems," to borrow René Char's title, poems that ironicize an anti-aura as part of their aura. A more transformational, comprehensive use of the same strategy by Charles Olson is sometimes taken for mere flatness.

As Adorno says further, "Value-free aesthetics is nonsense. To understand art works means . . . to perceive the moment of their logicality and also its opposite; and also their rifts and what they signify."[56] The most dominant exponent of "value-free" sociology was Max Weber, whose approach remained flexibly dialectical, like Adorno's own, but Adorno insists on more than that from an approach, even a sociologizing one, to the art work, and he does so with the ukase of an exaggeration. A "value-free" approach to the art work is not, strictly speaking, nonsense. It is a possible hermeneutic posture, to be found in Arnold Hauser's *Social History of Art* (in spite of Adorno's strictures on the limitations of that work), as well as in the other, more recent discussions that I am here trying to deemphasize—though not to discard.

For the most part the studies that center on relativizing the poetic experience by setting it in social context do offer valuable sitings on the poem. They continue the ongoing hermeneutic and critical enterprise of providing example, and the grounds for justification (even if in some cases by inducing counter-statement), in establishing what it is we find in poems that gives them the value they have. But we can empathetically ask for more from our accounts of poems, and we should do so, engaging ourselves thereby with the intimate subtlety of an account of the poem that approaches adequacy in addressing its wisdom by refusing to settle for the relativisms of situational description. We can proceed with the large, and still compelling task, of working out how the beauty and the wisdom in the poem are deeply intricated with each other. Terms like "beauty" and "wisdom," of course, are rich and unitary, and in some senses final. These are compelling reasons for building toward them (as I have here begun to do) and from them (as I have here taken the strategic liberty of doing), rather than avoiding them because under one set of constraints they may be characterized as vague. We should reach toward their richness. The relational analyses, however fine, incur the risk of losing sight of the force of the actual experience, just as the universal ones risk reifying that experience. But in a kind of binocular vision, it is possible to combine the two approaches simply by allowing the relationality of what is relational without letting it crucially impinge on the experience, while also not absolutizing the experience in an exclusionist way. In fact, so to overvalue the poem is effectually to undervalue it, to subject it to the very conditions it has the illusion of escaping (rather than integrating).

The redefinition of subjectivity in our time, even where it is asserted that the subject is some kind of illusion, so predominantly draws on literary materials for its validation that the procedure of doing so constitutes a sort of phenomenological demonstration of the existence of the subject. The interpreter, though, need not incur the loss of interplay in perceiving the literary work that accompanies the gain of extending its "intersubjectivity" along one or another set of lines, those of ego psychology, or the Lacanian imaginary and symbolic, or the various "differences" that "writing" evokes, in Derrida's terms or others. He or she need not enlist the attribution of the work to an overall *Weltbild* along lines begun in Hegel's *Aesthetics* and carried through by Foucault, Deleuze, and others. Nor need the interpreter account for the dialectics involved in "horizon-fusion" between reader and text. The interpreter, without bracketing these approaches, and without undertaking the considerable, wholly preoccupying task of redefining, qualifying, or combining them, may simply do so ad hoc by confronting the process rather than just the philosophical preconditions of the subjectivity inscribed into and evoked by a text.

2. "Most Take All": The Good and the Beautiful in Herbert's *Temple*

I

The poetry of George Herbert, considered in the light of how it at once highlights and denies its own fictiveness, offers a challenging case in which a seeming transparency is achieved by considerably poised construction. A subjectivity qualifies itself by transcending itself in the verbal act of dissolving in a God who is conceived of as already known from foregone theological positions and their psycho-spiritual derivatives. The good and the beautiful become derivatives of each other, and the reader can only accede to the wisdom yielded thereby by submitting to the process.

To ask about how this might work takes us beyond the elaborate reconstructive strategies of Jauss and Iser. What remains when the mechanisms of transmission through the "melting of horizons," through the effect or response of "Wirkung," have all been accounted for? Herbert's poetry can be taken to test such questions, a potentiality that may help explain why his work has drawn so much attention over the past three decades.

A devotional poet like Herbert, to begin with, raises problems other than those of suspending disbelief that may be brought to bear on a doctrinal poet like Dante, or even Milton—and even though the categories "devotional" and "doctrinal" are not made mutually exclusive. Herbert is, for one thing, a meditative poet in more than the technical sense of Renaissance meditation manuals, and not to participate in the goal of his meditation, at least putatively or virtually, is to slight a key dimension of the speech act which organizes his rhetoric. Still, an emphasis on other aspects of Herbert than this central one may itself contribute to understanding him. There is a hermeneutic yield to be derived from discussions that give attention to the seriatim presentation of Herbert's poems. But a proper interpretative, and evaluative, posture must keep in view the poet's own primary emphasis on a worship in the "temple" that aims for a good ultimately identifiable with a proposed union in God.

To ask how we respond to Herbert in such a way as to accord aesthetic value and wisdom to poems framed as invocations to religious virtue, goes beyond the question of our suspending, as we read, disbelief about the urgency of burial rites in *Antigone* or disbelief in the sudden apotheosis of Oedipus in *Oedipus at Colonus*. Even there, however, beyond our possible freedom from conscious or unconscious deference to Euro-centered or British-Empire–modified assumptions of the paramount value of Greek literature, there remains the very real question of the crossover we are effectuating when we make the profound leap of genuinely admiring Sophocles (or Pindar or Homer). It stretches the very notion of interpretive community to allow for such (not infrequent) cases.

Kant makes a distinction between a concept-free response to beauty in nature and a concept-involved response to beauty in the fine arts. But taste always begins as a conceptual experience because it is a response to a convergence of signs that are either managed by one human being in an art work or found in a nature itself inescapably laden with natural signs. The religious platitude, as it would seem, on which Herbert's poetry is based, poses at once the problem of how, given this base, we find it beautiful, and why we include it in the canon. Some fusion of intellect and emotion has taken place through the act of the poem that it is very difficult to separate out, nor are these elements easily definable. Theoreticians from Kant on have found the response to an art work to involve such a fusion, but it takes a fairly full epistemology—which Kant continues to offer for this problem in the *Critique of Judgement*—to rationalize the mechanisms of the intellectual content of the ordered signs. And so too for the emotions, the exhaustive study of a Suzanne Langer[1] offers a survey but, I presume, not a fully adequate explanation, any more than does the T. S. Eliot who evolves his own intricate theory of the emotions in poetry from prolonged study of comparable questions in the philosophy of F. H. Bradley.[2] We recognize the problem of the emotions, and their inescapable presence, but cannot separately account for them without recourse to the formidable rigor of such systems or of prior classifying codes like those of Freud and Lacan. We are reduced, perhaps necessarily, to taking our cue from Kant and finding that the aesthetic has affinities with the ethical (though belonging to different faculties in his account, the ethical to reason and the aesthetic to judgment). Consequently, in his formulation, the beautiful attests indirectly to the good by serving as an analogue to it and a symbol for it.[3] God is then for Kant the source and goal of the good, in a notion easily reconcilable with Herbert's.

This poetry offers a convergent experience in what Herbert regards as the plain sense of both the beautiful and the good, and to experience these poems is not only (or necessarily at all) to assent to the theology, even provisionally, but in the experience of the poem to flow with the ordering principle it presents and exemplifies. What Helen Vendler says of "The Windows" may be taken as characterizing the experience of his poems generally, "Alone man is brittle and formless ('crazie'), but God gives him a place both glorious and transcendent; God's light and glory grows, through the holy preacher, more reverend and winning. Doctrine joins with life, colors join with light, both combine and mingle, the result in the congregation is regard and awe."[4] Here the reader joins in the stated emotion, as a personal subject open to the wisdom of the poems. In this the reader of Herbert is distinct from the auditor of the Psalms, who in that act joins the collective persona of a worshipping people, fusing into the congregation, rather than a single conjectural devotee. The act of the poem unifies, as Vendler goes on to say of the poem "Justice": "However, by presenting two versions of a vision-through-a-glass—one self-regarding and the other God-directed—Herbert implies a third state, in which the medium will be dissolved and one will see without mediation. In that state, no names will be needed for attributes like 'justice' and 'mercy,' since those names are only human inventions, each one partial, for aspects of divinity, as Herbert says in 'The Glance'" (*The Poetry of George Herbert*, 79).

Stanley Fish impressively, and so far as that component goes, convincingly, traces a congruence between the progressions and metaphors in Herbert's poetry and discussions at his time of practices connected to the exercise of catechism.[5] Fish would go farther and characterize as "*radically* ambiguous" (italics Fish's; *The Living Temple*, 65) those characteristics of the temple metaphor and others that can in fact be described not as ambiguous but simply as aspectual. Fish's acutely learned tracing of congruences to discussions about catechism and his general overall description of the poems do hold. But they do not entail our allowing the poems to founder on their supposed contradictions, when their rhetorical aim is exactly the opposite. If they founder and also succeed, it might be asked what kind of success that could be. And if their foundering makes them failures, we might further ask why it is we should read them at all. "What is crucial is not the dialogue in the poem, but the dialogue the poem is in, and that, in turn, is a function of the way these poems characteristically engage their readers." Precisely. But Fish does not draw the right conclusion. Surely that way of engaging a reader cannot be one that would be regarded as repugnant by the intelligent, devout author. The "contradiction at the heart of Herbert's poetry" (*The Living Temple*, 68) can only be allowed if the discrepancy between processive presentation and ultimate rhetorical aim were to vitiate the utterance into a final paradox, just because it enlists paradoxes along the way. Again, like many literary products (all, some would maintain), this poetry can be seen to engage in an "equivocation between a structure that is precarious, shifting, and unfinished (work to be done) and a structure that is firm, secure, and complete (work already done)." Herbert at every point intentionally tilts his rhetoric toward the latter, and so the poems themselves, to state the obvious, are at once hortatory demonstrations and phase-sensitive assertions. It constantly, and perversely, misdefines these aspects of his (or other) utterances to call them equivocations, though Fish is right in his insistence that the interpreter must seek for a unity in the poems that integrates these two (seemingly contradictory) aspects in Herbert's poems, rather than lining up with the critics on either side who want to insist that the poems offer either a sequence of surprises or a simply coherent ordering.

Within the plain sequence of his assertions Herbert does master the contradictions he surveys; and for all these contradictions, the responsive reader can point, as he does, to their resolution under the sign of the cross in the poem of that title, where the difficulties of access to God and resolution of self are seen themselves to be redemptive within a Christian frame:

> And yet since these thy contradictions
> Are properly a crosse felt by thy Sonne,
> With but foure words, my words, *Thy will be done*.[6]

The whole rhetorical work of the identification between savior and worshipper, the whole intellectual understanding of what the sufferings, bewildering up to that point, really mean, has been carried through as the last four words are aimed to a doubling convergence. These four words are the direct statement of the speaker, functioning as the delayed succinct main clause of the sentence; and at the same time they stand in indirect discourse, a quotation, nested in their apposition to "foure words, my words."

First of all, catechism is not uniformly present as a discernible pattern in Herbert's poems and sometimes not present at all. Consequently, catechism is a subset of the general posture in this poetry. "Redemption" and several other poems ("Easter" among them) are not catechistical. The landownership metaphor organizes this poem to its end of simply asserting a Christian connection. The "rich lord," from whom the speaker-tenant seeks a new lease, is sought without any questions or cross-examination; he is finally and soon found undergoing the Passion. He "straight, *Your suit is granted*, said, & died." Though "Sinne (I)" speaks of the subject of its title, it only surveys the human situation. In its tight progression, one that approximates a cross-examination, "The Collar" is atypical; it composes for itself a special rhetoric. "Affliction" gives an autobiographical summary. "Faith" offers a nonprogressive series of reassurances based on theological inference, "Prayer" a résumé of sure and abundant definitions of this spiritual resource, "The Holy Communion" an assessment and alternative to prayer. "The Discharge" conjoins injunctions and definitions; "Longing" is an extended series of questioning prayers. "Peace" offers some wrong matches, and then a parable. It is not quite catechistical, but a matching by properties, using metaphors in which their resonance has a contributory grace rather than a mythicizing power. So, too, the nesting chests of "Confession" serve for correspondences, not catechism.

Moreover, the catechistical tradition is not the only general staple of theological rhetoric that Herbert draws on. As Louis Martz fully demonstrates, there is also the meditative tradition along the lines of Ignatius's *Spiritual Exercises* and the comparable literature of its techniques and strategies.[7] Martz finds Herbert adopting the techniques of meditation explicitly for the contemplation of death, but these techniques extend through his work generally. Now if we were to allow them to dominate, or wholly to contain, the poems, they would operate in some contradiction to the technique of catechism. For catechism requires of its very nature an interlocutor, a questioner who could be God or another person or the self in its divisions, or even some combination of these. Meditation, on the other hand, is of its very nature a solitary enterprise, of the self trying to collect the self (whatever subsidiary techniques it might enlist to that end). To allow for the dominance of one of these strains, then, would be to downplay the other; but both are demonstrably present, in a more expansive ordering, consequently, than an exclusive attention to either could allow.

As William Empson says in his discussion of "The Sacrifice," "Various sets of conflicts in the Christian doctrine of the Sacrifice are stated with an assured and easy simplicity, a reliable and unassuming grandeur."[8] Yet even so, Empson's concentration on "contradiction" here overplays this feature, which is his seventh and final type of ambiguity, even though he has just gone on to say that "the poem is outside the 'conflict' theory of poetry; it assumes, as does its theology, the existence of conflicts, but its business is to state a generalised solution of them." And this poetry states, as well as a solution, an act of verbal integration into the rich, if standard, typology that connects not only the psychology of suffering with the psychology of redemption but its historical counterpart of transposing the Old Testament into the New. "The Sacrifice" enlists such mechanisms when it recasts the rhetoric (and even more the assertions) of the book of Lamentations into the assertions of the crucified Savior. Since Lamentations proceeds under the figure of the prophet addressing a city, Herbert's poem involves a latent typological association identifying an afflicted Biblical Jerusalem with the Redeemer at the moment of highest eclipse. The close liturgical pattern is that of the *Tenebrae* in Holy Week. To describe this penitential meditation as either catechistical or Ignatian would be to overspecify it away from this liturgical framework. Still, all these rhetorical gestures work together, and the fundamental problem remains of how and why we find wisdom and beauty through the mere (as it might seem) dexterity of this attempt to recast standard devotional gestures.

If we ignore the rhetoric, we undo the poem. But if we dissolve the poem into its rhetoric, we leave out of account the fundamental force it carries off. This force centers the ethical so squarely in the poetic, and the devotional so squarely in the ethical, that the oriented reader cannot move, for all his castings about of psychological motion. He has the reassurance of rest, a haven after the enacted strenuousness, and this rest is offered as a yield, of a state imbued with a wisdom the poem has helped to bring about.

Take so paradigmatic and simple a poem as "Vertue":

Vertue.

Sweet day, so cool, so calm, so bright,
The bridall of the earth and skie:
The dew shall weep thy fall to night;
                        For thou must die.

Sweet rose, whose hue angrie and brave
Bids the rash gazer wipe his eye:
Thy root is ever in its grave,
                        And thou must die.

Sweet spring, full of sweet dayes and roses,
A box where sweets compacted lie;
My musick shows ye have your closes,
                        And all must die.

Onely a sweet and vertuous soul,
Like season'd timber, never gives;
But though the whole world turn to coal,
                        Then chiefly lives.

"Sweet day so fair, so calm, so bright" leans on the possibility, rather than the actuality, of a virtue-charged convergence between the public (shared day, rose, spring) and the private (the acts which amount to virtue), and so not just in rhetoric, but also in psychological possibility. The poem enacts the convertibility of a gather-ye-rosebuds-while-ye-may (or more generally a *carpe diem*) phrasal postulate into a postulate of the transience of all earthly things but virtue. Hence the achieved calm of the poem, a calm which governs and subsumes the rhetorical reversal, and the slight tonal emphasis, of the last stanza.

    It is not the local attributions in this poem but its overall compass that would be a strain if it did not draw on the predetermined ethos toward which the poet is writing, on which he is drawing. He performs an act of combination, so to speak, on what Kant would later resume as the two areas of human certainty, the starry sky above us and the moral law within us. The underlying similarity between the two as instances of God's creation allows the poet to assume the ease of pointing a moral by highlighting the difference. The poem is catechistical in Fish's terms; but it is also counter-catechistical in assuming that the reader will quickly follow it, since in its terms all the elements are prima facie the case. It is also post-catechistical, its rhetoric being aimed not at conviction but at action; the poem is set up rhetorically, and also set intentionally, as illocutionary and perlocutionary: it wants to induce a mood which will lead to kinds of action it nowhere mentions (and in that sense, too, it is extra-catechistical). As we read it there is a certain strain or violence between the first stanzas and the final one. A leap is required, and the attention is caught up into the austerity of abstract definition after having been permitted the delectation of beautiful transiences that instance our whole space and time: day, rose, spring. A stanza each, in calm equipoise, is accorded these three. "Vertue" can be the fourth of these only after a theological point which is easy to make but hard to assimilate—and in this way the poem can also be called subliminally catechistical.

In fact, as against Fish, this reader is oddly inert. He is not on the path of a catechized convert, but rather moves both to and from a state of psychic rest, because the poem is probing nothing and discovering nothing, only celebrating and affirming, even when it dramatizes tentatives and unveils conclusions.

II

A devotional audience is stipulated in the final couplet of Herbert's six-line "Dedication": "Turn their eyes hither, who shall make a gain: / Theirs, who shall hurt themselves or me, refrain." This blunt statement relegates to subordinate status much of the qualification involved in accounting for Herbert's mental play. The yield is unequivocally to be ethical-devotional as an assumption prior to reading, before the church porch of his overarching "temple" metaphor has even been approached. Such a distinction about audience the famous preacher Donne does not make for his poems. The simplicity for which Herbert aimed remains an overall ordering, tonal, and metrical, articulation of a posited concord. Take "Love (III)," the poem which, like many, reverts to a subject already treated, because the simple postulates of this key theological virtue are implicitly expandable enough, like the interpretation of Biblical verses,[9] to allow for further amplification under the same title:

Love (III).

Love bade me welcome: yet my soul drew back,
                Guiltie of dust and sinne.
But quick-ey'd Love, observing me grow slack
                From my first entrance in,
Drew nearer to me, sweetly questioning,
                If I lack'd any thing.

A guest, I answer'd, worthy to be here:
> Love said, You shall be he.
I the unkinde, ungratefull? Ah my deare,
> I cannot look on thee.
Love took my hand, and smiling did reply,
> Who made the eyes but I?

Truth Lord, but I have marr'd them: let my shame
> Go where it doth deserve.
And know you not, sayes Love, who bore the blame?
> My deare, then I will serve.
You must sit down, sayes Love, and taste my meat:
> So I did sit and eat.

FINIS

Glory be to God *on high*
> *And on earth peace*
>> *Good will toward men.*

This last, and capping, poem in *The Temple* can conclude by changing its meter and dropping its rhyme for the simple quotation of a phrase from the liturgy of Holy Communion, giving it no more modulation than a tripling, reminiscent of Biblical verse, into nearly equivalent clausulae. The poem's surface enchains a simple narrative in simply framed sentences, but these are based on a rich substructure of Biblical echoes and allusions, as Chana Bloch points out.[10]

As here between the speaker and Love, there are fixed antitheses throughout Herbert's poetry, between the visible world and Vertue, sin and salvation, "quickness" and "Dulnesse" in the poem of that title, man and the rest of creation; and both taken together in contrast to God ("Providence"), contrasting gifts between God and what the poet feigns to exchange with him ("Hope"). In "Time," the situation before the redemption stands in antithesis to the situation afterward. These antitheses tend to predominate over even progressive poems like "The Quip" or "The Collar." The progressions are structured into this contrastive equipoise, with all their dynamic internal backtrackings, through the regular containment (rarely run-over) of the individual stanza.[11]

As throughout Herbert's poetry, the antitheses are not completely balanced and the paradoxes do not finally hold, because they are at the service of the overriding devotional intention at which the rhetoric, too, aims the statement.[12] In "Sion" the title refers to both the earthly and the heavenly Jerusalem, and this reference embraces the antithesis between Solomon's temple and the temple within, that of the New Testament, but also of Herbert's embracing metaphor:

Sion.

Lord, with what glorie wast thou serv'd of old,
When Solomons temple stood and flourished!
    Where most things were of purest gold;
    The wood was all embellished
With flowers and carvings, mysticall and rare:
All show'd the builders, crav'd the seeers care.

Yet all this glorie, all this pomp and state
Did not affect thee much, was not thy aim;
    Something there was, that sow'd debate:
    Wherefore thou quitt'st thy ancient claim:
And now thy Architecture meets with sinne;
For all thy frame and fabrick is within.

There thou art struggling with a peevish heart,
Which sometimes crosseth thee, thou sometimes it:
    The fight is hard on either part.
    Great God doth fight, he doth submit.
All Solomons sea of brasse and world of stone
Is not so deare to thee as one good grone.

And truly brasse and stones are heavie things,
Tombes for the dead, not temples fit for thee:
    But grones are quick, and full of wings,
    And all their motions upward be;
And ever as they mount, like larks they sing;
The note is sad, yet musick for a King.

The relation between Old Testament and New is here not just typological. It is also theological; the poem makes a point between outer and inner devotion that is to be found in both Testaments. In its own terms Solomon's temple was a "glory," and so Herbert is not just reviving that veneration (though he is concessively doing that), and he is not even just repeating the idea of the body as a temple (2 Cor 6.16 and passim) or the "temple not made with hands" of the New Testament (Acts 17.24). The three stages of *The Temple* taken as a whole, and so specifically applied in this poem, can be taken to imply the three stages of the Christian life: conversion, purification, and salvation. And it can also be expanded to the patristic scheme in which the porch is the earth and the temple itself the heaven of the afterlife.[13] The fullness of attention given in the praise of the first stanza is not ironic; it is the thesis which will receive an antithesis and already implies a synthesis, a synthesis picked up in the last line as it reframes another antithesis, "The note is sad, yet musick for a King."

The turn of the second stanza, "Something there was, that sow'd debate," presents a temporal sequence in which the emergence of "sinne," the name for the "something," gives way to an overall condition, where the confrontation of sin in the events of the New Testament cannot here be taken to worsen the human condition. So "now thy Architecture meets with sinne" indicates not the ruination of the Temple but its redefinition, as becomes even clearer in the antithesis of the third stanza, where this friend of the King James translator Lancelot Andrewes touches on the "sea of brasse," a curious term for a ritual basin in the Old Testament account of Solomon's temple (I Kings 7.23–26), "All Solomons sea of brasse and world of stone / Is not so deare to thee as one good grone." Caesurae mark the emergence of antitheses, and they persist in the break of the last line. Yet antitheses themselves, the "grones" and "motions" are "musick for a King." And as Joseph Summers says, "Within most of the individual poems the emphasis is on construction rather than pilgrimage."[14]

Speaking of the "resolutely dialectical" nature of Herbert's poems, Barbara Harman points out that "the speaker of 'The Reprisall' sunders himself from the text in an act of self-relinquishment, but also binds himself to the text in an act of self-generation."[15] But these opposing motions are not contradictory. Self-generation supervenes over and rewards self-relinquishment. The poem starts and ends from the security of doctrinal adherence, and all the processes of self-qualification are grace notes on the ground of that fundamental and many-dimensioned assumption. The many dimensions are theological, and to the degree that they aim at an enlightened orthodoxy, they are catechistical, as Fish insists; but also they are devotional. Not just conviction is their aim, but also a state of "heart," to use Herbert's habitual term. In this they give a direction, at once special and conventional, to their poetic character, which remains stubbornly, but also triumphantly, inaccessible to the mere unpacking of the poem's propositions. Their effect must be allowed for their message to be coordinately understood.

III

Such a process is envisioned in the poetics that can be extracted from Herbert's poetry. As Arnold Stein says:

> As the visible church stands truly, beautifully, but imperfectly for the invisible church, so do the "sweet phrases, lovely metaphors" express imperfectly the "True beautie" on high. In its plainness the essential expression, "Thou art still my God," will fulfill the end of expression, "And if I please him, I write fine and wittie." The essentiality of the expression, when one contemplates its meaning, by itself and in the context of the poem, would seem to be better established than the poet's assurance of writing "fine and wittie." That claim one may perhaps regard as a little assertive, markedly different from the persuasive tact with which art demonstrates the limitations of art in the argument of the poem. . . . We may perhaps regard "Thou art still my God" as a symbolic plainness, an ideal to which his poetic art of plainness may aspire, but it is not itself an expression of that art.[16]

"The Quidditie," beginning with what a verse is not, first limits poetry and then enigmatically expands it:

> My God, a verse is not a crown,
> No point of honour, or gay suit,
> No hawk, or banquet, or renown,
> Nor a good sword, nor yet a lute:
>
> It cannot vault, or dance, or play;
> It never was in *France* or *Spain*;
> Nor can it entertain the day
> With my great stable or demain:
>
> It is no office, art, or news,
> Nor the Exchange, or busy Hall;
> But it is that which while I use
> I am with thee, and *most take all*.

John Middleton Murry's gloss reads the enigma of the last three words as meaning that poetry embraces all the activities of which the poem is a census, but only via God. One can also take it the other way; it is poetry that enables the orientation toward God of which the census of other activities is then an ordered corollary that would otherwise find them scattered, as they are separate in the enumeration here. The power is evidenced in the leap to generalization that the maxim abruptly caps, "Most take all." The maxim, as though quoted for proverbial force, can be given the general force of a proverb, so that what is excluded from poetry can be finally included in it, "Most take all."[17] But also, *"Most,"*—if read as a noun and subject of a subjunctive "take" instead of (alternatively) as an adverb modifying "[I] take"—may also refer to the supreme topic of this poetry, God, who is not paradoxically different from it because the poetry leads up to Him. In that application of the proverb, included in its generality, both poetry and all other activities that are legitimate and human would be taken by the "Most," which is God. The simplicity of the convergence in the language here need not resume any logical train, because first the initial act of devotion, and then the poetry, have done that work. The scholastic essence, the "quiddity," of the poem's title, disappears into the very function it names, that of bringing poetry close to God.

A smoother reading of this line would have the verb "take" not as the imperative, with "Most" as the subject, but as the first person singular, setting it in parallel to "I am with thee," a reading which would continue Herbert as the speaker at the center of the activity. In this reading "Most" becomes an adverb. Still, the comma before "and" and the italicization of "Most take all" would endorse reading the phrase in the separate, proverbial sense, as I have done. But whichever of these readings, both ambiguously present in an Empsonian sense, may be taken as predominant, they enrich the poem by their interaction if both are allowed to be present: God takes all, and therefore I follow him in having poetry do so.[18]

The term "fiction" in "Jordan (I)" abjures a long tradition, rooted even in a religious poetry, as exemplified by Dante's description of his *Comedy* as a fiction, a *fictio rhetorica musica composita*, a rhetorical fiction put together with music. While Herbert does aim for his poetry to be *musica composita*, it would be alien to his act to stress the element of *fictio rhetorica* in it. Fiction is inescapable, as inherent in the modalization of any successful poem. But fiction is not foregrounded here, and no Stevensesque reflexivity names as a fiction Herbert's denial of fiction.

The self-instantiation of the thinking and phrasing that issue in a poem is not fictionalized or reflected, but rather devotionally offered as an instance of God's grace. Or, as Herbert says in "The Thanksgiving," "If thou shalt give me wit, it shall appear, / If thou hast giv'n it me, 'tis here."

In Jordan (I) the notion of poetry begins with a challenge, whose rhetorical questions do not abjure beauty for religious poetry, but rather assert it:

> Who sayes that fictions onely and false hair
> Become a verse? Is there in truth no beautie?

In the tribe of poetry, he demands inclusion while allowing for variety:

> Shepherds are honest people; let them sing:
> Riddle who list, for me, and pull for Prime:
> I envie no mans nightingale or spring;
> Nor let them punish me with losse of rime,
>   Who plainly say, *My God, My King.*

"Jordan (II)" enters the same area of definition from a different angle:

> *Jordan (II).*
>
> When first my lines of heav'nly joyes made mention,
> Such was their lustre, they did so excell,
> That I sought out quaint words, and trim invention;
> My thoughts began to burnish, sprout, and swell,
> Curling with metaphors a plain intention,
> Decking the sense, as if it were to sell.
>
> Thousands of notions in my brain did runne,
> Off'ring their service, if I were not sped:
> I often blotted what I had begunne;
> This was not quick enough, and that was dead.
> Nothing could seem too rich to clothe the sunne,
> Much lesse those joyes which trample on his head.
>
> As flames do work and winde, when they ascend,
> So did I weave my self into the sense.
> But while I bustled, I might heare a friend
> Whisper, *How wide is all this long pretence!*
>
> *There is in love a sweetnesse readie penn'd:*
> *Copie out onely that, and save expense.*

The view that metaphor is a hindrance to the truth rather than an aid, working "to clothe the sunne," is not only a rhetorical pretense. It is also a principle of communication, odd for poetic communication but central to it in this particular poetry, which is singular for pretending to confine itself ideally to the "plain intention" and to an automatic fluency, "a sweetness readie penn'd," that is a sign of love. The gesture begins as a derivation from what could be called the sincerity trope, to be found persistently in Shakespeare's Sonnets and in Sidney's "Look in thy heart and write." But it does not end there. For this love is one which is not conditioned by the vagaries of the object, as in the sonnet tradition, but exclusively by those of the subject.

The music of this poem aims its rhyme scheme toward stepped convergences of simplicity: first it drops feminine endings in the second stanza, and then it drops any assonantal variation in the third. These stepped rhymes go to the expense of saving expense by a fluency whose economy would have to have been achieved by a sort of calculation. And the relation between the title and the poem modifies the poem's main goal—since that title, arbitrary and wilful enough, is a rich addition, an allegorical extension of *The Temple* into the Biblical landscape—but does not at the same time enlist it directly. The Jordan, nowhere hinted at or figuratively worked over in the text of the poem, serves obscurely as an instrument toward plainness. Reach the Jordan, it is saying, and the sense of Jordan will be plain.

The desired effect of this poetry draws on and names a range of effects that depend on the religious effect for their frame. "Let the wonder of his pity / Be my dittie," Herbert says in "The Banquet," and the bounty imagined at that table is a delicious one:

> O what sweetnesse from the bowl
> >   Fills my soul,
> Such as is, and makes divine!
>
> Is some starre (fled from the sphere)
> >   Melted there,
> As we sugar melt in wine?

Herbert links the power of a religious poetry to the choice of eschewing the secular love lyric, where Dante conflated the two, and Donne, like Marvell, sees no need to press the question to a decision. As Herbert says in a sonnet quoted from Walton's *Life* (and not in *The Temple*), "Cannot the Dove / Out-strip their Cupid easily in flight / Or since thy wayes are-deep, and still the same / Will not a verse run smooth that bears thy name?" Here the two attributes gained are "smooth" and "deep," but these depend on each other not exactly as literary goals, or not exclusively. They derive as a possibility that can be actualized after the subject matter has been chosen. This amounts to an exclusion on Herbert's part of the deep connections between secular love and its various religious counterparts, an exclusion that radically revises the possibilities of fusion that had operated since the troubadors and of which Dante's inclusion of Beatrice in the *Divina Commedia* is a supreme example.

In Herbert's immediate background the fusion remains still present; the line between the earthly Venus and the heavenly, as in Italian Renaissance Neoplatonism, can be taken as so endemic to the poetic perception that it can shade over into a generalized Christianity. Even the Virgin can be mentioned equivocally in this odd connection. Such is the case of the "Virgin Queene" not only of Spenser's *Faerie Queene*, but of the figure, mainly Platonic, for which he produces effusions in his "Hymn in Honour of Beauty." Spenser offers the full form of this demotic expression that by his time has become endemic to Renaissance poetry, and which Herbert is emphatic in avoiding. Its minimal form, in a simplicity akin to Herbert's—but these are the words of a song—is well illustrated in Jonson's "To Celia":

> Drink to me only with thine eyes,
> And I will pledge with mine;
> Or leave a kiss but in the cup,
> And I'll not look for wine.
> The thirst that from the soul doth rise,
> Doth ask a drink divine:
> But might I of Jove's nectar sup,
> I would not change for thine.

The second stanza of this poem presents a matching eight lines in which a wreath sent to the beloved seems not to wither, but to grow and smell of her because "thou thereon did'st only breathe." This fictive biology is, of course, a conceit on Jonson's part. It is what Herbert means by "fiction," and for us, as for the Renaissance, it is the very stuff of poetry, allowing for the substitution of a potion strictly speaking impossible for the wine of the cup, and for a comparison with the nectar of a Jove in whom the poet advertises the fictiveness of his belief, since here we cannot make Jove any sort of analogue to the Christian God. At the same time "The thirst that from the soul doth rise, / Doth ask a drink divine" puts in simple form much of Spenser's Neoplatonism. This poem delectates in its ironic, and again demotically minimalist, adoption of the false-fictive as conventionally true, by way of what can be at least three turns of assertion and counterassertion from the rough early Roman faith in Jupiter.[19] This poem, so to speak, is framed as a compliment, a match for the kiss left in the cup, an adjunct to the returned gift of the breathed-upon wreath. In such trifles does the courtly lover-as-singer glory. And the possibility of such trivialization does the austere Herbert abjure, so that a gravity impels Herbert's "bowl" in "The Banquet," controlling and expanding his conceit of a star melting in the divine drink as sugar melts in wine.

"Herbert's interpretation of his experience of relationship to God is revealingly analogous to the act of interpretation performed by the reader of his verse."[20] This is so if by "interpretation" we include what resists interpretation, the whole act of apprehending the poem. Like all poems, it has a bright (or, if one wishes, dark) presence that resists interpretation, but in Herbert's poems that presence converges with the doctrinal as well as with the devotional. Donne's religious poetry refers to the doctrinal and the devotional, but it does not enlist them in this way; it is not exactly aimed toward them. And the poetry of Vaughan is aimed even further toward the devotional, that of Crashaw toward exuberance about the devotional.

For Herbert, poetry derives directly from the Savior's act of redemption. As he says in "Easter," "His stretched sinews taught all strings, what key / Is best to celebrate this most high day." The metaphors in his poetry often meld the extravagant and the conventional:

The Bunch of Grapes.

Joy, I did lock thee up: but some bad man
                Hath let thee out again:
And now, me thinks, I am where I began
                Sev'n yeares ago: one vogue and vein,
                One aire of thoughts usurps my brain.
I did toward Canaan draw; but now I am
Brought back to the Red sea, the sea of shame.

For as the Jews of old by Gods command
                Travell'd, and saw no town;

So now each Christian hath his journeys spann'd:
     Their storie pennes and sets us down.
     A single deed is small renown.
Gods works are wide, and let in future times;
His ancient justice overflows our crimes.

Then have we too our guardian fires and clouds;
     Our Scripture-dew drops fast:
We have our sands and serpents, tents and shrowds;
     Alas! our murmurings come not last.
     But where's the cluster? where's the taste
Of mine inheritance? Lord, if I must borrow,
Let me as well take up their joy, as sorrow.

But can he want the grape, who hath the wine?
     I have their fruit and more.
Blessed be God, who prosper'd *Noahs* vine,
     And made it bring forth grapes good store.
     But much more him I must adore,
Who of the Laws sowre juice sweet wine did make,
Ev'n God himself being pressed for my sake.

This poem aims a range of nonce metaphors out of the accepted situation of the transforming power of the New Testament on the Old, culminating in the one of the title (which is therefore held in suspension through the poem), a metaphor at once traditional for the Old Testament and daringly conceited for the New, since Christ is the wine of the communion. But to see that wine as pressed from a bunch of grapes is an innovatively vivid use of a central theological identification. It is vivid, shocking, and confirming, all at once. The first-named entity in the poem, "Joy," is an abstraction. The initial motion is to go backward after having gone forward, and the spatial result of the "theft" of joy after seven years expands into the Exodus metaphors that are a favorite of the Biblical prophets. The backward motion entails a counter-Biblical one; the speaker goes back (metaphorically) from Canaan to the Red Sea. This in a situation that the congruent metaphor of the next statement controls, with its new contrast between the "Jews of old" who "saw no town" and the individual "Christian" whose journeys are "spanned."

Contemplating this situation, and its power in the wide justice of God to "let in future times," the speaker and his like return to a proper Exodus, with fires and clouds, manna, sands, tents, and even shrouds. The question about wine at first separates wholly from the image of a promised land and its produce, "But can he want the grape, who hath the wine?" "I have their fruit and more," and the question has introduced the juxtaposition, unusual if still typological, between Noah and Christ, with the crucial difference that Noah has the grape, whereas Christ, being Testament and Produce and Person all in one, conflates and focuses the whole process: "Who of the Laws sowre juice sweet wine did make, / Ev'n God himself being pressed for my sake." This is indeed new wine in new bottles (Matt. 9.17; Mark 2.22; Luke 5.37–38), so comprehensively that there are no bottles. The phantasmagoria of the "bunch" in the title is now blurred into theological condensations; but the metaphoric properties highlighted by the special twist of this identification between Christ and the bunch of grapes stand, as always in Herbert, at the service of a doctrinal deduction, whose climactic force is included in the overall rhetoric. The homeliness added to the sacrament by the "bunch" of the title as it carries through to the end, twists the significative structure, lightening it and riddling it at one stroke.

As Vendler says (*The Poetry of George Herbert*, 97) of "The Pilgrimage," "The conquering of allegorical narrative by lyric dialogue, the transformation of past-tense recapitulation into present speech, the abandonment of manned stations in favor of anonymous encounter, all make this poem a very peculiar example of 'allegory'"—but also a very transparent one. For as she goes on, at the same time, "any allegorical or emblematic form, in Herbert's hands, is undergoing a constant critique of its own possibilities comparable with, but not identical to, the continuing critique of his own feelings so pervasively conducted in the lyrics" (99).

So, keeping metaphor and psychological process in tandem, "The Forerunners" begins with an elaborate metaphor whose terms do not twist the syntax in Donne's fashion. Rather they are simply packed into the statements: the harbingers who go before a royal progress into a town chalking the doors where the monarch will be staying are compared to the signs of approaching death. In the metaphor then, the unmentioned royal presence is God, but it is also death, and at the same time the body is the town. All these metaphoric connections are traceable to standard religious figures or to poetic ones (notably for the last, Phineas Fletcher's *The Purple*

Island, in which the body is also presented under a geographical figure). But the combination is Herbert's.

This first stanza dwells not on intrications of the metaphor but of questioning psychological consequences: will the harbingers take over?

> The harbingers are come. See, see their mark;
> White is their colour, and behold my head.
> But must they have my brain? must they dispark
>
> Those sparkling notions, which therein were bred?
>   Must dulnesse turn me to a clod?
> Yet have they left me, *Thou art still my God*.

The full, reassuring answer to whether the white hair means that the harbingers will "have my brain" is given in the last couplet: "Let a bleak palenesse chalk the doore, / So all within be livelier then before."

After speaking of a "dittie" in which "I write fine and wittie," Herbert once again exalts the plain style and confirms the rejection of love poetry, so that his "sweet phrases, lovely metaphors" he has "Brought . . . to church well drest and clad." But beauty is not exactly abjured, or the relation between truth and beauty. Rather, it is redefined:

> True beautie dwells on high: ours is a flame
>   But borrow'd thence to light us thither.
> Beautie and beauteous words should go together.

Since the attributes and direction of his poetry have been the main subject, the word "livelier" must refer immediately to them: the "drest" religious verse is more vivid, as verse, than another kind would be. It is more vivid because more devotional. But the "sparkling notions" of the first stanza, matched here against the speaker's fear that "dulnesse" will turn him to a clod, are a more general activity of his "brain"; poetry is a main but still subsidiary effect. And to be "dis-parked" complicates all the other metaphors with a light reference to Eden. Since human life and the aging process have been the continuous topic, "livelier" must also include them, and the devout speaker will be fuller of life at the moment that death has chalked his door. Beyond all this, he is livelier because he expects the promised heightening of the afterlife. Superior verse, superior thoughts, an improved condition in this world, and the superlative condition in the other, are all included in the single world "livelier," in the comprehensive convergence which it at once names and illustrates.

Indeed, when Herbert says, "Lovely enchanting language, sugar-cane, / Hony of roses, whither wilt thou flie? / Hath some fond lover tic'd thee to thy bane? / And wilt thou leave the Church, and love a stie?" he implies not the abandonment of ornamental embellishments to a poem but a rhetorical direction for them. The very fact that he equivocates in this matter—and "Sion" among other poems can be adduced as a counter-example—means not that he contradicts himself, but that in the last analysis embellishment is indifferent one way or the other. The plain, unornamented style notable in "Discipline," "Antiphon I," "Antiphon II," and "Praise II" (these must be among the simplest successful poems in the language) serves only as a ground bass for extravagances like the metaphorical structure of "The Forerunners," which is Donne-like in its underlying, but not in its surface, intrication.

The dialectic is omnipresent but the elements are not in suspension. They are calm. The integrity of faith—the intended yield of the poem first for the dramatized poet and then for the reader—preponderates, as appears in its very metric.[21] Here the strenuousness of Donne's logic has been transposed into the meter, but then muted. We can see these motions at work through the entire poem:

The Forerunners.

The harbingers are come. See, see their mark;
White is their colour, and behold my head.
But must they have my brain? must they dispark
Those sparkling notions, which therein were bred?
              Must dulnesse turn me to a clod?
Yet have they left me, *Thou art still my God.*

Good men ye be, to leave me my best room,
Ev'n all my heart, and what is lodged there:
I passe not, I, what of the rest become,
So *Thou art still my God*, be out of fear.
              He will be pleased with that dittie;
And if I please him, I write fine and wittie.

Farewell sweet phrases, lovely metaphors.
But will ye leave me thus? when ye before

> Of stews and brothels onely knew the doores,
> Then did I wash you with my tears, and more,
> > Brought you to Church well drest and clad:
> My God must have my best, ev'n all I had.
>
> Lovely enchanting language, sugar-cane,
> Hony of roses, whither wilt thou flie?
> Hath some fond lover tic'd thee to thy bane?
> And wilt thou leave the Church, and love a stie?
> > Fie, thou wilt soil thy broider'd coat,
> And hurt thy self, and him that sings the note.
>
> Let foolish lovers, if they will love dung,
> With canvas, not with arras, clothe their shame:
> Let follie speak in her own native tongue.
> True beautie dwells on high: ours is a flame
> > But borrow'd thence to light us thither.
> Beautie and beauteous words should go together.
>
> Yet if you go, I passe not; take your way:
> For, *Thou art still my God*, is all that ye
> Perhaps with more embellishment can say.
> Go birds of spring: let winter have his fee;
> > Let a bleak palenesse chalk the doore,
> So all within be livelier then before.

The motion of query and reply governs the regularity of the progression here. In addition, there is an extravagance in the motion that permits the dialogue-key shift of the last line of the first stanza as it introduces the refrain, "Yet have they left me, *Thou art still my God*." There are comparable key-shifts in the recurrence of the refrain. One could go through the metrical ordering of the poem noticing the syllabic exactness of this music. Overriding that exactness, the rhythmic correlative of certitude, a wondering and stretching is operative—and what the poet endows with an air of questioning is actually well known. The whole metaphorical structure, mysterious in the title, is revealed at once in the first two lines, while at the same time the effects of the forerunners linger. Nor is it entirely a fancy; "must they have my brain" surely indicates what we now know as Alzheimer's disease, though the actual poet, as distinct from the speaker of the poem, died too young to have been much at risk. The reprise of the second stanza broaches a politeness perhaps covering an anxiety, the normal attitude to royal officers who are making demands. This attitude is sustained in the voiced thought that "He will be pleased with that dittie"; and this first fillip of a feminine ending circles back to the question of the religious direction of a poetry which, with a proper attitude, may have grace notes accorded it that are signs of grace, "And if I please him, I write fine and wittie."

Yet in the next stanza he first relinquishes the "sweet phrases, lovely metaphors," and then regrets their absence, going on to contemplate their proper use and dwelling on it in a still further lingering that aerates this tone of pause and wonder. The next stanza restates the opposition between secular love poetry and this sacred verse by abjuring the former. In the dramatic progression here, this gesture induces and occasions a third and last statement of the refrain. There is a return of the governing metaphor that has been hovering over the poem, and the "white" of the second line of the poem returns as the "chalk" at the end. The increase of liveliness that is wished for has also been mimed; the psychological motion and the intellectual-theological constructions of the metaphor fit together, but not neatly. Their relation is actually loose, just as the progressions are seemingly random. Their security in the devotional adherence and evocation of the poet permit and even celebrate such looseness: in devotion, his powers wax; they do not wane. And the whole is a foretaste of what by definition cannot be concretely known, the life of final union with God that cannot come in this world.

Even the lightness of the "aspergings" in the very long, gnomic poem *Perirrhanterium* are firmly devotional-prudential, a long series of recommendations for behavior in the rhetorical set of the nearly contemporary Spanish aphorist Gracian, but with virtually no play of worldly cynicism. As Herbert says at the end of the first of these seventy-seven sestets, "A verse may finde him, who a sermon flies, / And turn delight into a sacrifice." These recommendations are expansions of proverbs, or else sub-proverbial, in that they sound like proverbs but elide the proverbial point into a ratiocination sometimes obscure. Proverb itself is not only a Biblical form but a rhetorical staple for poetry in the West at least since the time of Theognis; and it implies in itself not one rhetorical gesture but a converging rich set of rhetorical constraints and social-philosophical assumptions.[22] If one may conceive of the single abstraction of a title as related to the proverb through the slightly different enunciation of a single principle, then comparably do many of his poems anchor themselves on the simple, direct, single, theological noun of their titles: "Vertue," "Peace," "Love," "Redemption," "Repentance," "Confession," "Divinity," "Faith," and so on.

"The Forerunners" speaks not only of death but of the good death often broached at the time, an expectation related to the circumstance that these poems and Donne's, as well as many others, were published posthumously.[23] The transmission of Herbert's book is linked with his good death, as Izaak Walton recounts it in his "Life of Mr. George Herbert": "Sir, I pray deliver this little Book to my dear brother Farrer [Nicholas Farrer, founder of Little Gidding], and tell him, he shall find in it a picture of the many spiritual Conflicts that have past betwixt God and my Soul, before I could subject mine to the will of Jesus my Master: in whose service I have now found perfect freedom; desire him to read it: and then, if he can think it may turn to the advantage of any dejected poor Soul, let it be made publick: if not, let him burn it: for I and it, are less than the least of God's mercies." Yet Herbert's very confidence in God allows him the sort of freedom that a familiar language evidences, as later with Emily Dickinson. He takes for granted that death is a gain for those who benefit from the Salvation. In his statement (from "Death"), "But since our Saviors death did put some blood / Into thy face," there seems to be no strain, and not any triumph, but simply a notion of death as the portal to resurrection, a notion which the tone and direction of the poetry accommodates and masters.

IV

In the academic setting where he had reached easy success in his youth, Herbert mastered the professional rhetoric of his time to the degree that he was appointed to the post of Public Orator at Oxford, which he held for seven years, earning the praise of the king. This role was often a stepping stone to a post as Secretary of State. When he gave up these illustrious prospects to become a homely country parson, Herbert set the conditions for a relation to the public world that, on the evidence, allowed him firmly to purge from his poetry a manifest relation to politics.[24] He turned that relation, which was a long and varied one for such predecessors and contemporaries as Sidney, Spenser, Donne, Milton, and Marvell, into one of simple and austere negation. His step followed a pattern to be found in many societies, of retreat from the world, the most spectacular example in the Renaissance being the retreat of Emperor Charles V—on one of whose religous counsellors Herbert commented at length—from his lofty position to a monastery. The Anglican religious community of Little Gidding became a main reference point for Herbert's devotional life, as well as for the literary activity based on it. This capital move gives his poetry the boundary-definition we associate with pastoral, but as Annabel Patterson and others have shown us, even pastoral echoes into and refers to politics. Vergil's *Eclogues* all have a political dimension that appears variously in the poetry and in the careers of Dante, and also of Spenser, Donne, and Milton.[25] Even Marvell, for all his lightness, felt that pressure, often lightly. And the mix of lightness entered into his most explicitly political lyric poem, the *Horatian Ode*.[26]

In Herbert, that worldliness is present only through the poet's sensitivity to the psychological motions that are the stock-in-trade of the courtier. And perhaps also, if we follow Marion White Singleton, there is a congruence between his posture toward God and the posture that he once entertained toward the king and has eliminated, except in its formal traces, from his poetry. "A poem like 'Discipline'," she says, "enacts a reconstructed relationship to God: here the self maintains identity because God's courtier has rewritten his speech to God and thereby revised the roles both God and self are to play."[27] While there is no obvious reference to the courtly in this poem, Singleton is able (*God's Courtier*, 190–93) to characterize its marked simplicity as an embodiment of a courtly ideal for expression, and to trace similarities between Herbert's relation to God and the courtier's relation to a monarch.

The social gesture of the Orator has been made to disappear into the poem, in any case. The seriousness of the Anglican Herbert wholly foregrounds the conceptual-theological; so the resonance of his work lies not preponderantly in the metaphors he uses, for example, but beyond them in the underlying devotion, a source conceived of as inexhaustible. This reliance permits many of the poems to have the same title: they take the posture of aiming toward an infinitely expansible core of doctrine. In that rhetorical disposition they are distantly akin to Midrashic commentary on Scripture. The repose underlying his expressed certitude endows this poet with a freedom from modulating his relation to the mythic. He can take his Christian picture for granted—window, rose, altar, and so forth, are harmonized both as fiction (the Temple) and as realities (the congruent devotional life, the Church).

The base of a scriptural and theological matrix to draw on as source and reference makes for a "classical" style, as Donald Davie has shown for the hymns of Watts and Wesley.[28] But these hymns, like the psalms to which Herbert's work is often compared, posit a collective and not an individual speaker. The singer, imagined or real, resonates into a group, and the poetic experience is socialized into the religious experience directly. Herbert's poems, though his speaker in contradistinction to the speaker of a hymn is intensely individual, in some ways do resemble the best hymns, in ways that differentiate both from an exploratory poetry, even a religious poetry like that of Dickinson, which attempts original theological definition,[29] or Hopkins's attempt to turn visual perception to the intensification of theological commonplace.

V

Barbara Herrnstein Smith draws some sharp and convenient distinctions between the intention to write a poem and the function of an actual published document, as in the case of "greeting card" verse, where the (possible) poetic intention is nullified by the use of the text as a phatic greeting on Mother's Day or a birthday; and also, contrariwise, the "message" adaptation of separate sentences from whole poems as carriers of proverbial wisdom: "Frailty, thy name is woman," "Neither a borrower nor a lender be," and the like.[30]

The Temple is a sort of intermediate case. As edificational, it is confirmatory, and so it has not left the phatic "greeting card" message wholly behind. But it is also a repository of aesthetic value. It aims to be good and beautiful together, as well as happening to be ethically good—or our having to assume it is good in order to read it properly. In this sense, however deeply its rhetoric enlists the catechistical, it is finally counter-catechistical: the edificational is celebratory, and the celebration acts to confirm by engaging a mood of uplift or exaltation for which the traditional term is "the sublime."

As for the distinction Kant used, superficially one could contrast Donne to Herbert as sublime to beautiful, except that the convergences effectuated by Herbert make him both sublime and beautiful at once. The surface of "Vertue" is beautiful, but the conclusion, and the very title, aim at the sublime. Or one could say generally, staying with Kant's usage, that the poems use the proportionality of the beautiful as a means to attain the vastness of the sublime. Continuing such an arbitrary schematism, it can be said that for Herbert man apprehends, organizes, and creates a set of beautiful gestures (or learns to reject those that are not beautiful) in order to gain access to the sublime in God, which at the same time, in its immensity of adaptability, meets him more than halfway continually. The sublime stretches and validates the human capacity.

As much recent discussion has shown, the effort, praiseworthy if inescapably arbitrary, to give a name and find a crucial territory for a sense of the sublime, can result in powerful phenomenological, philosophical, and psychological extrapolations. Harold Bloom touches, if too simply, on the relationship between the sublime and a belief system similar to Herbert's in its constituents, if differently oriented in its presentational logic, that of Wordsworth:

> When Wordsworth speaks of the workings of his spirit, he describes not a believing that something is so but a trusting in a covenant, a covenant made between his adverting mind and a subsuming presence not wholly distinct from his own best aspect. What the spots of time testify to is the astonishing extent of the mind's mastery over the universe of death.[31]

In Wordsworth, actually, believing is operative just as trusting is. For Herbert the trusting goes still deeper; allowing for belief, in both cases, one could substitute his name for Wordsworth's, and Bloom's statement would hold.

The force of conviction, imputed if not held, is necessary to the force of the poetic effect. And Herbert's mechanism is both normative and distinctly his own. So, by contrast, on his own doctrinal ground, the *persona* in union with God is differently visualized in Vaughan as fading into the mystery, "O for that night! where I in him / Might live invisible and dim." (These are the last lines of "The Night.") Neither of these adjectives accords with Herbert's aims. Wordsworth, by contrast, looks not just back in his elaborate strategy for looking back; he also looks forward to "something evermore about to be," a resolution from his expressed tentatives into a future stability through the informed recollection of a past stability. We have learned to hear the tonality of these tentatives resonating with the sublime, or with a poetic force for which "the sublime" is as good a term as any other. Herbert's assumption, at once conventional and daring, conceives of a persona who is distinct in finding himself by losing himself in God. It is the exclusive reliance on this assumption that endows Herbert's poems with their tone of resolution, a deep ground to which all the gestures of self-doubt and strenuous definition can return.

The persona of the speaker, as it undergoes the mutations that recent commentators have diagrammed, gets subsumed into a steadying, unifying and transfiguring presence that he identifies with God. The sublime comes about as the beautiful converges upon the good. Here, in Herbert's poetry, a version of the complex dynamics can be rediagrammed that Joel Fineman shows for Shakespeare's sonnets, starting at the point of the "deictic" use of the pronoun "I." As Fineman says, "In a very formal sense deictics are *always* 'self-conscious' because these 'shifters' as Jakobson calls them, these 'egocentric particulars,' as Bertrand Russell called them, acquire their reference, i.e., they identify their referent from the point of view—personal, temporal, spatial—of the speaker who employs them."[32]

Love, in Shakespeare's hands, however, is vested in shifting persons changeable as to sex, to pairing, and to the responsiveness of both parties in the love, so that the strain is toward a validation of the "powerful rhyme" which "not marble nor the gilded monuments / Of princes" can outlast. For Herbert, on the other hand, the beauty of the poems in one sense disappears into the goodness that is its object, an object unitary, unchanging, and perfectly identified with Love. As Herbert says in "Clasping of Hands," 157, "If I without thee would be mine, / I neither should be mine nor thine." Here identity is not lost or strained by dialectical divisions, but rather fulfilled and pacified by its crucial dependence on moving toward union with God. And as he says in "Whitsunday," "Lord, though we change, thou art the same." At one extravagant point of appeal to God, the poet speaks of himself as cruder than his poem, a division, again, that a response to his prayer will presumably heal: "Verses, ye are too fine a thing, too wise / For my rough sorrows" ("Grief"). All fragmentations, pairings, dialectical postures, are qualified and resolved there, and the poetry enjoys a putative modesty which can become an actualized virtue in itself through the process of going through the sequences it mounts. The fears of aging bring not Shakespeare's "tann'd antiquity" but a presence on the threshold of death "livelier then before." The identification of the good and the beautiful resolves, celebrates, and enlivens all questions. Most has taken all,[33] and the reader has been brought to the wisdom inherent in carrying out this identification.

3. Heidegger and the Wisdom of Poetry

The wisdom of Herbert cannot reside in the standard doctrine on which it bases itself. It must inhere in the whole process, and act, of envisioning the state of peace of which this doctrine is the posited fundament. To begin with, we would want to know what the positive yield of wisdom was for someone not sharing Herbert's beliefs, after this reader had suspended disbelief—a question which would be the same for the admirer of Beckett who did not share the encompassing despair of his works. For both Herbert and Beckett the yield would bear on a newly vivified understanding of psychological processes. But this just characterizes the wisdom, rather than allowing us to define it.

In seeking an answer to the fundamental question of where the wisdom in poetry might lie, Heidegger, still more powerfully than the distinct thinking of Maurice Blanchot, R. P. Blackmur, Jacques Maritain, and Leone Vivante,[1] gets into the clearing (what Heidegger would call a *Lichtung*; also "lighting") by meeting poetry halfway in his language, allowing it and his own philosophical thinking the relaxedness, the *Gelassenheit* that will let it happen the way the poetic language does. This difficult strategy both utilizes and evades the combinatory approach of predicative, enchained propositions. Hermeneutic gambits are substituted for propositions, and left somewhat unfulfilled. The marks of their tentativeness, their double affiliation to ground (*Grund*) and abyss (*Abgrund*) remain in themselves unmediated, so that both ground and abyss can come into play, but without the short circuit of endless supplementing play.[2]

Heidegger locates himself at the paradox between the ineluctable kernel of the poetic statement and the expressive-philosophical utility of the word, between *physis* and *logos*, between the immediacy of the word as an access to Being and the mediation of its evasions from the *Grund* and *Abgrund* that constitute the earth (*Erde*). These paradoxical expressions both mime and evade, in their exaltation of dif-ference (*Unter-schied*), the fixity of the wisdom of which they are a means for giving account. They are indeed on the way to speech, *unterwegs zur sprache*, and they cannot be arrested in the easy refutations of Paul de Man or the comfortable formulations of many early Heidegger advocates, as Gerald Bruns stresses.[3] And from an open Heideggerian point of view even the open approach of Derrida's *différance* arrests the power of the *Unter-schied*, though Derrida has been able to approach poetry in the quasi-Heideggerian method of his books on Francis Ponge and Paul Celan and his address of Trakl.[4] Heidegger's terms, and his procedures, permit (as well, to be sure, as standing to warn against) such extrapolations ahead and backward from them as I am offering here. And what is true of them is true of the wisdom encoded into the poems they house their being in. It is also true of the evasive splitting characterization of truth as a non-forgetting and dis-closure, the *Unverborgenheit* that, after his "turn," Heidegger both repeats and gets beyond, as he says in his dialogue with the Japanese.[5] As he says there of the consistency between his earlier views and his later practice, "That which stays in thinking is the way. And ways of thought secure themselves in secrecy, so that we can go backward and forward, so that even the way back first leads us forward."[6]

Heidegger's identification of the result of thought with the process of thought, and his anchoring of thought in the energy-atoms of the words brought to light by the most skillful usage in poetry and philosophy, at once identifies the two activities, allowing an essence of wisdom to poetry, and separates the two activities through the *Riss* (rift) or *Unter-schied* (difference) that he would assert has characterized all aware usage since Plato's insistence on the One and Aristotle's counter-gambit of insistence on the corollary of twinning or doubling. As he puts it in "Was Heisst Denken" ("What Does Thought Mean?" or "What Calls for Thinking?")—thereby moving beyond the key Cartesian postulate for poetry as well as for philosophy, and in the context of a discussion of Hölderlin—"What is said poeticizing and what is said thinking are never identical. But the one and the other can in different ways say the same thing. This succeeds, however, only when the cleft between poeticizing and thinking splits cleanly and decisively."[7]

Resting on an unarticulated assumption about the authority of the poet as well as about the poem, Heidegger early and late follows the procedure of pressing the words of a few poems, or else of quotation of a poet's remarks, in order to flesh out his own thinking. So the lengthy and central late essay, "The Essence of Language" ("Das Wesen der Sprache") builds itself out of a repeated questioning of separable statements in a poem of Stefan George, and then of other poems.[8] In "Hölderlin and the Essence of Poetry" ("Hölderlin und das Wesen der Dichtung"), he constructs a socio-historical siting and an epistemological-anthropological grounding for both speech and poetry out of five propositions drawn from both prose statements and poems of Hölderlin: "poetry is the most innocent of all occupations"; "speech is the most dangerous of all goods given to man"; "We are a conversation / and can hear one another"; "What abides do poets found"; "Full of profit, and so poetically / does man dwell on the earth."[9] And so, consistently, he reads his way in others of these essays at great length through the separable assertions in Hölderlin's poems "Wie wenn am Feiertage" ("As When on the Holiday") and "Andenken" ("Remembrance").[10]

His longer disquisition on "Andenken" contains a "warning against the mere admiration for the beauty of the poem," and this warning implicitly draws a line between the beauty of the poem and the statements in the poem from which Heidegger extracts the wisdom of philosophical import, as well as between all the other features of its composition and its sited utterance. Still, I am asserting that if his readings of the statements can hold, then indeed, as the "formalists" assert, the other features are contributory to that wisdom, and one cannot divorce Hölderlin's discovery of apt phrasings from his attentiveness to adaptive sounds and his sense of the reaches and boundaries of his utterance. Hölderlin manages to build his poem from a voice that is at once ruminative and declamatory, pulling the phrases forward that float just a shade over the merely descriptive. Still, the shade beyond the descriptive in "Andenken," and the sounds that embody it, preserve a buoyancy in the poem, and also the modality of its possibilities. Indeed it is that sense of welling up from the depths that seals and measures the statements themselves, in his profound attunement to the Romantic access to something other than the tightly fixed lyric that Goethe practiced.[11] Beyond his separable statements, then, there is a content in Hölderlin's assumption of what Heidegger calls, citing a poem of Rilke, the daring of the poet, a standing forth that allows the sense of affirmative excess, wondering acquiescence, and deep doubt to meld in the words and rhythms of his poems.

Hölderlin, as he interweaves a wondering reach of commentary with his descriptions and evocations of a particular event, manages to strike a rhythmic fullness out of the momentary pullings-apart and pullings-together of urgency and contingency. Thus he distances his subject, the holiday of "Wie wenn am Feiertage," as he is producing the participatory voicings that will bring it into the consciousness of the achieved poem. And at the same time he makes the remembrance and religious memorialization of "Andenken" itself a thrust into a future rather than a recollection, an affirming question rather than a resigning answer. In the conclusion of that poem, much-quoted by Heidegger, "What abides, however, do poets found," there is a revelatory abruptness that Heidegger does not mention. This conclusion can be taken as revelatory not only of the pressure on Hölderlin's expression brought into verse but of the "rift" (*Riss*) that Heidegger finds generally in the most expressive language:

> Nun aber sind zu Indiern
> Die Männer gegangen,
> Dort an der luftigen Spiz'
> An Traubenbergen, wo herab
> Die Dordogne kommt
> Und zusammen mit der prächt'gen
> Garonne meerbreit
> Ausgehet der Strom. Es nehmet aber
> Und giebt Gedächtniss die See,
> Und die Lieb' auch heftet fleissige Augen.
> Was bleibet aber, stiften die Dichter.

> Now, though, to the Indians
> Have the men gone,
> There on the airy peak,
> on vineyard mountains, where down
> comes the Dordogne
> And together with the majestic
> Garonne broad as the sea
> The stream moves out. The sea, though, takes
> and gives remembrance,
> And love, too, holds our zealous eyes.
> What remains, though, do poets found.

The mark of the shift is the logical transition implied, but never fully broached (and not mentioned by Heidegger) in the small word "aber," "though," a word that holds the rift in place and also reveals it as it lets the voice break and elide into the fullness of its expression. The very abruptness of the last line is both anticipated and brought to a crest with this word, which appears three times in the stanza and eight times in the poem, always as a parenthetical expression rather than in its usual function as an introductory conjunction.

Spanning the whole of Europe in his memory, and recalling the vine-covered slopes of French mountains, Hölderlin locates the friends, one of whom he names (Bellarmin) as distant from him. The culminating "aber" puts the fact that poetry abides above the majesty of nature in its everpresent but transitional waters, and also even above love's fixity for zealous eyes. This hierarchy, not mentioned by Heidegger, might be questionable if it were itself fixed into place rather than an instance of the ongoing flow. But poetry is not really separated from nature and love; it is just separately accounted for. Thus is permitted the modality of the understanding this poem attains, which removes the last line from the platitudinous in a way similar to the comparably abrupt ending of Keats's "Ode on a Grecian Urn": "Beauty is all / Ye know on earth, and all ye need to know."

The remembrance and memorialization of "Andenken" is what the poem classifies as its embracing subject. This "Andenken" implies, as Heidegger does say, by its reference to "founding" and "abiding," an inclusion of the future in its present address to the recuperated past (*Erläuterungen zu Hölderlins Dichtung*, 83–84). The assertion leads to an implied address to a deep time beneath the "ordinary" Aristotelian time that already extends and re-fuses the connection between Being and time in *Sein und Zeit*.[12]

As Maurice Blanchot says of Heidegger's reading of Hölderlin, "The poem, by its speech, makes that which is unfounded become foundation, so that the abyss of the day becomes the day/light that makes something arise and that constructs. *Das Heilige sei mein wort*, he acts so that the Sacred is speech and speech sacred."[13] Here Blanchot emphasizes the resurgence into the function of poetry of addressing the numinous that Heidegger honors and reconstitutes by at once addressing and evading terms like "the holy," which here of course Hölderlin avails himself of, and versions of *Geist*, that large term which can be translated both "mind" and "spirit" and is sometimes used in opposition to *Natur*, though Heidegger, like his poets, tries to move onto ground that allows for both terms. Doing so allows for them modally, however, just as in his own practice, throughout his career, he at once programatically avoids such terms for discussion and keeps returning to them for use.[14] Here it should be noted (as once again he does not) that Hölderlin has modalized the frame of his approach to such subjects. The poem being quoted is entitled not "Holiday," but "Wie wenn am Feiertage" ("As When on the Holiday"). The poem quickly gets to the heights of such speculation:

> Drum wenn zu schlafen sie scheint zu Zeiten des Jahrs
> Am Himmel oder unter den Pflanzen oder den Völkern,
> So trauert der Dichter Angesicht auch,

> Sie scheinen allein zu sein, doch ahnen sie immer.
> Denn ahnend ruhet sie selbst auch.
>
> Jetzt aber tagts! Ich harrt und sah es kommen,
> Und was ich sah, das Heilige sei mein Wort.
>
> So when she seems to sleep at times of the year
> In the heaven or among the plants and the peoples,
> So do the faces of the poets mourn,
> They seem to be alone, they have always a foreboding.
> For she herself too rests in foreboding.
>
> Now, though, day breaks! I waited and saw it coming,
> and what I saw, let the holy be my word.

Both the poet and Nature ("she") are in a state of foreboding, *ahnend*. But the poet is alone, and his ability to express the holy is connected to his solitude and derives from it. The melding of absence and presence in the power of his utterance is rooted in the identical situation of his posture toward nature. As Blanchot says, "Both nature and the poet, in the reciprocal implication [and intrication] and because of the reciprocity of their absence are already carried toward one another and in this movement surpass their solitude and their sleep."[15] Again, the reaching of the poem licenses Heidegger to press the term Nature, and to ask what time is meant by "Now" in "Now, though, it is day," or, literally beyond what English will allow, "Now, though, it days," "Jetzt aber tagts!" The poet is sad, but this exclamation point indicates an elation, the fusion of sadness and elation which is a topos in Romantic poets like Keats, Wordsworth, and Leopardi. The "aber," as Heidegger remarks of another occurrence (*Erläterungen zu Hölderlins Dichtung*, 101), seems to indicate an antithesis but transcends its own nascent antithesis in the trans-Hegelian adaptive fusions of the poem, which will sustain in the strength of its utterance all our deductions.

Heidegger not only ascribes truth to just the statements in the poems, and to the combinatory power residing in them that he chooses to exercise. Their truth is a laying bare, in his reading of the Greek term, an *a-letheia* or non-forgetting, an *Unverborgenheit*, an attainment for the poetic utterance that gives it a crucial character in man's awareness of himself, and therefore of access to wisdom.

It would be a mistake to think that Heidegger only listens for the echoes of key words: *Abgrund*, for example, can be found in Rilke, and *Abendgrund* in Trakl, but this is incidental.[16] His area of strategic intervention is the single proposition, which is not exactly detachable, since he locates it in the poem, and not exactly enchained, since he matches it to its other statements, only loosely deducing sequences from it. Yet the question remains, or rather the preponderant conviction, that those features of the poem, some incidental and some global, that he does not discuss will fall in line as acts of Thinking and Saying, along with what he does talk about.

Now, an account that addresses the correspondence of an experience to a complex reality will of necessity be circular; and it will be subject, like any account, to endless supplementation. So Heidegger in *Sein und Zeit* offers one set of descriptive accounts for human existence in general, which later he keeps returning to when he expands on the wisdom in the speech act (*die Sprache*) at its highest, in poetry. Being in time involves an existence that indicates a care-filled awareness that being in the world must be revealed as a being toward death. (*Sorge, In-der-Welt-sein, Seiendes, Dasein, ontisch, ontologisch, Unverborgenheit, Geworfenheit*, are some of the terms Heidegger combines to flesh out this situation, for a *Sein* or being that he says is so inclusive as to be undefinable.) But however much importance we attribute to Heidegger's turn away from such terms, to his "Kehre," he does later supplement them with still others in "The Origin of the Work of Art," where *Erde* is added to *Welt*, *Ding* takes on a special meaning, and *Er-eignis* is adduced to combine the notion of actualization with those of individuation and event.

Suspending the question as to how far one can go with the identity of poetry and philosophy, and of the related question of the power of naming in natural language, Heidegger resorts in the discussion of the broadest category possible, the Being (*Sein*) that even includes "nothing" in its reference, to a poetry that will shed wisdom on, and therefore in some ways implicitly define, the essence of the human condition. His *Introduction to Metaphysics* rises to an explication of the final verses of Sophocles' *Oedipus Rex* and of the first chorus of the *Antigone*, but he easily adduces a verse of Goethe in offering a trans-Aristotelian census of meanings for the verb "to be":

> "Über allen Gipfeln / ist Ruh"; the "ist" cannot be paraphrased, and yet it is only this "ist," tossed off in those few lines that Goethe wrote in pencil on

the window frame of a mountain hut near Ilmenau (cf. his letter to Zelter of September 4, 1831). Strange how we hesitate in our attempted paraphrase and in the end drop it altogether, not because the understanding is too complicated or difficult but because the line is spoken so simply, even more simply and uniquely than any of the other familiar "ists" that are forever dropping unnoticed into our everyday speech.[17]

Heidegger has also risen to this quotation by distinguishing it in a group of others that he astonishingly begins with the simple and most far-reaching theological affirmation (and therefore can have applied to it, from a different angle, his whole survey of the modalities of what it means for Nietzsche and for us to say "God is dead"):[18]

> "God is"; i.e., he is *really present*. "The earth is"; i.e. we experience and believe it to be permanently *there*; "the lecture is in the auditorium"; i.e. it *takes place*. . . . "the peasant is to the fields"; he has gone to the fields and is *staying there*. . . . "Over all the summits / is rest"; that is to say ??? Does the "is" in these lines mean it is situated, is present, takes place, abides? None of these wants to fit. And "ist" is the same simple "is." Or does the verse mean: Over all the summits peace *prevails*, as quiet prevails in a classroom? No. That won't do either. Or perhaps: Over all the summits lies rest—or holds sway? That seems better, but it also misses the mark.[19]

By insisting on the special comprehensiveness, and even on the special mystery, of the commonest words when they occur in poetry, Heidegger points in a direction that bars access to the poem unless one has accepted the premise of wisdom governing the special conditions inherent in the caution against the heresy of paraphrase. This procedure preemptively turns the tables on a deconstructive reading by making such a reading itself part and parcel of the special enlightenment that poetry provides.[20] All the other features of Goethe's poem that might be surveyed in the various hermeneutic approaches to it would thus be subsumed under this general condition and redirected toward this meaning, this *Reden* that is an essentially heightened *Sagen*, as he had originally asserted in his essays on Hölderlin.

Goethe's poem is itself a mysterious counterpart to the Romantic absorption in landscape and to the investment of landscape with numinous power. The simple poem moves to a laconic evocation of the sacred places that go back to Greece and can be found all over the world in cultures like the Japanese and the Navajo:

Über allen Gipfeln
Ist Ruh,

In allen Wipfeln
Spürest du
Kaum einen Hauch;
Die Vögelein schweigen im Walde.
Warte nur, balde
Ruhest du auch.

Over all peaks
Is rest,
On all treetops
You trace
Scarcely a breath.
The little birds are still in the wood.
Just wait, soon
You too rest.

(From *Gedichte der Ersten Mannesjahre*)

Insofar as he intensively extrapolates out of the single word, "ist," Heidegger continues the practice of his earlier readings in Hölderlin. But insofar as he has chosen an example of seemingly casual effusion, written in haste on a window and become classic, he is overriding the sharp distinction in *Sein und Zeit* between *Rede* and *Gerede*, between utterance and casual speech. Here is what appears to be a casual and momentary effusion, arrested into a finality that will bear the weight of the wisdom it is asked to provide. The strength of Heidegger's reading itself permits an extension into the very weight of the individual words here, the rhythms that let the stillness of each individual syllable seem to issue into accent and rhyme, they are so lightly held, like the scarce breath named in the poem. The rhythms seem to be tripping lightly, but also to be pausing, as these short lines suggest in the hush of their progression, as well as in the hush that is their central subject, a rest. By the last line, this *Ruh* has doubled the number of syllables for the line where it makes its assertion, while still occupying exactly half the line as before, and the chiastic order turns the sense and desirability of rest easily upon itself, "Ist Ruh" / . . . / "Ruhest du auch." These two lines also can be heard to produce an effect of whispering, since in them the individual words—four of these five are monosyllabic—are held at a nearly even level of accentuation, the greatest difference of intonation hovering in the "st" of each line, "Ist Ruh" and "Ruhest." The lightness and pause on each of the words of the poem generally, as for the longest of them all, the trisyllabic *Vögelein*, feeds them back into a central experience into which they seal the auditor, word by word, totally.

This poem, indeed, itself constitutes a horizon-fusion, since it is itself an imitation and partial translation of a poem by Alcman (which so far as we know may itself be a fragment):

> There sleep peaks and ravines of mountains,
> Headlands and gullies,
> Creeping tribes, all those black earth nourishes,
> Mountain beasts and the clan of bees,
> And monsters in the depths of the purple sea.
> There sleep the tribes of birds that stretch out their wings.

We cannot say that Goethe has either understood Alcman or misunderstood him. He has merely transposed him, Romanticizing his words by turning the perceptions back to the intimate "du," selecting from Alcman's vast and populous nature only the peaks and the birds (which Goethe miniaturizes), adding the treetops. And the poem of Alcman will retain its force even in the face of our radical inability to orient a reading of it which would locate it in a seventh-century Spartan context. The horizon fails to fuse, far more than with Homer or Hesiod. Nor can we even confidently locate its distances and proximities of semantic field to the other (and for us itself only partial) repertory of poems by Alcman. We could read it as an entire poem, but there is no evidence to its being other than a fragment. It was transmitted in the context of an entry under *knôdalon*, "sea monster," in the Homeric lexicon of Apollonius the Sophist, a figure who lived a good seven hundred years after Alcman. So Apollonius may not have known, but certainly does not transmit, the evidence on which we could approach it hermeneutically.

We cannot even know whether or not it has the religious reference that poems of Alcman do sometimes have. And indeed, at this early date, there is a possibility in this poem, if elsewhere too in Alcman, of the very philosophical reference that Heidegger makes much of in the Pre-Socratics.[21] And it is not clear that the census of creatures of underground, mountain, sea, and lower and upper air is meant to be especially inclusive, the way Apollonius takes it, quoting the lines to locate the *knôdalon* firmly in the sea, where, in Homer's single use, the word had been more general. Is there a stretched significance to the same verb, repeated in the first and last lines, *heudousi*, "they sleep," when it is applied first globally to rugged-

Heidegger and the Wisdom of Poetry

features of landscape and then to varieties of animals? Is there any significance to the exclusion of men and domestic animals or other land animals from the list? We cannot even know they have been excluded, having no evidence to say that the lost text would not have continued to list them (assuming the lines to be a fragment).

Yet we can still respond to the power of the achieved poetic utterance here in the light of Heidegger's insistence on the force of such utterance, even though we cannot fuse our horizon with its, in Gadamer's terms. There is not enough linkage from one horizon to another to effectuate a transformation, for us to "reconstitute its horizon of expectancy," in the terms of Hans Robert Jauss.[22] There is a minimal kernel of poetic energy, an essential one, that transmits into the sense of a wisdom in default of fulfilling such other hermeneutic conditions. Heidegger's approach permits us to read Alcman's "sleep" intensively, the way he has read "ist" in the short poem of Goethe—the very word Goethe has used to translate "sleep," or at least to substitute for it. And the act of speaking encoded into poetry legitimizes our finding the sublimity of wisdom in this poem, an access to some feeling of nature that inheres in the words and rhythms but cannot be fully defined beyond our locating it with reference to various topoi, most of which come later and so are themselves not firmly inclusive of Alcman's lines. We need not point the words out to religion, to the rapture inherent in naming sleep, for the poem to express that rapture.

As we have it the poem moves in assured and varied logaedic rhythms, matching its first two words of the first line, εὔδουσι δ' ὀρέων, to the first two lines of the last, εὔδουσι δ' οἰωνῶν. Before the poem moves into its census of the fauna on these mountains, it has offered a somewhat different description of the mountains themselves, the jagged terrain that strongly in Laconia, and throughout Greece, was felt to be an especially appropriate siting for temples.[23] The heavily formulaic diction of the poem here, at what for us is the outset, avails itself of the reduplicative formulae found especially in the parallelism of Biblical and other religious poetry, though not especially in Greece. Is it significant here that Alcman's traditional birthplace is in the Near East, in Sardis?

εὔδουσι δ' ὀρέων κορυφαί τε καὶ φάραγγες,
πρώονές τε καὶ χαράδραι.

There sleep peaks and ravines of mountains,
Headlands and gullies.

Peaks match headlands, ravines match gullies. The *charadrai*, the gulleys, imply torrents of water swirling through them—or having swirled. The black earth and the purple sea are more generic in nomenclature, as though the poet were focusing on a long view as he gets into the poem, picking up the generic adjective "mountain" for the beasts of the fifth line, a revision of the particular features of mountains with which he had begun. To glory in these skilled variations through varied wisdom is surely to lay claim to the very act of naming that Heidegger celebrates and Apollonius records. The poetic function is a constant under the closely traceable Romantic circumstances of Goethe and under the circumstances of Alcman—so remote they cannot be traced, though Goethe can imitate them.

Throughout his career, either side of the "Kehre," or turn, Heidegger inspects poems for nuggets that are proposition-like. Insofar as he goes on from one such quotation to another, whether early with Hölderlin or late with Trakl, he matches these nuggets one against another. The same could be said of his handling of individual nugget-words, the central technique of many of his essays. For him, as Beda Allemann says, "The structure and the major interconnections of the poem are comprehended with reference to the central word."[24] In this sense, he enchains the key words, concatenating them in a fashion that resembles his practice in the much more expansive *Sein und Zeit*, though he would subcategorize the logical enchainments of the various empiricisms he abjures for their evasiveness. In a characteristic relaxedness toward the assertiveness of the thrust of the individual, resonant words and their interconnections with other words, he effectually asserts—in a way that takes us beyond the merely technical descriptions of Jakobson's projection of the axis of selection on the axis of combination—that the achievement of poetry is to lay bare the possibility for language to have all the resonances and the interconnections. Furthermore, poetry can have these in a way that exhibits a wisdom that need not be parsed, or even deconstructed, in the logical relations the process seems to be implying.

"Language is the world-pathbreaking uttering of the relation of all relations. It relates, converses, reaches and enriches the opposite in the world regions, holds and protects languages while it itself—the uttering—keeps to itself."[25] And as for the relation that obtains between reference and referent, Heidegger bypasses all the intricacies of a Peircean or other analysis of this question that has occupied the intention, and stalled the intentionality, of so many recent commentators. "This relation is not a connection between the thing on the one hand and the word on the other. The word is itself the relation, that at any time so comprises the thing that it itself 'is' a thing."[26] What results is not a simple connection between word and thing, but rather a greater resonance even than the individual word can be made to carry, an indwelling of the speech-act of the poem in the situational rightness of what it has expressed, and so not a solipsistic evasion of reality but a triumphant capturing of it. "The uttering is in no way the expression in speech after the fact of appearances. Rather do all appearance and off-appearance reside in the pointing of uttering. It frees the present into a presence for every case, releases absence into its absence in every case."[27] The large questions of presence and absence are not addressed, nor does Heidegger come down in favor of either. Rather, characteristically, he allows both presence and absence their situational function in the large human situation of finding themselves in a proper apprehension of the poem, which preserves the features of the situation down to, and especially including, what seem to be such contradictions. The contradictions are included positively through the assertion of difference (*Unter-schied*) as a boundary that is enabling as well as restricting, moving word and its object in a connection that allows for both likeness and difference: "The dif-ference for world and thing *locates* things in the gesturing of the world, *locates* world in the favoring of things. The dif-ference is in the fullest case a dimension for world and thing."[28]

The procedure here, while not so different from the one that Heidegger used in the Hölderlin essays of the thirties and forties, including some volumes of his courses up to 1942–1944, does raise problems about the modality of the statements in the poems, and beyond those the question of how we can use this powerful practice for criticism. If we take these procedures at full value and then amplify them, or at least interpret them, we can use them in ways that would allow us to understand more deeply the expressive-communicative procedures issuing in either poetry or philosophy.

We can remain faithful to Heidegger's injunction that we stay open and still carry forward his own speculations about the nature of the word in poetry and in discourse, the discourse of philosophy particularly. While his own discourse strains beyond philosophy, it remains at the same time in the region of decidability. "*Die Sprache spricht*" ("speech speaks"), is tautological, but still propositional, at one end of the discourse. At the other end, the gradual accumulation of key words produces its own *Ereignis* (en-owning, achievement, enactment, identification, appropriation), as an accumulation of inter-reverberant meanings. Yet the relations that obtain among them—among *Sage, Sagen, Welt, Riss, Abgrund, Ding, Wort*, and *Denken*—are proposition-like, while evading the propositional. This is in fact the character that, in whatever circular fashion, Heidegger emphasizes as he draws poetry close to philosophy in ways that Gerald Bruns has carefully sketched. To discriminate further, though, the special strength of the Heideggerian *Denken* and the special singularity of his *Dichten*, still do not "thicken" the poem into a full version of thinking alone, nor does Heidegger's use of language, after the fact, make the philosopher himself into a poet. The poem insists on what it gets beyond, and this insistence is the mark of its wisdom. "Finally the expression men exercise is a demonstration and representation of the real and unreal."[29] "Language in its essence is neither expression nor an activity of man. Language speaks. We seek now the speaking of language in the poem."[30] "What is purely spoken is that in which the completion of speaking, that which comes to identification, is for its part a beginning. The purely spoken is the poem. We must let this proposition stand first of all as a bare assertion."[31] "The language of the poem is a manifold speaking-out. Language shows itself indisputably as expression. What has now shown itself, however, stands against the proposition, 'Language speaks,' granted that speaking in its essence is not an expressing."[32] And yet, "First and last is speaking an expression."[33]

In his later work, Heidegger continually uses a centering on poetry to define speech and language generally (*die Sprache*) as both using and transcending reason. "We do not want to bring the essence of language to a single concept whereby this would provide a notion about language everywhere useful to put all demonstration to rest."[34] "Reason is language, *logos*," he says, quoting Hamann, " . . . I await always an apocalyptic angel for a key to this abyss."[35]

Thought, I have argued to some degree along with Heidegger, is only one of the ways of the poem, inescapably a chief way when words are used. But neither the *Erfahrung* (experience) of the poem nor its *Ereignis* can be confined to thought. In his terms, the act of speaking darkens itself in a poem, but that darkness does not lose the portent of its wisdom. In my terms, Image and Story will also play a role, if no more than the residual sequence inherent in the poem which is the skeletal or implied story of the mind going through it.[36] Heidegger's *Sage*, if it be taken for "legend," buries the legend in the crusted word or words that stand for it, without full sequence, and prevents the discrimination of layers in the paleosymbols they constitute. In the light of his sense of the wisdom in poetry, that wisdom does call into play images that remain images, distinguishable from the thought they do not fully embody in some variant of the Aristotelian analysis of the propositions concealed in metaphor.

Where then do we go in the poem, taking these cues as marks on the way but wishing to proceed further? What can be said of the poem on which Heidegger dwells, the evening poem of Trakl?

Ein Winterabend

Wenn der Schnee ans Fenster fällt,
Lang die Abendglocke läutet,
Vielen ist der Tisch bereitet
Und das Haus ist wohlbestellt.

Mancher auf der Wanderschaft
Kommt ans Tor auf dunklen Pfaden.
Golden blüht der Baum der Gnaden
Aus der Erde kühlem Saft.

Wanderer tritt still herein;
Schmerz versteinerte die Schwelle.
Da erglänzt in reiner Helle
Auf dem Tische Brot und Wein.[37]

A Winter Evening

When the snow falls on the window,
Long does the bell of evening ring,
For many is the table laid
And the house is well set up.

Many a one in wandering
Comes to the gate on dark paths.
Golden blooms the tree of graces
From the cool sap of the earth.

Wanderer, step still inside;
Pain turned the threshold to stone.
There flashes in pure brightness
On the table bread and wine.

Trakl's revision broadens the reference of bread and wine from the altar of the first draft also to the house. A state of being is contemplated and bodied forth in which the holiness of the ordinary has the effect of welcoming the stranger. Pain, in some past to the present of the poem, has turned the threshold to stone; and Heidegger notes that *versteinerte* is the only verb of past tense in the poem. Heidegger does not comment on the transformation itself, though his terms, the real and the unreal, can easily be made to apply: "Poetry sees the real and the unreal at the same time."[38] It involves an unreal transfer, since in the real world, where houses connected to the age-old neolithic landscape, even if they are palaces, have thresholds of stone. That literal sense blurs a physical architecture into a psycho-spiritual one, since labor may involve pain and it takes labor to set stone thresholds in place, but pain of itself does not do so. Psycho-spiritually, the world (in the sense of Heidegger's *Welt*) comes into a sort of fixity and numbness that at the same time both afflict and define the human condition, where a connection to earth (in the sense of Heidegger's *Erde*) may quarry a threshold, psychological and actual, from the hard matter of earth—from stone.[39] Thus does "speaking speak," "*die Sprache spricht*," and thus for Heidegger can this poem be said to broach what he calls the quartet, "*das Geviert*," "gods, mortals, heaven, and earth."[40]

Heidegger sees the dark paths as reaching to a death not mentioned here, but in tune with Trakl's symbology, with the Christian sacrifice that has been included, though in a fullness the revision blurs, in the last lines, and with the Biblical echoes of the twenty-third psalm ("Yea though I walk through the valley of the shadow of death"). This retains its power by refraining from specific evocations. Heidegger's comment is not a hermeneutic act exactly—and he points out that he has redefined the term hermeneutics.[41] Yet at the same time he claims a broader use of hermeneutics than that to be found in Schleiermacher or Dilthey. As Bruns says, for Heidegger "hermeneutics is not a method of treating texts but is rather a tradition of reflection, say upon a family of questions having to do with what happens when anything occurs in language at all."[42] Heidegger's act is a location within a reticulation of his own terms, one that the force of the poem legitimizes. So *Welt* and *Ding* assert their connection by namings.

The stretching of *versteinerte* and *Schwelle* does not generalize these words, "petrified" and "threshold," —the past tense of a simple verb and a noun—into an incantatory rapture. To stretch these terms makes them contain the very opening into wisdom that Heidegger's extrapolations imply. If, in his claim, the term Being is as wide as possible and for that very reason undifferentiated (much like the God of Spinoza), then the widening of terms has the effect of bringing the hearer close to a sense of Being. Speech speaks, *die Sprache spricht*. A modalization has occurred for "graces" (*Gnaden*), when "golden blooms the tree of graces," as well as a stretching, where a super-Romantic transfer has taken place in which the kind of participation of the self in Nature that Wordsworth (and, differently, Hölderlin) evoked is taken for granted and fused into a religiosity. It is so modalized that the application of the Christian story from these lines remains the faintest of traces, though our justification for reading that into *Gnaden* comes from the six lines of the conclusion in the first draft:

> Seine Wunde voller Gnaden
> Pflegt der Liebe sanfte Kraft
>
> O! des Menschens blosse Pein.
> Der mit Engeln stumm gerungen,
> Langt, von heiligem Schmerz bezwungen,
> Still nach Gottes Brot und Wein.
>
> His wounds full of grace
> Does love's soft power tend.
>
> O! man's sheer pain
> Which, with angels wrestling dumbly,
> Stretches, pressed by holy grief,
> Still, toward God's bread and wine.

Heidegger claims that the poem brings stillness to sound; it names stillness as part of the manner of the stranger. "Naming does not distribute titles and does not apply words but calls to the word. Naming calls. Calling brings the called nearer."[43] And further, "The poet calls into trusted appearances the strange as that in which the invisible sends itself in order to remain what it is: unknown. . . . 'poetically does man dwell.'"[44]

In the essay succeeding his use of "Ein Winterabend" to illustrate the act of speaking, Heidegger interweaves terms from several of Trakl's poems. Still, he stays close enough to his own goal of searching for wisdom to keep from merely building a phenomenology of the particular poet in the manner of Otto Bollnow for Rilke or Jean-Pierre Richard for Mallarmé.[45] "Gewaltig ist das Schweigen im Stein" ("Powerful is the silence in stone"), is a line from another poem that could be read back to *versteinerte*. "Nothing is clear; but all is significant."[46] So in his unsystematic system he can offer a depth-reading of color terms generally (*Unterwegs zur Sprache*, 74–75), giving us a ground for ourselves expanding on the many blues in Trakl: *blue deer, blue soul, blue bells, blue smile, blue of night, blue moment, holy blue, blue spring*.[47] The considerable conceptual extensibility of these terms reaches them into a naming that permits connnection to Heidegger's other terms, to *Geschlecht* and *Geist*, to *sterben* and also to *Schmerz*. Thus does he achieve a sort of "placement" which is an opening for "debate," an *Erörterung* that also suspends debate in a satisfaction of having been brought into articulation.

The poem empowers the possibilities of these connections, a deep sense that allows these acts of construction an independence that at the same time remains faithful to the experience of the poem—but also, and no doubt deliberately, stops short of that experience by never speaking of its overall formal features, its cumulative effect, the rise of its music, or its formal existence as a rounded statement. Heidegger's location of its concerns allows us not to lose sight of the wisdom it amounts to, its deep justification and ground of being.

Taking a cue from Heidegger, one could continue to extend his extrapolations from poems by attending to the integral differences that he elides. The short Trakl poem is complete in itself, along with the mysterious openness and ellipses that Heidegger does not discuss. In his long essay mostly on Rilke, about the poet "in a needy time,"—the quotation coming from Hölderlin—[48] he again elides the considerable differences among the poems he quotes, while empowering us to orient those differences toward, and out of, the wisdom in the poems:

>   Schwerkraft
>
> Mitte, wie du aus allen
> dich ziehst, auch noch aus Fliegenden dich
> wiedergewinnst, Mitte, du Stärkste.
>
> Stehender: wie ein Trank den Durst
> durchstürzt ihn die Schwerkraft.
>
> Doch aus dem Schlafenden fällt,
> wie aus lagernder Wolke,
> reichlicher Regen der Schwere.

Gieb mir, oh Erde, den reinen
Thon für den Tränenkrug;
mein Wesen, ergiesse das Weinen,
das sich in dir verschlug.

Dass sich Verhaltenes löse
in das gefügte Gefäss.
Nur das Nirgends ist böse,
alles Sein ist gemäss.[49]

Gravity

Center, how from all things
you draw yourself, even from what is flying
you win yourself back, center, who are strongest of all.

A standing man: as a drink through thirst
does gravity plunge through him.

So from the sleeper falls
as from a low-lying cloud
a rich rain of heaviness.

Give me, Earth, the pure
clay for the jug of tears.
My essence, pour the wine
that got lost in you.

That what holds itself unloose
in the offered vessel.
Only nowhere is evil,
All being is in measure.

What has awakened Heidegger's particular attention here, perhaps, is the air of tentativeness, of creating the poem as it goes along. This tentativeness mingles into the air of assuredness, the mastery of the speaker who draws his definitions of gravity (not to be confused, Heidegger reminds us, with the topic in the science of physics) out of his own formulation, as though there were an orphic, or at least a vatic, finality in the words, a finality that can allow him to leave the traces of tentativeness marked by the uneven lines, the caesurae, and an absence of rhyme that in the context of 1925 would be more striking than after free verse had become the norm.

The poem returns to, attains to, regular rhyme and meter, but for whatever reason Heidegger does not quote that part of it. From "Gieb mir" on, Heidegger does not quote the poem. He deals with it in an earlier, more fragmentary form. That first section does strongly evince the existential probing of an imagined flying, of drinking and thirsting, standing and sleeping, sluggish clouds and rich rain either physical or psychological and so both. All these features are testimonies to and evidences of the super-Kantian conditions of living, the a priori mastered by finding a poetic expression.[50] The two quatrains which follow take permission, and a rest from the strenuousness of the opening lines, to set up an allegory, the "jug of tears," and to conclude with an aphorism that would seem to return the conception of gravity to physics, were it not that the experience of the poem is already there barring the way to mathematical formulae and asserting a perception that would subclassify the formulae under itself, as Heidegger's mode of interpretation can be said to have taught us and licensed us to assert.

In his essay as a whole, Heidegger does not attend especially to the differences in poetic percept, and in achieved wisdom when it comes about, that obtain of the different modes of the poems he is here quoting: first, the gradually evolved fragment; then a framed dedication, the second poem he quotes; and then his third quotation, the high-pitched facet of an elaborate sequence, a single sonnet from the *Sonnets to Orpheus* which in fact he discusses at less length than he does the passages from the two "slighter" poems.

The center here expands into an extrapolation by Heidegger that is comparable to the psychological insight that Rilke exhibits in this poem.

> And yet—beyond what is, not away from it but before it, there is still something else that happens. In the midst of beings as a whole an open place occurs. There is a clearing, a lighting. Thought of in reference to what is, to beings, this clearing is in a greater degree than are beings. This open center is therefore not surrounded by what is; rather, the lighting center itself encircles all that is, like the Nothing which we scarcely know.[51]

The Sonnet to Orpheus is balanced into a more even rapture:

Wandelt sich rasch auch die Welt
wie Wolkengestalten,
alles Vollendete fällt
heim zum Uralten.

Über dem Wandel und Gang,
weiter und freier,
währt noch dein Vor-Gesang,
Gott mit der Leier.

Nicht sind die Leiden erkannt,
nicht ist die Liebe gelernt,
und was im Tod uns entfernt,

ist nicht entschleiert.
Einzig das Lied überm Land
heiligt und feiert.
                Rilke, *Die Sonette an Orpheus*, I:19

Even if the world changes as fast
as the shapes of clouds,
all perfected things at last
fall back to the very old.

Over what's passing and changing,
freer and wider,
your overture is lasting,
god with the lyre.

Pain's beyond our grasp,
love hasn't been learned,
and whatever eliminates

us in death is still secret.
Only the Song above the land
blesses and celebrates.[52]

The Sonnet to Orpheus, as Rilke's numbering and even his exclusion of some works from the series would tell us by themselves, inheres as a statement linked to many others in a large system-like structure, of which I will only begin to point out the linkages and correspondences. The late poem is a draft, so tentative that Heidegger has not had access to the fuller version (which I give). And the dedication, while published by Rilke as a complete poem, belongs firmly to a rhetorical form that is as fixed in its way as the Greek epigram (to which it is akin), going back to the Album verses of the eighteenth century.[53]

Heidegger's predilection for these particular poems, across their boundaries of rhetorical distinctiveness, shows his instinct for what Rilke himself would seem to have felt to be most Rilkean in his work, the depth-psychological manifestation of "*heart-work*" instead of the "*sight work*" to be found in poems about Gothic cathedrals or Picasso paintings, panthers or blue hydrangeas,—or the Roman wells included in the *Sonnets to Orpheus* (II, 15), on which Heidegger does also remark.

The extrapolability of the poetry means that it could join a proper formulation of wisdom at any point. So in the *Sonnets to Orpheus,* to go no further in Rilke's work, the groundedness of the peasant on the earth from *The Origin of the Work of Art* also finds expression:

> Selbst wenn sich der Bauer sorgt und handelt,
> wo die Saat in Sommer sich verwandelt,
> reicht er niemals hin. Die Erde *schenkt*.
> (I, 12)

> Though he works and worries, the farmer
> never reaches down to where the seed turns
> into summer. The earth *gives*.

And the very next poem is like a hymn embodying Heidegger's doctrines of existence and language:

> Voller Apfel, Birne und Banane,
> Stachelbeere . . . Alles dieses spricht
> Tod und Leben in den Mund . . . Ich ahne . . .
> Lest es einem Kind vom Angesicht.
> (I,13)

> Banana and pear, plump apple,
> gooseberry . . . all these reveal
> life and death inside the mouth. . . . I feel . . .
> Read it in the features of a child.

The speaker of the first sonnet of the second part speaks of a counterpoise in which he attains a rhythmic individuation, using a key word that Heidegger might therefore have got from Rilke, "Gegengewicht, / in dem ich mich rhythmisch ereigne." Soon he will be saying, as though in summary of Heidegger:

> Sei—und wisse zugleich des Nicht-Seins Bedingung,
> den unendlichen Grund deiner innigen Schwingung,
> dass du sie völlig vollziehst dieses einzige Mal.
>
> Zu dem gebrauchten sowohl, wie zum dumpfen und stummen
> Vorrat der vollen Natur, den unsäglichen Summen,
> zähle dich jubelnd hinzu und vernichte die Zahl.

> Be—and at the same time know the implication
> of non-being, the endless ground of your inner vibration,
> so you can fulfill it fully just this once.
>
> To nature's whole supply of speechless, dumb,
> and also used up things, the unspeakable sums,
> rejoicing, add yourself and nullify the count.

In the particular sonnet that Heidegger quotes, cited above, "Wandelt sich rasch auch die Welt," the dwelling on a permanent condition overridden by transience is at once mirrored in the speed of the dactylic trimeter lines pushed to a greater speed by the dimeters, and it is also overcome once that speed has become song. In this phase of the sequence, it anchors its utterance on an audible contrast between its rushing rhythms and the long-range view of life and death at once evasive of and mastered by the blessing and celebration of a song, played on a lyre by someone who is putatively identified with the archetypal cosmic poet Orpheus. As in the poems of Hölderlin, celebration and consecration are felt to merge in the "blesses and celebrates" of the sonnet's last line, "heiligt und feiert." The death of the dedicatee, the young woman who has died, recedes from its oppressiveness as it proceeds rapidly into a turn of the rapt incantation. As for the rushing it does name, "the world changes as fast," such evasions and difficulties lie in the human situation, and in the modern situation, as Heidegger sketches them out, but here quite allusively. What he chooses to write about instead— and we should admire the wisdom-orienting strategy of his choice—is the daring of the poet-utterer, something not mentioned in this sonnet. Daring, rather, is praised in his earlier quotation, the occasional dedication to a friend, first a sort of daring in nature, a state conveyed by the noun, *das Wagnis*, and then the encompassing of man in this process verbally, in Rilke's tensed aphorism, "*er wagt uns*" ("it dares us"):

> Wie die Natur die Wesen überlässt
> dem Wagnis ihrer dumpfen Lust und keins
> besonders schützt in Scholle und Geäst:
> so sind auch wir dem Urgrund unseres Seins
> nicht weiter lieb; *er wagt uns*. Nur dass wir,
> mehr noch als Pflanze oder Tier,
> *mit* diesem Wagnis gehn; es wollen; manchmal auch
> wagender sind (und nicht aus Eigennutz)
> als selbst das Leben ist—, um einen Hauch
> wagender. . . . Dies schafft uns, ausserhalb von Schutz,
> ein sichersein, dort wo die Schwerkraft wirkt
> der reinen Kräfte; was uns schliesslich birgt
> ist unser Schutzlossein und dass wir's so
> in's Offne wandten, da wir's drohen sahen,
> um es, im weitesten Umkreis, irgendwo,
> wo das Gesetz uns anrührt, zu bejahen.[54]

> As Nature abandons beings
> to the daring of their dull pleasure and guards
> none especially in clod and branch
> so are we too no dearer to the prime guard
> of our Being; *it dares us*. Only that we,
> even more than plant or animal,
> go *with* this daring; will it; often are
> more daring (and not from selfishness)
> than even life is—by a breath
> more daring. . . . This shapes for us, outside protection,
> a safety, there where the gravity works
> of pure forces; what finally covers us
> is our unprotectedness, and that we so
> turned it into the Open, where we saw it threaten,
> so as, in the widest orbit somewhere
> where the law touches us, to affirm it.

Some of the modality of this occasional poem would have to situate it in the circumstances of its occasion. It was inscribed in a copy of *Malte*

Laurids Brigge (at the request of the sculptor who was Rilke's divorced wife) that was given to a nobleman, Helmuth Freiherr Lucius von Stoedten. He at that time was German ambassador in The Hague. "Daring" must include, then, diplomatic as well as poetic daring, nor could nobility and even matrimony be excluded from its purview.

Heidegger, in the preterition of a full attention he does later partially engage, says that "we" are not ready to lay out the profundities of the elegies and the sonnets.[55] Thus does he approach them by indirections—disquisitions on Nature, Being, the Open, and animals, all of which enter the Sonnets and the Elegies, but not this particular sonnet, and only obliquely this particular dedication.

The "alike-and-different" of Heidegger's assertion about poetry and philosophy, and about poetry and ordinary language, suspends the issue between Derrida and Searle vis-à-vis Austin's question of whether or not literary language can be characterized as "parasitic." It suspends such questions into a *Gelassenheit*, a more relaxed version of bracketing that does not close out the consideration but allows it to float in the consciousness as part of a whole situation. The relaxedness becomes an ideal disposition of the self, and a self we can confidently expand into the full "Romantic" consciousness, in spite of Heidegger's strictures against the subject-object distinction that allowed him to get beyond Husserl for the situational formulations of *Sein und Zeit*.[56] It is at the same time a sort of pre-contract rather than a position that is logically extrapolable. But to give our attention exclusively, even as philosophers, to the logical extrapolations, would arrest our addressing the possibility of how the wisdom in poetry works. Heidegger returns to the Romantic questioning of language, in the philosophy of Hamann and the theoretical linguistics of Humboldt, to orient himself toward keeping these questions open. As he says, "For Hamann the abyss consists in the fact that reason is language. Hamann returns to language in the attempt to say what reason is. Attention to reason falls into the depth of an abyss. Does this consist in the fact that reason resides in language, or is language itself the abyss? We speak of an abyss in the situation where we depart from the ground and a ground fails us, insofar as we seek for a ground and depart in order to reach a ground."[57] In an opening of an intentionality that will include the languages of both philosophy and poetry does he press his insistence: "Questioning is not the genuine gesture of thinking but a hearing of the pledge for that which is supposed to come into the question."[58] Otherwise, if we translated poetry simply into philosophical language, we would have slighted both domains and distanced ourselves from the true situation. "We would have degraded poetry into a cover-term for thinking and taken thinking too lightly and also have already forgotten what it is to have an experience with language."[59]

Attending to these amplifications along the lines of distinctions that are not allowed to take over a narrowing of the field, we obviate a turning away from the wisdom in any achieved imaginative language, in any *Dichtung*, a term in which the ordinary-language term of German can be pressed for a comprehensiveness that admits all of this, whether poetry or prose: "The opposite to the purely spoken, to the poem, is not prose. Pure prose is not 'prosaic.' It is as poetic and so as rare as poetry."[60] The modalization of poetry cannot simply be ascribed to fiction, since it is a chief means for indicating powerful, elusive, and comprehensive, states of affairs. We go to what is poetry, in the largest and strictest sense, so as to attune ourselves to these states intellectually and, it can well be said, spiritually.

4. Finalities of Utterance and Modalities of Expression

I

When we go to the whole poems from which Heidegger has detached the nuggets of wisdom on which he puts such great weight, the poems are found to resonate by fixing these nuggets into a precise place in the text and at the same time to modulate their doing so. The shift through the light "abers" of Hölderlin's *Andenken*, the unique turn toward the past tense in the "versteinerte" ("made stone") of Trakl's *Winterabend*, betoken not only a mastery of the various formal features the analytic critic attributes to poems. These features also, in the rhetoric of their presentation, betoken a handling of logical turns. The turns, through the rhetoric, present and reorient their qualifications.

Metaphor, in context, constitutes one large kind of qualification, as well as an identification. In a poem, the modality of the leap in a metaphor is as important as its propositional structure. This modalization begins as an enlistment of the fiction that tags and situates it initially, and modally, with respect to other utterances. But if we accord a preoccupying attention to the fictive element in metaphor, we tend to neutralize it, or even to vitiate it, by failing to attend to the power that the fictive element enables, the state of (what I have been calling) wisdom. This stands forth once the truth-resemblance has attained realization as what Hesiod already called "lies similar to truth." The graveyard of history teems with examples of poetry that has shed the illusion of providing wisdom. But poems that stand free, at whatever time, carry the aura of managing such modulated communication. They do so in many ways, often in the strength and purity of a focus that implies mastered exclusiveness. This happens early on in Greek poetry, in Hesiod and in Homer, great focalizers both; and in Sappho, Alcaeus, and Alcman.

The awareness of fictiveness, if given a definition that aligns it with philosophical structures, can be seen as a method for effectuating an "epoché," a suspension that serves the Stoic philosopher to organize logical expressions and has been taken by Hegel, Husserl, and others as a key term in the mind's relation to its management of perceptions. For poetry, as John Baker says, "epoché is not the abolition of reference but its suspension. By suspending the question of reference, fictional or poetic language does not render it otiose but gives it instead a new ontological pertinence."[1]

But with such modalizations, and with the rationale for such exclusions, if there is a wisdom in poetry the very nature of the poetic act, by capacitating itself, incapacitates the commentator from grounding that wisdom, except through the circuitous route of the hermeneutic circle. Kant, just to bring himself to the point of accounting for judgments that include aesthetic judgments, is obliged to combine the categories of two entire previous critiques, those of pure reason and of practical reason, and to interlock their terms so as to produce what remains a psychological description. And going from that to the presence of the sublime, which modern writers then apply from his system to poetry, involves a leap of further psychological description. The sublime is recognized, and its absence is recognized, but it persists while not being accounted for.[2] Heidegger's careful, subtle, and deep attribution to achieved poetries of what amounts to the sublime bases itself on the self-revealing congruity of single utterances or short-term sequences in poems by Hölderlin or Trakl to key aspects of his own world view. But such expression comes off only in the after-ring of the interactive wise statements: in their sublimity.

In one more particular approach, the theoretical questions about metaphor, much discussed in our time, are brought to bear on poetry, with results that nearly always reveal a facet of the wisdom in poetry but none of which can be taken for a grounding of poetry as its own domain of wisdom, especially in cases where no distinction is made between utterances in poetry and utterances in ordinary language. What if the expression "Was bleibet aber, stiften die Dichter" ("What abides, do poets found"), were itself not a sentence in a poem, concluding a poem by Hölderlin, but were simply a prose aphorism? Heidegger does not really raise this question, and he can be said implicitly (and justifiably) to dodge it by aligning quotations of prose remarks by Hölderlin with such verse quotations. The arresting utterances of Heraclitus, I have argued, work, in ways picked up by René Char and others, to fuse poetry and the prose aphorism in such a way that a poetry to the second degree results. That this poetry is identical with a form of philosophy is not surprising, if the wisdom inhering in poetry is bared by being given this subsumptive turn.[3] So from Aristotle through the modern conferences on metaphor the propositional structure of the metaphor is inspected; and usually it is found to yield usable propositions or self-limiting ones,[4] without any necessary reference to poetry, even if the illustrations of metaphor are drawn from poetry. In another move, surprisingly congruent with that of Heidegger, the metaphors inhering implicitly in the common language are found by George Lakoff and Mark Turner to be put to deft and condensing use in poetry. As they say,

> Take a quatrain from [Shakespeare's Sonnet 73]:
>
> In me thou seest the twilight of such day
> As after sunset fadeth in the west;
> Which by and by black night doth take away,
> Death's second self that seals up all in rest.
>
> As we saw before, there are at least five conventional conceptual metaphors sculpted into the composite metaphorical conceptions of death we find in this quatrain. They are LIGHT IS A SUBSTANCE, EVENTS ARE ACTIONS, LIFE IS A PRECIOUS POSSESSION, A LIFETIME IS A DAY, and LIFE IS LIGHT.[5]

Metaphors, in their implementing account, turn out to be deeply rooted in implied assumptions that govern any utterances in language, and poetry is notable for an ability to condense and intricate such assumptions. So far so good, but the question "Why poetry?" remains, even if the question "Where is the wisdom?" has been answered, at least for that element in wisdom which draws, as it must, on prior assumptions.

Metaphors often, and characteristically, involve not just propositions that enlist bold or intricating leaps of logic. They involve images, and images are arresting in many ways that cannot be unpacked with anything less than attention to a whole system.[6] The images may begin as what Habermas calls "paleosymbols," thus seconding Lakoff and Turner's insistence on the rootedness of metaphors in deep social habits of language and definition. But a paleosymbol also exceeds these habits. It allows the poem to tap into myth, or an equivalent for myth, and myth itself is undefined, a question to which we do not have an answer.[7]

Going further along the lines of the propositional character of metaphor, but necessarily begging the question of the necessity of poetry to wisdom (and vice-versa), Samuel Levin proposes that the poet bodies forth an utterance that contains a self-consistent and truth-correspondent vision of a "possible world" in conformity with Aquinas's theory of analogy as well as with Kant's constructions about reason and understanding as they enter into an act of judgment. Levin says of Wordsworth:

> Unlike the standard Kantian challenge, therefore, in which the imagination must be spurred to approach a rational idea as a limit, the intellectual task for Wordsworth was, rather, to overcome an impression of nature that disaccorded with deep and strongly held intuitions. . . . What overcame this conflict for Wordsworth and produced for him a condition of finality was the conception of an "active" universe . . . "a soul divine."

Between the unitary view of Levin's whole possible worlds and the constructive view of Lakoff and Turner that poetry carries off a combinatory presentation of deeply ingrained social propositions, there is an accord in principle: both extend the propositional character of metaphor, Levin by characterizing the end result, Lakoff and Turner by analyzing the propositional constituents. But there is a difference between them that can only be bridged by standing laterally aside and raising (even without hope of answering) different questions. Levin emphasizes what we may continue to call the originality of the poet, in the face of all the recent discourse about how the writer tends to efface himself into precisely the preformed composites of expectation and expression that Lakoff and Turner are analyzing. Levin's possible worlds are actual new worlds, provided by the "culture hero" (the phrase is Delmore Schwartz's) who has brought them forward from his stock of conceptions. The sources of Wordsworth, and his accord with contemporary thought even beyond specific traceable sources, have engendered elaborate commentary. But we are faced with the fundamental fact, unprovable but experiential, that what makes Wordsworth Wordsworth cannot be traced to any combination of sources.

Two approaches to how this could be the case can be made, laterally, through the modality of his or another successful poet's utterance; or through his success at mounting and preserving a possibility or contingency in the very poems themselves, quite apart from their density or complexity. So, for example, the elegies of Tibullus are quite simple, more so than the more complex poetry in a related tradition, the sonnets of Samuel Daniel. If one succeeded in demonstrating this difference, it would still not entail assigning a superiority of poetic force to the more complex Daniel. And if not, there would be something in the modality of Tibullus's utterance that gave him at very least a parity of utterance, which we would accord a parity of wisdom, with Daniel.⁸

William Elford Rogers, under the aegis of a questioning rigorous enough to put easy generic definitions at a remove and open enough to attempt a metasystem where both the probes of Heidegger and the strictures of E. D. Hirsch could find a place, aligns the generic dispositions under one of the categories of Kant (quality, quantity, relation, and modality), that of relation.⁹ He proposes

> that each of the traditional broad genres—epic, dramatic, lyric—be associated with one of the Kantian relational categories—substance, causality, and community [which in Kant's definition means reciprocity between agent and patient or commutability—A.C.], respectively. . . . Every interpretation of a literary work, if the relation between mind and world in the work is interpreted in terms of one of the categories, must also be an interpretation of the category.

That is to say, such works (when successful, I would emphasize) are intrinsically metalinguistic. As such, they engage another of Kant's categories, if we may go further in adapting them to this specific use, the category of modality. Indeed, I have taken this term modality, somewhat confusingly if we were obliged to stay with Kant, to cover all the self-qualifying sleights built into or derivable from a poem, including those of the Kantian modality more narrowly defined: possibility or impossibility, existence or non-existence, and necessity or contingency. In his own study, Rogers (*The Three Genres*, 57) puts us on a ground "transcendental" enough to permit our defining other attributes of literary works than just their generic adherence: "The genres are modes of relation between the mind of the work and the world of the work."

In the light of modality, in the sense I expand from Kant's sense of the term, the difference between Wordsworth and Herbert, for example, is not the fact but the modality of belief, their different ways of modalizing the language of the poem—which would include meter as a content (as well as a form) both received from the tradition and welded to a particular utterance or set of utterances. The evidence for such modality, and its relation to feeling, must of course be retrieved from what is coded into a poem, and the transfer from writer to reader involves the sort of epistemological problems that demand the protracted treatment given them in recent discussions of "reading." Those problems can be bracketed, but even if they are, the intricacies of belief engaged in a poem do not admit of a simple solution, even if, as in the case of Herbert, simplicity is the assumption and goal of the poet.[10]

The sublimity of Wordsworth hinges not on a prior belief, like the set of beliefs that Herbert sets into his own particular fictive combination, but on the recuperation of belief from sets of circumstances in which the poet feels his way verbally and perceptually to their presence. Poetry, I am arguing, inescapably modalizes. At Wordsworth's particular juncture, his sublimity must come through considerable modalization, a modalization that for the poets of this time—for Keats and Hölderlin, as well—poses a radiant problem.[11] The modalization is already there in Herbert, as it must be in the modality of any successful poet's utterance. For Herbert, this can be seen in the high poise—by contrast with the work of some devotional versifier—residing in the fictive element of such conceptions as "The Collar" or "The Forerunners," which are metaphorical, but also in the broadening of the central conception inhering in the title of "Jordan," which can be called metaphorical only by extending or arresting Herbert's usage. For Wordsworth, the modalization can be traced in a sort of fading in his vocabulary. By contrast with Wordsworth's handling of words, the flat statement of notions sounds prosy, even when accompanied by fading, nostalgia-evoking rhythms, in such works as Matthew Arnold's "Stanzas at the Grande Chartreuse" and "The Scholar Gypsy."

The Arnoldian touchstones, slightly longer instances of the weighty phrases of Heidegger, are in my terms the one or two lines that can be taken to reveal a modalization carried through into an achieved modality. They are often absent in Arnold's own poetry. Without subjecting them to analysis here, it can be said of such poems as Arnold's that the substructure of self and ego prior to the utterance has not been mastered, so that in failing to be fully adequate to the sort of modalities that Wordsworth and Keats did master, the speaker is too present in the work in one sense and not present with the proper fullness in another. Or, to put it differently, the transcendence of self-referentiality in the subject has not been effectuated, so that the modality of possibility closes down on the utterance. There is a sense that the utterance has not been fully launched, even though the poems establish a success in their coherence of tone. As Adorno effectually cautions while making the declaration, "With the categories the materials, too, will have lost their a priori obviousness, and thus the words of the poetic act. The decay of the materials is the triumph of its [Hegelian] intersubjective purposiveness."[12]

And as he says elsewhere in the same work, "Art is based on truth, but not without mediation. To that extent is truth its content. Knowledge is through its relation to truth. Art itself knows this, while truth comes forward in it. However, its knowledge is neither discursive nor is its truth the mirroring back of an object."[13]

The thought in Arnold's poems is offered sequentially and full-blown, locked into its mood, whereas Keats and Wordsworth have in common the traces of an exploratory conception of the poetic utterance, where the air of being on the way to discovery invests the very words. "No, no, go not to Lethe," Keats says, in the "Ode to Melancholy," but he is there offering an elusive substitute for Lethe, the notion of embracing melancholy. All the narrative is modalized by a future possibility that is also a kind of past. When Arnold enjoins the Scholar Gypsy to "fly our paths, our feverish contact fly!" he writes from a supposition similar to that of Keats about the nightingale: in Arnold's case, in "The Scholar Gypsy," a human being instead of a bird is fancied to be deathless. But the range of Arnold's poem, rich as it is, is limited by the mere notion of the difficulty of modern life. Not just for reasons of rhythm has he fallen short of Keats's resonance and depth.

At another turn of modulation the religious subject in its modality entails a denial of religion. For such a poem as Wallace Stevens's "Sunday Morning," the crescendo he finally sets for the last lines of this poem fuses nostalgia and affirmation. The attitude verges on the satiric, but the submersion of the satiric possibility in turn verges to the sublime:

Deer walk upon our mountains, and the quail
Whistle about us their spontaneous cries;
Sweet berries ripen in the wilderness;
And, in the isolation of the sky,
At evening, casual flocks of pigeons make
Ambiguous undulations as they sink,
Downward to darkness, on extended wings.

The resonance here lies not so much in the metaphoric extensibilities of the images as in the underlying tonal fusions of this meditation, at once sharing and distancing itself modally from the sentiment of the woman meditating on Christian history as she refrains from worship while "she hears, upon that water without sound, / A voice that cries, 'The tomb in Palestine / Is not the porch of spirits lingering. / It is the grave of Jesus, where he lay.'" Here Stevens's often dominant philosophical modulations are traceable, if at all, only faintly in the commas. The strain of affirmation takes over in the rhythms from the declaration of denial, but that affirmation is not an affirmation of faith. Rather it is a displacement of faith. But a similar tone infuses the *Four Quartets* of T. S. Eliot, whose *Ash Wednesday* attains its modality by relying much more on deep images, the paleosymbols of Lady, leopard, and juniper tree, and on syntactic disjunctions, than does this early Stevens. Eliot's orientation performs its modulations from a base within Herbert's own church. The same base serves for the work of John Wheelwright, which both expresses and reduces its energy of fuller reference by failing to evolve a modulation equivalent to the strength of its imaging:

Rococo Crucifix

Guarded by bursts of glory, golden rays,—
Christ, when I see thee hanging there alone
in ivory upon an ebon throne,
like Pan, pard-girded, chapleted with bays;
I kiss thy mouth, I see thee in a haze,
but not of tears, and not the briar crown . . .
Is it, O Sufferer, my heart is stone?
Am I, in truth, the Judas who betrays?

> To hang in shame above a gory knoll,
> to die of scorn upon a splintered pole,—
> this was not beautiful, I know, for thee . . .
> Would I have whispered upon Calvary,
> "An interesting silhouette, there, see!"
> while God groaned in the dark night of his soul?[14]

As a kind of defence against the strained directness of this poem, its failure to invent a modality, Wheelwright appends a note to it: "contradicts the axiom and corollary of Keats, 'Beauty is Truth: Truth, Beauty,' and recalls the silence of God's Father when God died." This remark does map an area of affirmation and denial; it leads directly to Adorno's famous declaration that there can be no poetry after Auschwitz. There are—or are there?—domains where beauty or the thought of beauty is a scandalous intrusion. What does one do with a beautiful poem that must be in some way making such an assertion? One wonders what Wheelwright conceived to be the domain and intent of this prose remark, as it summarizes the bare assertions of the poem. Beauty and truth only find their expression in Keats through a disjunction between this statement and the rest of his poem. It would be hard to make those terms, whatever their function in Keats's ode, cover either Wheelwright's devotional-imaginary act here or the topic in general.

Strain and modulation would overmaster the later Emily Dickinson, were her supreme capability at alert modalization not overmastering them, as can be seen, for example, in her Poem 1216:

> A Deed knocks first at Thought
> And then—it knocks at Will—
> That is the manufacturing spot
> And Will at Home and well
>
> It then goes out an Act
> Or is entombed so still
> That only to the ear of God
> Its Doom is audible—

Dickinson does not rest on a prior theology—hence the impossibility of defining her affiliation. Instead she relies on the force of using poetry to deduce theology. Modulation comes not from the fictive set of the poem, as in the best of these modern examples, but from the ratiocination that is at once rigorous and ineffable, an attained modality. As in Wordsworth and Keats, though her compositional principles differ as much from theirs as they do from each other, she keeps the wondering, exploratory possibilities open at every line; her dashes indicate as much. The pitch of speculation is never allowed to relax in a set stand. Consequently expressions like the repeated metaphor or catachresis of "knocks"—at this depth it is impossible to define the rhetorical figure—shift easily to the different near-set of "manufacturing," then to the strange "Will at Home and well" with the puzzle of capitalization for "Home." This puzzle is the greater for the inclusion of the word in an adverbial phrase. In that modifying posture, the phrase is out of parallel with the three capitals preceding it, "Deed," "Thought," and an unmodified "Will." Life and death come into her oracular sense of their proximity in the metaphor of "entombed," since she is talking about life but adduces "God" and "Doom." The last word, "audible" stretches the speculation once more, raising the question in almost Heideggerian fashion of what hearing means and how it works if it is seen "sub specie aeternitatis." At some level, it would seem, thoughts and wills and acts and deeds are scored into a communicative sound for final definition, but the poem offers an intimation of such almost inconceivable finalities by tracing the depth-sequences of a psychological process.[15]

A more thoroughly aestheticized modalization, of an admiration for faith in what amounts to the absence of faith, appears in such poems as Yeats's "Byzantium." A history put into periodization by a reliance, itself problematically modalized, on the occult, governs this poem, whose first two stanzas attain instantly a raptness dependent on the mechanisms of these evasions:

> Byzantium
>
> The unpurged images of day recede;
> The Emperor's drunken soldiery are abed;
> Night resonance recedes, night-walkers' song
> After great cathedral gong;
> A starlit or a moonlit dome disdains
> All that man is,
> All mere complexities,
> The fury and the mire of human veins.
>
> Before me floats an image, man or shade,
> Shade more than man, more image than a shade;
> For Hades' bobbin bound in mummy-cloth
> May unwind the winding path;
> A mouth that has no moisture and no breath
> Breathless mouths may summon;
> I hail the superhuman;
> I call it death-in-life and life-in-death.

A great deal of keen hermeneutic attention has been given during the past half a century to the proportions, beauties, and implications of this startling poem (from which, of course, I quote only the first two stanzas). If the unpurged images have receded, to ask what a purged image might be raises at once the whole anthropological history of religious purgation and the whole romantic symbology of the image, which here serves to illustrate, to evade, to exemplify, and to deepen this Byzantium, itself a composite image unresolvable back to, or for that matter away from, the actual history or actual theology it might be shown to involve. It cannot be said that art serves theology here (as with Wheelwright) or that theology serves art, so thoroughly do they modulate one another. "Man or shade" will also not resolve, and the "death-in-life and life-in-death" wants to come at a Christian eschatology from an angle that will not accommodate it, as the "bobbin" is an image not out of Byzantium but out of Yeats's deep and radically equivocal reliance on the spinnings of an occult history, derived ultimately from the spindles at the end of Plato's *Republic*. The correlation with "the superhuman" seems to bring "death-in-life and life-in-death" under something like the long tradition, Western but also generally human, of mystery at the border between life and death, expressed early in the aphorism of Heraclitus, "Mortals are immortal and immortals mortal, living their own death, dying their own life" (Fragment B62). But the juxtaposition immediately reveals the essentiality of the imaginary and imaginal to Yeats's propositions, as these could not be taken in such an aestheticizing way for Heraclitus, or for anyone with an actual doctrine in mind.

The structure of this Byzantium is at once firmly poised and evasive in its resonances. Such good as obtains of this beauty would require a great deal of derivation. There is no simple external source, as with the theology of Herbert. And even if there were, the fusion would not necessarily hold, as witness the failed Byzantium epic segments by a younger contemporary of Yeats, Charles Williams, in *Taliessin through Logres* and *The Region of the Summer Stars*. Williams possessed great critical and historical imagination, and his mastery of the historical sequences was such that he wrote a strong history of the Church from the point of view of a doctrinal adherence close to Herbert's. He had, furthermore, a complicated overriding conception that did not depend on Yeats's arbitrary and extravagant connection with mediumship. Yet, as close analysis might show in the very rhythms he has chosen, he has not wrought his poem to Yeats's mastery of modalities, and it does not come rapturously together. Whatever the good might be, the beautiful has faded to a trace:

> The Acts issue from the Throne. . . .
> the household inscribes the Acts of the Emperor;
> the logothetes run down the porphyry stair
> bearing the missives through the area of empire.
>
> Taliessin walked through the hither angels,
> from the exposition of grace to the place of images.
> The morn brightened on the Golden Horn; . . .[16]

Intellectually, this is a great deal more intricate and informed than Yeats's presentation of his Byzantium. But the vast gaps are not really breached in imagination between the Byzantine theocracy and the England of Arthur, here conceived as an outlying domain of the Byzantium that the Welsh poet Taliessin is visiting. A comparable failure to modalize saps Tennyson's *Idylls of the King* of a wisdom and power sought where Milton, "long pondering," had decided not to seek it, in the Arthurian legend.

To find these connections made in a wrought fusion that brings a sort of inevitability to all these matters, we could well turn again to the *Cantos* of Ezra Pound, where the Arthurian matter is brought in at the subtle angle of the legendary king's long line of descent through complicated politics going back to the discovery of Britain by a pre-Roman "Brutus." The hinge is the worship of Diana—a worship modalized by Pound as emotionally valid through an Actaeon paralleled to others of his key figures. All this is distortedly mirrored through Layamon's *Brut*, which Pound quotes in his usual nodes of condensed multiple matching:

> Heye, Diana, help me to neode
> Witte me thurh crafte . . .
> 'Merlin's fader is known to none.'
> Lay me by Aurelie, at the east end of Stonehenge
> where lie my kindred.
> (Canto 91; 613)[17]

Here the many-dimensioned reticulation, constantly modalized in its relation to various doctrines (some of them incompatible, like residual anarchism and rampant fascism), is brought into relation with China and England. It also exhibits historical links of an occasionally microscopic accuracy, with Byzantium, which waits in the wings for condensed integers of bureaucratic connection, Heraclius, Justinian, and Leo the Wise's *Edict of the Eparch*.[18]

In Eliot's *The Waste Land*, the grail legend becomes an underlying armature also, and a panoramic history is grazed, but without the confusion of allowing history to permute a simply falsifying fiction. The convergences are faithful not to an actual religious feeling but a nascent one, as is indicated by the movement to the Upanishad injunction in Sanskrit—"Give, sympathize, control"—in the concluding words of "What the Thunder Said," the last section of the poem, ending in a "Peace" that is also modalized through the quasi-ritual repetition of the Sanskrit term for it, "Shantih shantih shantih."

II

Related to this modality is a second characteristic, a communicated sense that there is a finality in the utterance which, in the case of metrical poetry, the meter seems to seal—but it will do so only in the case where there is also a finality in the utterance. The sense of closure in the finality is a balancing counter-twist to the openness of the modality. It takes the whole of the "Ode on a Grecian Urn" to give finality, and wisdom, to the otherwise virtually inexplicable, but ringingly wise, conclusion, "Beauty is truth, truth beauty; That is all / Ye know on earth and all ye need to know," though one is tempted to find the locus of intensity not in the commutable proposition of the first clause but in the conjunction of "know" and "need" in the capping one. If we were to do so, we would be borrowing Levin's unitary approach, and also Lakoff and Turner's constructive one; but we would also keep in view the urn, itself an imagined and secondary object not distinct from the images of men and maidens upon it, and the patterns said to compose it, independently, as it happens, of any actual classical or classicizing artifacts.

The census of the formal features of a poem will still not really account for the mysterious rightness that the poet works toward, the click of the box of which Yeats spoke, and which all poised poems, whether their music offers an exact design or not, are felt as aspiring toward. Toward this click of rightness tend the constant reshaping revisions of Whitman, no less than those of Yeats, though in Yeats we tend to "hear" the click through the formal meter and in poets like Whitman the openness of the form makes it not only inaudible but questionable. Finality in such poets is itself a modalized possibility rather than an actually attained goal—or can be; Pound's processes tend, over a long time, to zero in on precise formulation, to the click, no less than do Yeats's. And part of what the poet finds his way to is a proper management of the modalities that will make the "Heideggerian" nuggets of utterance fall into the managed rightness, the finality, that allows for the combinations, avoiding the flatness of the prose summary, or of Wheelwright's poem above.

The last stanza of Stevens's "Sunday Morning," the end of which I have quoted above, was originally the first stanza as late as the first published version of the poem. The crescendo toward which Stevens found his way by putting that stanza last is not just a musical gesture; it is also tonal and thematic. It mysteriously readjusts the relationship between the good and the beautiful by setting the proportion of just this emphasis of affirmation against the tonic insistence on denial, and with the finality of

94   Chapter 4

the order that brings it to closure. This was a process that took longer than a decade for the Pound who was evolving the *Cantos*, in the large and in the small, working his way to a rightness that is a mysterious, indirect testimony of how the language must often be shaped and reshaped to yield up its wisdom. And indeed it took him over a decade just to work his way through the many drafts and slowly evolved condensations of Canto 4.[19] William Carlos Williams worked through some one hundred and fifty versions to arrive at the first few lines of *Paterson*.

For Yeats, indeed, his idea, and even his symbolic identifications within it, may have come at a very early state, and he worked his way toward a proportionality and rightness that could come at a stroke to another poet (or possibly on occasion to Yeats as well). Take the startlingly bald beginnings, and the impressively long reworkings, of "Byzantium."[20] At first, there is merely, but also for the ideas almost entirely, the noted subject, and Yeats puts his conceptual frame succinctly in his notebook:

> Subject for a poem
> Describe Byzantium as it is in the system towards the end of the first Christian millennium. (The worn ascetics on the walls contrasted with their [?] splendour. A walking mummy. A spiritual refinement and perfection amid a rigid world. A sigh of wind—autumn leaves in the streets. The divine born amidst natural decay.)

No one would give to these notes the artistic status even of a painter's sketch. The elements that will become poetry are there, but there is a something deeply necessary that is entirely not there. There is no hint of the mysterious necessary formulation. Modalization may already hover over this note: finality does not.

Some of these details will get incorporated in the companion poem "Sailing to Byzantium," but there is no sense of a possible separation of elements in this note. As he worked on the idea, Yeats, probably later, canceled the passage Bradford places in parentheses and wrote over it:

> A walking mummy flames at the street corners where the soul is purified. Birds of hammered gold singing in the golden trees. In the harbour [dolphins] offering their backs to the wailing dead that they may carry them to paradise.

The drafts cast about with a tentativeness so extreme it is hard to see how the poet will arrive at the peerless utterance we know: Yeats throws his net

Finalities of Utterance and Modalities of Expression 95

wide in the process of working through four entire versions in order to reach this point, one still far from final (Bradford's X's indicate canceled lines):

  X This Danish merchant on a relic swears
  X That he will
  X All this afflicts me, but this merchant swears
  X To bear me eastward to Byzantium
     But now this pleasant dark skinned mariner
     Carries me towards that great Byzantium
  X Where nothing changes
  X And ageless beauty
     Where age is living [word undeciphered] to the oars
     That I may look on St. Sophie's dome / on the great shining
        dome
  X Of Phidias' marble, or a / or upon marble stairs
  X Or mirroring waters where a glint
  X On mirroring water, upon sudden foam
     On gold limbed saints and emperors
     After the mirroring waters and the foam
     Where the dark drowsy fins a moment rise
     Of fish, that bear / carry souls to paradise.

After four more drafts Yeats splits off the separate poem "Sailing to Byzantium" and shapes it through eight further versions. He then turns his attention to the other poem, "Byzantium."[21] And the drafts of this poem continue in his notebook:

  When all that roaring rout of rascals are a bed
  When every roaring rascal is a bed
  When the last brawler's tumbled into bed
  When the emperor's brawling soldiers are a bed
  When the last brawler tumbles into bed
  When the emperor's brawling soldiers are a bed
  When the last
  The last robber
  The last benighted robber or assassin fled
  When the last
  The last robber or his

> The night thieves latest victim / last benighted traveler dead or fled
> Silence fallen
> When starlit purple [?]
> When deathlike sleep destroys / beats down the harlot's song
> And the great cathedral gong
> And silence falls on the cathedral gong
> And the drunken harlot's song

And then, after at least a dozen further versions, the poem itself comes to a finality, the box clicks:

> The unpurged images of day recede;
> The Emperor's drunken soldiery are abed;
> Night resonance recedes, night-walkers' song
> After great cathedral gong;
> A starlit or a moonlit dome disdains
> All that man is,
> All mere complexities,
> The fury and the mire of human veins.
>
> Before me floats an image, man or shade,
> Shade more than man, more image than a shade;
> For Hades' bobbin bound in mummy-cloth
> May unwind the winding path;
> A mouth that has no moisture and no breath
> Breathless mouths may summon;
> I hail the superhuman;
> I call it death-in-life and life-in-death.

I am raising the question, as bearing on what the emotional-intellectual effect of a poem entails, not of what beauties may be noted in the final version, but what the bearing of our sense of finality may be on our sense of the poem, of Yeats's, but also of Herbert's, or anyone's.

The traces of such efforts, often extreme and prolonged, give evidence of how rare and elusive the rightness of poetic statement is, beyond the formal beauties of the poem as they may be detailed by careful attention. To master the modalities often requires the sort of search exemplified here, to come into the clear of an utterance whose constituents could bear the weight of such attention as Heidegger's. To ask what this rightness is brings us to the heart of the question of what is brought into expression by any poetry, since its absence is detectable and even ascertainable in segments of poems where the supreme achievement is not fully carried through, as in segments of Whitman—for all his procedure of lifelong revision. The poet not only stretches his words on the one hand, so that they apply widely, with an approach to gnomic finality. He also raises the possibility of a modal stance, a possibility found not only in the way modern poetry handles its access to religion, as in the examples with which I have begun, but the way he orders his stance toward all the constituents of what he says. Such a skillful ordering can be found in Sappho and Pindar, and in individual chapters of Isaiah, as well as in what has come through as the equipoise in poets like Cavalcanti and Arnaut Daniel, or Jonson and Herbert. In such poets, the formal features that are the external signs of a finish induce to a sense of rightness, but also to a something deeper, a rightness in which the last trace of modality, and of assuredness and indeed of wisdom, lies in the fictive condition that any poetry must not only use modally but must embrace in a way that turns the fictive toward the real.

Clearly the movement of revision brought Yeats (and differently Pound) to a greater abstractness, a greater condensation, a greater richness, a greater intensity, in a way that must have some kinship with the way a shaman warms up to the exercise of his powers. We move from documented details about Byzantium to burning images. So in "News for the Delphic Oracle," the title at once effectuates the modality of reversal. The Delphic oracle emits news rather than receives it, and that massive turn nests the further modality of the religious inaccessibility of the Delphic oracle to the modern speaker or hearer in any case. The news is about sexuality, and sexuality in alien mythic traditions, and the sexuality of the old:

> There all the golden codgers lay,
> There the silver dew,
> And the great water sighed for love,
> And the wind sighed too.
> Man-picker Niamh leant and sighed
> By Oisin in the grass;
> There sighed among his choir of love
> Tall Pythagoras.
> Plotinus came and looked about,

> The salt-flakes on his breast,
> And having stretched and yawned awhile
> Lay sighing like the rest.

Love and the sea, love and the grass, would that be news for the Delphic oracle? If in one aspect of her ambivalence she is ageless and sexless, in another there is always a sexual and fertilizing connection when any seasonal religious system comes into play. A priestess figure in a cult with fertility connections cannot be divorced from a hieratic connection to sexuality, even if at the (characteristically ambivalent) remove of personal chastity. In this first part, there seem to be only men, but in the next part "Innocents" of indeterminate sex ride "brute dolphins" and "pitch their burdens off." The term "innocent" itself has both a Christian and a sexual tinge, and these are combined, as well as permuted into the afterlife. Capitalizing the term turns it from a description into a title. These innocents are "Innocents." Have they become innocent, or were they always so? Did they just become so as they pitched their burdens off (which for Plotinus would be the burden of the body)? If so, they can participate in an untrammelled sexuality only after the instrument of sexuality has been, in an earthly sense, taken away from them: so that, for the heightening that comes after a divestment from the body, they are super-Plotinean after all, even if Plotinus in this non-Apollonian afterlife joins in "with the rest." And what is the breast on which a salt flake rests? While the poem does not point in any unmodalized fashion to some equivalent for an astral body, it presents us with the inextricable mystery of a bodily figure, Plotinus, who after he has attained his desired bodilessness goes through what we know as bodily actions, having bits of salt cake to his breast, stretching, yawning, and sighing. All these are a prelude to the culmination of some bodiless inversion of intense bodily activity, participation in (an equivalent for?) sexual congress. An afterlife is envisioned all-embracing enough to include legendary Irish lover-heroes along with Greek philosophers and Greek demigods.

The second part modalizes beyond sexuality: "Those Innocents relive their death, / Their wounds open again." The Peleus and Thetis of the third and last part, as it once again focusses on sex, respond with eye and body to the sexuality of others, and in this context the whole resounding conclusion is further modalized by a disjunction cryptic in the very bluntness of its emphases:

Slim adolescence that a nymph has stripped,
Peleus on Thetis stares.
Her limbs are delicate as an eyelid,
Love has blinded him with tears;
But Thetis' belly listens.
Down the mountain walls
From where Pan's cavern is
Intolerable music falls.
Foul goat-head, brutal arm appear,
Belly, shoulder, bum,
Flash fishlike; nymphs and satyrs
Copulate in the foam.

What these final lines say is as easy as what they mean is difficult. They withdraw into a super-oracularity labeled as antipodal to the oracularity of the sacred Apollonian source.

The poem also forms a distant, reverberant commentary on its source, Porphyry's *Life of Plotinus*, and a rewriting of it that is in some sense a reversal. The very iconography is obsessive and evasive in Yeats's hands, while rapt and eulogistic in Porphyry's. Indeed, toward the climactic end of this short "life," Porphyry quotes an oracle of Apollo to Plotinus which is a eulogy that predicts an afterlife with a personnel that may be included in the "golden codgers" of the first stanza: Rhadamanthus, Aeacus, Plato, and Pythagoras, complete with "the choir of immortal love." These figures are involved in activity very different from Yeats's sexual congress. They perform a union of the soul with other souls in a vision of divine truth once the soul had not fulfilled the body but divested itself of it; and much of Plotinus's own writing stresses the ideal of the bodiless purity of the soul. The first sentence of Porphyry's *Life* states how Plotinus "seemed ashamed of being in the body." So Yeats contradicts the other oracle, while using it as a grid for modalizations, and of course adds to it the Irish mythological figures. The sea mentioned more than once in Porphyry's account of Apollo's oracle is not the afterlife, and not even the "sea of time and space" of Porphyry's own doctrine, but just the welter of this life.

The nymphs and satyrs of this poem are in the pastoral tradition still followed, with all its intensifications, by the Mallarmé of *L'Après-midi d'un faune*. This tradition sets these figures in a tree-bordered dale of some sort, and not in the foam that suddenly emerges here. And Yeats's prior reference in the poem had been to a landscape more accordant with Delphi: "Down the mountain walls / From where Pan's cavern is / Intolerable music falls." Pan is Dionysus, and in Greek as well as Nietzschean tradition he is the opposite of Apollo, the sponsor of the Delphic oracle. But Greece offers various fusions of Apollinian and Dionysian perspectives. Whether Yeats does so here may resist explanation ultimately, as it certainly does initially. But the presentation of high modality in the lucidity of a song-like directness will assert its own finalities in any case.

5. Sound, Sense, and Religion in the Dialogized Context of Donne's Poetry

Beauty accompanies poetic wisdom. It accompanies other wisdom too. Why this should be so is not clear, but it is often experienced. The beauty that lingers over wisdom comes about, as Kant can be taken to have implied, because of the deep reassurance in the achievement and expression of control over an area of the otherwise bewildering world. So the beauty underlying the elegance of a mathematical proof or the heightened sense of mastery (even if surrendered in further argument) that comes about in the apprehension of the sequences in a dialogue of Plato, the condensations in an aphorism of Heraclitus or Wittgenstein. The fact that the natural beauty of a man or a woman is culture-bound connects it to similar reassurances, even if wisdom is not involved. The sight of a beautiful person reassures the continuance of a line within society through reproduction, or just through the inclusion of the beholder and the beheld in the same group. And the beauty in physical nature, of which Kant and others have made much, of seas or trees, shells or flowers, fields or mountains, contains, if again not wisdom, a sense of reassurance which merges into a sense of pleased repose—a sense that it is the wisdom of the painter sometimes to transpose and organize into a communication not distinct from wisdom. In Kant's complex presentation, beauty is a symbolic analogue to the good.[1]

Just as in Freud's analysis of wit a pleasure indicated by the discharge of laughter accompanies the management of complex, sometimes paradoxical material in the economical condensed fashion of the joke, so the poised condensations of the poem (or story, or enacted play) bring with them a sense of completed satisfaction, of getting into the clear. Experience, in John Dewey's terms, has been organized, and the achieved act of organization brings pleasure. Such pleasure, again for Kant, stands as an analogy, distinct but loose, to the sense of the moral good. The aesthetic is an analogue to the ethical, and entails wisdom from that angle as well. The work of visual art, too, organizes: something is apprehended and structured, necessarily with respect to conventions of seeing, but those conventions of themselves are not sufficient to complete a fulfilling act of organization. And music, drawing on a conventional set of sounds, organizes them not only to charm but also to penetrate to a satisfied sense of something deeply correspondent to the truth of emotions.

Such organization is the cognitive side of form. The formed poem reminds of its form, and organizes its utterances into sound patterns. It tends to do so also in a poetic diction, a conventional pre-selection from the whole lexicon of words, a selection charged for the poetic function. It may also play with the fact of its own forced inclusions: it may be witty in a twentieth-century sense as well as in a seventeenth-century sense, as in the poetry of Pope and Herrick. Cleanth Brooks in "The Language of Paradox"[2] gets something of the pressure to organize incongruities in poetry into his characterization of poetry as paradoxical, even though a poet like Herbert will not easily fit his categories. Herbert, and Pushkin, and Sappho, and many another, cannot be made to exhibit either the subliminal kind of paradox Brooks finds in Wordsworth's "It Was a Beauteous Evening," nor the more pointed kind found in Pope and Donne. Yet, to begin with, the wrenching of assocation necessary for a metaphor to be a metaphor at all can be described as a paradox. And metaphor has in common with conversational wit an economical flash of perception at the service of combining associations.

The wisdom in Donne's wit seemed for centuries to be a merely gratuitous display of associations. And, correspondingly, its beauties, the beauty of its achieved modalization, were lost on Samuel Johnson and many others. But the force of its particular mix of the fictive and the real has come through. It only begins as an enlistment of the particular wittiness of interchange in the legal discourse of the time.[3] The poems of Donne mount themselves as the sort of dialogue that posits much more interchange than in the prayerful poems of Herbert. The poet Donne, by a shock engagement with his readers, forces them to the exercise of reproducing his modalities; he is "hard."

The poetry of Herbert, by contrast, while no less modalized, is more intimate in its conception of a private devotee working his way through the psychological motions of coming toward a quiet in harmony with God. It seeks not Donne's dramatic definitions, and not his robust affirmations, but a drawing together of the worshipper and the Worshipped. This makes the surface, and the depth, of the poetry more pellucid. Traherne and Vaughan are comparably pellucid, though Traherne, for all his pellucidity, engages profundities of theological definition. These, on Leigh

De Neef's showing, are a fair match for the modern epistemological speculations of Heidegger, Lacan, and Derrida.[4] A philosophical theology governs the smoothly modalized celebration of doctrine in Traherne. As De Neef says,

> For the center of that poetry is not a text in the students' normal understanding of that term. It is rather a textual gathering of a particular saying of language, the site of a dialogue in which man questions his own being and nature's by attempting to converse with all things exterior to him.[5]

On another construction, we could follow De Neef's lead and structure Donne's dialectic about his relation to God, and to a beloved or a friend with some relation to God, to the systems of these later thinkers. So when Donne says in a Sermon "God's own name is *I am: Being* is God's name, and nothing is so contrary to God as to be nothing."[6] Here a proto-Heideggerian construct links a man's sense of his identity to the Being of God. The light self-canceling implied in the irony of the *Songs and Sonets* could easily be subjected to the regresses of a Gricean structure of implication: the addressees (we) know that he knows that his approach to the rhetorical addressee (the beloved) is wholly governed by the intent both to celebrate the beloved and to seduce her and is not to be taken "seriously." Donne has it both ways, modally controlling the implications through his irony. The very extravagance of the self-presentation and the arbitrariness of the ratiocination announce their existence as seduction-rhetoric. They are, in Lacan's terms, merely "imaginary." In Derrida's terms, the advertisement of a perpetual supplement—"you see I can go on like this"—amounts to its arising from an already existing plenitude announced by being aspired to. But at the same time these poems bracket the imaginary and celebrate the plenum. In a comparable but different strategy the *Anniversaries* push extravagance so far that the utterance is obviously far-fetched in a pejorative sense. But that very extremity serves as a compliment to the rhetorical addressee: "See to what lengths I am willing to go to praise you and your family."

Traherne, by contrast, is quieter. He all but subverts metaphor.[7] But at the same time he can become still more intricate: "An Object Seen, is in the Faculty Seeing it, and by that in the Soul of the Seer, after the Best of Maners. Wheras there are eight maners of In-being, the In-being of an Object in a Faculty is the Best of all."[8]

Without either Donne's or Herbert's different engagement of the speaker and the interlocutor, Traherne strikes off inferences from his doctrine with a seemingly inexhaustible abundance. So in the conclusion to

"The Recovery" he does not at all dramatize the experience implied in his title:

> Tis not alone a Lively Sence
> A clear and Quick Intelligence
> A free, Profound, and full Esteem:
> Tho these Elixars all and Ends to seem
> But Gratitude, Thanksgiving, Prais,
> A Heart returnd for all these Joys,
> These are the Things admird,
> These are the Things by Him desird.
> These are the Nectar and the Quintessence
> The Cream and Flower that most affect his Sence.

We may imagine how Donne or Herbert would have handled such a "recovery." But Traherne more straightforwardly casts his ratiocinations into verse. As De Neef says,

> Traherne's glimpse of this truth is spoken in the wit of God's own "Beatifick Vision." The "response" of beings to Being, as that of Being to beings, Traherne names, at the conclusion of "The Recovery," as "One Voluntary Act of Love." And he does so in an interesting tautology:

> One Voluntary Act of Love
> Far more Delightfull to his Soul doth prove
> And is abov all these [effects] as far as Love.
> (ll. 68–70)

> The tautology may return us to what we have already called the reflexivity at the heart of Traherne's thought. Love is the center and the sphere, means and end, essence and act, Being and beings. God loves in order to grant the power of loving, the inclination to love, and the act of love itself.[9]

As Traherne says in "The Demonstration":

> The Highest Things are Easiest to be shewn,
> And only capable of being *Known*.
> A Miste involvs the Ey,
> While in the Middle it doth lie;
> And till the Ends of Things are seen,

> The Way's uncertain that doth stand between.
>   As in the Air we see the Clouds
>   Like Winding Sheets, or Shrouds;
>   Which tho they nearer are obscure
> The Sun, which Higher far, is far more Pure.

This principle in fact permits him an occasional metaphysical flight, as in this stanza from "Love," where the classical background of Jove's homosexual abduction of Ganymede is exhibited in the modalized pretense of the metaphor. It is swiftly put (in Derrida's terms) effectually "under erasure" by the solemnity of the utterance and the very speed of the ratiocinative procedure:

>   His Ganimede! His Life! His Joy!
> Or he comes down to me, or takes me up
>   That I might be his Boy,
> And fill, and taste, and give, and Drink the Cup.
>   But these (tho great) are all
>   Too short and small,
> Too Weak and feeble Pictures to Express
> The true Mysterious Depths of Blessedness.
>   I am his Image, and his Friend.
>   His Son, Bride, Glory, Temple, End.

As Traherne says:

> And every Thing is truly Infinite,
> In its Relation deep and exquisite.[10]

In a more relaxed mode, Traherne mounts the associativeness of Whitman in combination with something like a Biblical-prophetic tone—a further testimony to the range possible within the sphere of this modalizing devotional verse:

>   But above all, O Lord, the Glory of Speech, whereby thy
> Servant is enabled with Praise to celebrate thee.
>   For
>   All the Beauties in Heaven and Earth,
>   The melody of Sounds,

> The sweet Odours
>   Of thy Dwelling-place.
> The delectable pleasures that gratifie my Sense,
>   That gratify the feeling of Mankind.
> The Light of History,
>   Admitted by the Ear.
> The Light of Heaven,
>   Brought in by the Eye.
> The Volubility and Liberty
>   Of my Hands and members.
> Fitted by thee for all Operations;
>   Which the Fancy can imagine,
>   Or Soul desire:
> From the framing of a Needle's Eye,
>   To the building of a Tower:
> From the squaring of Trees,
>   To the polishing of Kings Crowns.
> For all the Mysteries, Engines, Instruments, wherewith the World is filled, which we are able to frame and use to thy Glory.[11]

Yet another modalizing organization of sound and posture—one that fuses light melancholy with visionary calm—is found in Vaughan, as can be seen in this last part of his "Ascension-Hymn":

> They are all gone into the world of light!
>   And I alone sit lingring here;
> Their very memory is fair and bright,
>   And my sad thoughts doth clear.
>
> It glows and glitters in my cloudy brest
>   Like stars upon some gloomy grove,
> Or those faint beams in which this hill is drest,
>   After the Sun's remove.
>
> I see them walking in an Air of glory,
>   Whose light doth trample on my days;
> My days, which are at best but dull and hoary,
>   Meer glimering and decays . . .

If a star were confin'd into a Tomb
    Her captive flames must needs burn there;
But when the hand that lockt her up, gives room,
    She'l shine through all the sphaere.

O Father of eternal life, and all
    Created glories under thee!
Resume thy spirit from this world of thrall
    Into true liberty.

Either disperse these mists, which blot and fill
    My perspective (still) as they pass,
Or else remove me hence unto that hill,
    Where I shall need no glass.[12]

This contemplation of the deceased puts them at the remove of the third person while simultaneously holding them in the closeness of a fixed contemplation. These dead are figured as the speaker's only source of light, as the accentual emphases of the first line underscore, "They are áll góne into a wórld of líght." He has a "cloudy breast" and is as in a "gloomy grove" among "mists," "dull and hoary." Their memory, "fair and bright," "glows and glitters like stars." The poem proceeds by an intensification of this central contrast: the "light" of their "air of glory" "doth trample on my days." The culminating "star confin'd into a Tomb" creates such pressure that the poem breaks into the second person of an address to God to resolve the contrast one way or the other: either to "disperse these mists" and bring that light into this world, or else to transport the speaker to heaven so that he will no longer need the "glass" of his "perspective" or telescope. In the afterlife he will, it is implied, fulfill the words of Saint Paul, on which the stanza, and by extension the whole poem, is a gloss: "Now we see through a glass darkly, but then face to face" (1 Cor 13.12).

    Crashaw, like Donne, pushes the mind's confrontation with God to the point of extravagance, to the "Baroque."[13] "Love, thou art Absolute sole Lord / Of LIFE and DEATH. To prove the word." Here the long syllables exhibit not Herbert's equanimity but a controlled intensity.[14] God, as the outside addressee, grounds and extends and validates and individualizes this poetry, much like the psychoanalyst in Lacan's system whose presence as a virtual silent other guarantees his role as the Other that will circulate all the communicative possibilities through the "symbolic." Here the poem, as if in deference to this principle of a split in naming induced by the dialectic of communication, has two titles. It is "A Hymn to the Name and Honor of the Admirable Saint Teresa," but it is also a *Carmen Nostro Deo*, a "Hymn to our God" in the underlying language of Crashaw's Roman Catholic devotions. God, even as a bare notion, is more inclusive and still more dialectical than Lacan's analyst, since in the Christian scheme he is posited not as withdrawn but intimately identified with the worshipper ("the kingdom of heaven is within you") and lodged but also infinitely reverberated in the mystery of the Trinity. Consequently, the Son is posited to assume an equivalence to the worshipper, as the worshipper by a membership in the Christ who is the body of the Church can desire and will a participation in which need and demand no longer must be bifurcated. Not to give the full functional weight to this overpowering felt presence—independently of the particular beliefs of the critic—is to fritter all such poems into the "Imaginary" (to stay with Lacan's terminology).[15] Dissolving them out of the "symbolic" that God as a named presence or a stated interlocutor provides, leads to a dissolution also of the person whose integrations are being conceived and carried through in the statement of the poem.

None of these poets dynamizes the dialogue of the speaker with his audience in Donne's manner, and so for all their various profundities they fall short of the pointedness that might have been a source of ambivalence in the poet, as Donne himself declares when he looks at poetry in its aspect as obsession:

> Sir; (though I thank God for it) I do hate
> Perfectly all this town, yet there's one state
> In all ill things so excellently best,
> That hate, toward them, breeds pity toward the rest.
> Though poetry, indeed, be such a sin
> As I think that brings dearths, and Spaniards in,
> Though like the pestilence and old fashioned love,
> Riddlingly it catch men; and doth remove
> Never, till it be starved out; yet their state
> Is poor, disarmed, like papists, not worth hate.
> (*Satire* 2, 1–10)[16]

Here Donne castigates not just bad poetry, though he also does that in passing. This is the topos of Catullus and Horace before him, of Dryden and Pope afterward. He castigates all poetry, thereby setting up a paradox for the assumed speaker himself. He has written "A Fit of Rime Against Rime," but more radically than Jonson, whose title provides a platform for the speaker. Donne's only platform is the extravagance of his voice, which is taken to carry the day; its very forthrightness is felt to exempt the speaker. Moreover, in a further unusual turn, poets are in this satire linked with lawyers, and at one moment of the poem genetically: the lawyer could well once have begun his life as a miserable poet. But also they are linked as misusers of words, the lawyer for power, the poet for illusion-sapped self-expression. To step forward and claim no illusions, as the writer of this satire does, is also implicitly to exempt oneself from the stated inescapable trap of using words to further illusion—but in a poem this is a self-reflexive, modal turn.

Here not the addressee but the central conception engages Donne's dialectic, which, by including all poetry and linking it to legal writing, validates the turn and allows the speaker to come forward more triumphantly because what grounds his utterance has been stated as canceled. It is the force of such a central conception that links the satires to the epistles, and both to the divine poems, as well as all to the *Songs and Sonets*.

The stir and liveliness, the play of sound and sense, which is immediately apparent to the reader of Donne's poems, can be attributed most directly to his sensitivity, or anxiety, toward the communicative act he is entering, and to the context of poetic utterance that he is invoking. The modalizing mix of rhetoric and logic in his poems is strong and subtle enough to allow for the abundance of rich commentary that has been accorded them without much attention to their communicative acts, even when the recent techniques of setting logic against rhetoric are not employed.[17]

Donne's own attention to the act of communication in his poems is apparent, very often, in their pointed enlistment of interrogative and imperative modes and in their strong and immediate address to one or more addressees: "I wonder, by my troth what thou, and I / Did, till we loved" ("The Good Morrow"); "Little think'st thou, poor flower" ("The Blossom," an address to a flower followed by an address to the beloved, and then an entreaty phrased as a command, "Meet me at London, then"); "For God's sake hold your tongue, and let me love" ("The Canonization"); "So, so break off this least lamenting kiss" ("The Expostulation"); "Oh do not die, for I shall hate" ("A Fever"). And there are more—"Mark but this flea" ("The Flea"); "Send home my long strayed eyes to me" ("The Message"); "Busy old fool, unruly Sun / Why dost thou thus?" ("The Sun Rising"); "Take heed of loving me" ("The Prohibition"); "Whoever comes to shroud me, do not harm / Nor question much / That subtle wreathe of hair" ("The Funeral"); "Stand still and I will read to thee / A lecture" ("A Lecture upon the Shadow"). Not to mention "Go and catch a falling star." In his *Obsequies*, and elsewhere, Donne begins a poem by addressing abstractions like death: "Death, I recant"; "Death, be not proud." He addresses faith, "Look to me faith, and look to my faith, God"; and language itself, "Language thou art too narrow and too weak." He also addresses the dead, "Fair soul, which wast not only, as all souls be, / Then, when thou wast infused, harmony."

So far as the addressee of such emphatic communicative acts is concerned, our conjecture that some large group, but certainly not all, of these poems is addressed to the woman who became his wife does not much affect our ascertainment of their sound and sense, germane as it is to our ascertainment of his sexual behavior in life. It can be said, indeed, that the very lack of information about the addressee of the poems especially in the *Songs and Sonets* and the *Elegies* throws into relief the importance of their addressee, and often of the action of their addressee, where characteristically from the early troubadours through Shakespeare the addressee is either inert or arrested in a posture of inertness after an action that the poem accounts for. Donne modalizes the interaction between addresser and addressee. His access to the rhetorical device of apostrophe here, and his heavy dynamic reliance on it, functions in the poem as a counterweight to its self-preoccupation with its own ratiocinative procedures, as though to ensure the modal balance in an utterance that measures to an ideal, an utterance only gradually, intermittently, and privately exposed to the possibility of publication. Keats, indeed, takes access to similar ratiocinations through a poem, and to a similarly heavy use of apostrophe—"No, no, go not to Lethe"; "Thou still unravished bride of quietness"; "Where are the songs of spring. Aye, where are they?"; "Thou wast not born for death, immortal bird." But Keats centers his poem in an advertised subjectivity, rather than in a dialectic with an imagined auditor.

In one public face, the literature reflecting Donne's society is gloriously histrionic and celebratory, turning its displayed glories into a celebration of themselves. The attention to surface in both verse and dramatic presentation well abets such celebration. Thus the side of Spenser, and of Jonson's masques, or even in some ways of Shakespeare, that has been finely discriminated in our own time.[18] Donne was attentive to the power such a celebratory note might have, but his awareness of underlying contradictions displays itself even in the "Epithalamium for Somerset," where the emphatic and even-rhythmed fortissimo of celebration has been introduced by a dialogue between Idios and Allophanes about the comparative virtues of city and country:

> Allophanes:
> Unseasonable man, statue of ice,
> What could to country's solitude entice
> Thee, in this year's cold and decrepit time?
> Nature's instinct draws to the warmer clime . . .
> Most other Courts, alas, are like to hell,
> Where in darke plotts, fire without light doth dwell:
> Or but like Stoves, for lust and envy get
> Continuall, but artificiall heat;
> Here zeale and love growne one, all clouds disgest,
> And make our Court an everlasting East.
> And can'st thou be from thence?
> Idios:
>   No, I am there.
> As heaven, to men dispos'd, is every where,
> So are those Courts, whose princes animate,
> Not onely all their house, but all their State.

The emphasis, finally, on exclusive celebration, and the strong meter as well, skirts as well as overrides the circumstances of this marriage. This bride, not named in the headnote, who may have tried to poison her first husband, is very soon to be implicated in Somerset's murder of Sir Thomas Overbury. Elaborate legal preparations were necessary to prepare the bill of nullity, the divorce that would permit them to be married, and the Donne who was to write the "Epithalamium" for them would seem to have spent much of the period, during which he was contemplating Holy Orders, in serving as a legal consultant on the bill of nullity. That Somerset was the chief patron for this unemployed family man entering his forties gives point, and indeed bite, to the discussion in this quoted opening dialogue about the court intrigues on which Donne perforce based his own persistent and often frustrated applications for permanent employment. That these court intrigues were resolved by the King's steering him toward Holy Orders sets the secular and the religious into the tight intrication always present, it would seem, as a pressure on Donne's expressions, in whatever genre.[19]

A solution to these intrications in poetic terms is to express them while modally containing them. In ideological terms, the paradox, and also the connection, between eroticism and religious devotion, often noted in the *Songs and Sonets*, is only one dimension, and one particular mix. Seen not just as expressing and ordering the feelings of his own consciousness but as modalizing these feelings in their communicative matrices, Donne's poems of various kinds, and also his sermons, are notable for stretching and strengthening that communicative link, a link that is virtual when the poems were mostly unpublished and actual for the sermons. The more vibrant communicative link, actual in the sermons and virtual in the poems, distinguishes them from his more formally objectified earlier prose treatises, *Ignatius His Conclave*, *Biothanatos*, and *Paradoxes and Problems*.

The prophets, whom Donne frequently quotes and praises, combined the poem and the sermon. Donne split his access to the prophets into public sermon and private poem—poems so private that the poems were only occasionally published during his lifetime, an extreme version of the personal attitude toward poetry in the Renaissance, since Shakespeare and Spenser and Ben Jonson, and before them Wyatt and Sidney, did publish their poems both in collections and in separate volumes. At the same time the approaches are not free of interplay between public and private. Donne did publish the *Anniversaries* at once, and he circulated his poems in such a way that Jonson was aware of them. Donne, as late as 1627, equates poems and sermons in some respects, when he speaks of showing his poems, presumably still in manuscript, to the reader par excellence, the king: "The King, who hath let fall his eye upon some of my Poems, never saw, of mine, a hand, or an eye, or an affection, set down with so much study and diligence, and labour of syllables, as in this Sermon I expressed these two points."[20]

Erving Goffman's fine-tuned discriminations of the social constraints on normal oral interchange throw into relief not only the richness of poetry in general, but its strategic exclusion, whether it be oral or written, of cues noting those constraints,[21] "set alignment," "projection," and "continuity." Goffman's "footing" does not have to be established in poetry between poet and auditor. It is often suspended in poetry, since it exists as a pre-condition. But Donne sets up the poem, often, along the lines of invoking such a footing. As for Goffman's "bracketing of liminal roles," a two-person arrangement can be set up, when the addressee of a poem is pulled rhetorically, and fixedly, into it, and Donne does this with notable bravura. The poet sets himself off by suppressing and channeling some of the features of ordinary conversation. Such a suppression casts him in the role of poet, which he defines as well as sustains by the thrust and coherence of his performance, oral or written. As Donne says, in a memorable description of the scattering of the ego prior to utterance:

> I am not all here, I am here now preaching upon this text, and I am at home in my Library considering whether *S. Gregory*, or *S. Hierome*, have said best of this text, before. I am here speaking to you, and yet I consider by the way, in the same instant, what it is likely you will say to one another, when I have done. You are not all here neither; you are here now, hearing me, and yet you are thinking that you have heard a better Sermon somewhere else, of this text before; you are here, and yet you think you could have heard some other doctrine of downright *Predestination*, and *Reprobation* roundly delivered somewhere else with more edification to you; you are here, and you remember your selves that now yee think of it, this had been the fittest time now, when every body else is at Church, to have made such and such a private visit; and because you would bee there, you are there. I cannot say, you cannot say so perfectly, so entirely now, as at the Resurrection, *Ego*, I am here; I, body and soul; I, soul and faculties; . . .[22]

This passage is evocative of the reflexive splitting of the self, as it engages self and other, in his poems. Yet, there is a "steadiness" in a poetic utterance with respect to normal conversation, and this shows up normally in the regularity of the poem's sound and sense. Donne's poetry subverts this steadiness by the overlay upon the harmonious text of the phenomenally sensitive tuning of disruptive rhythmic modulation, deprecated by Ben Jonson as "not keeping of an accent" and elaborated by Arnold Stein into four alternating and conflating metrical types.[23] The "Epithalamium" for Somerset notably abjures such "rough" rhythmic variation, its own counterassertive power showing in the contrast between its unqualified affirmation and the oppositions in the "Eclogue" that introduces it, as well as in the force of assertion, so strong as to be constantly hyperbolic, with which Donne characteristically thrusts his poetic utterance on an imagined auditor.

Within his discourse, the counterpart for the strong apostrophes and for the high hyperbole is the ratiocination that feeds them, with its comparable binariness of deployment into constantly formed and reformed paradoxes and antitheses.[24] This, and the accompanying extravagances of metaphor and imagery, have drawn much attention in the large literature about Donne in the last fifty years or so.[25] But their overall form even more arrestingly complements, as it enlists, such internal structures.

Along with the intensity of an individual ratiocination, often built upon a metaphor, there comes in Donne the modalized density of a sequence of metaphors, which thrusts itself on the attention of an imagined auditor and rivets him. This intensity can only be intermittent on stage, for example, in Shakespeare—or in Lope de Vega. In one interesting instance, Lope has a character tell a moral tale about a horse frightened by a lion.[26] Then, much later in the play, as the plot intricates, one character brings an extravagant metaphor about sex to bear on his son (1216–1219):

> Según eso, ni tu quieres
> vivir, Conde, ni morir
> que entre morir e vivir
> como hermafrodita eres.

> According to this, Count, you seek
> neither to live nor to die,
> but between living and dying
> you are a hermaphrodite.

Donne is far more condensed than this in his poems; there is rarely so much space or extension over an image. And he is even more condensed than Góngora. But Donne, who declares that Spanish books dominated the foreign section of his library, is too early to have been likely to see the poetry of Góngora. He might have known the work of Lope, and as it happens, Lope's metaphor is curiously paralleled in the last lines of Donne's "Epistle to Mr. Tilman after he had taken orders":

> And so the heavens which beget all things here,
> And the earth our mother, which these things doth bear,
> Both these in thee, are in thy calling knit,
> And make thee now a blest hermaphrodite.

Here is not only Lope's metaphor, but almost exactly its same application. Yet the application is accompanied by energetic modalization and by far more ratiocinative quickening.

Donne in the concluding lines of his elegy "Change" much condenses, and also extends, the "Mutabilitie Cantos" of Spenser, "Then are they [waters] purest; change is the nursery; / Of music, joy, life and eternity." The name cut in the window, the shortest day of the year, the blood of lovers commingled in the innards of a flea, "A bracelet of bright hair about the bone"—these and myriads of other intensifications are robustly held in place, and themselves testify, to the special complexity of a communicative act that conceives of them as necessary to stave off a sort of communicative dissolution. They are the opposite of and hold off from the self-scattering of ego vividly evoked in the sermon quoted above. A fortiori, they are far removed from the self-consumption they are in fact managing to stave off.

The predominance of the act of combination in Donne over the particular acts of thematic statement can be highlighted by contrasting two poems from the *Songs and Sonets*:

The Good Morrow

    I wonder by my troth, what thou, and I
        Did, till we loved? were we not weaned till then,
    But sucked on country pleasures, childishly?
        Or snorted we in the seven sleepers' den?
    'Twas so; but this, all pleasures fancies be.
    If ever any beauty I did see,
Which I desired, and got, 'twas but a dream of thee.

    And now good morrow to our waking souls,
        Which watch not one another out of fear;
    For love, all love of other sights controls,
        And makes one little room, an every where.
    Let sea-discoverers to new worlds have gone,
    Let maps to others, worlds on worlds have shown,
Let us possess one world, each hath one, and is one.

    My face in thine eye, thine in mine appears,
        And true plain hearts do in the faces rest,
    Where can we find two better hemispheres
        Without sharp north, without declining west?
    What ever dies, was not mixed equally;
    If our two loves be one, or, thou and I
Love so alike, that none do slacken, none can die.

Song

Go, and catch a falling star,
    Get with child a mandrake root,
Tell me, where all past years are,
    Or who cleft the Devil's foot,

> Teach me to hear mermaids singing,
>   Or to keep off envy's stinging,
>   And find
>   What wind
> Serves to advance an honest mind.
>
> If thou be'est born to strange sights,
>   Things invisible to see,
> Ride ten thousand days and nights,
>   Till age snow white hairs on thee,
> Thou, when thou return'st, wilt tell me
> All strange wonders that befell thee,
>   And swear
>   No where
> Lives a woman true, and fair.
>
> If thou find'st one, let me know,
>   Such a pilgrimage were sweet,
> Yet do not, I would not go,
>   Though at next door we might meet,
> Though she were true, when you met her,
> And last, till you write your letter,
>   Yet she
>   Will be
> False, ere I come, to two, or three.

Setting these two poems together will bring out their contradictory postures: one poem assumes the realized goal of a full constancy, the other assumes that it is impossible to find a constant woman. These are both conventional attitudes, the first of someone deeply in love, the other of someone willing to take worldly sophistication at full value. It is clear from the contradiction that the speaker pretends his enunciated notions, but it would also be oversimple, of course, to see him as falsifying the positions. Each time they are virtual and dialogic, tried on for their aspectual relevance and so both modalized and given their full head in the strong assertive thrust, with the sense of achieved finality that Donne himself prized in a poem.[27]

"The Good Morrow" begins with a remarkable set of hyperbolic characterizations of an imaginary past, as it comes up, finally, in the second stanza, to a shared, all-encompassing present. In the third stanza, it comes up to the "morrow" which continues that absorption in a proximate future so full that it easily falls into a macrocosm-microcosm metaphor, with the couple rather than a single person forming the microcosm. "Were we not weaned till then" hyperbolically equates the actual entrance of the infant into the world with the entrance into sexuality, erasing all the time between the two events, as a reinforcing reference to the emptiness of a time not given to love. As for the alternative, "Or snorted we in the seven sleepers' den," this pre-coital grossness of breathing, a sort of permanent condition equal to the lovers' spiritual, as well as their physical, absorption in each other, is not especially a metaphor. It is, if anything, an anti-metaphor: the snorting is the opposite of their absorption in one another. It calls into play an intense range of associations by its setting the lovers in the context of legend, through a gigantism of physical effect that continues the hyperbole. The seven sleepers slept through several lifetimes. They are extremely old, as a suckling babe is extremely young. These extremes are adduced, and then removed, as states only possible before the love that the poem celebrates.

If explorers and map users are seeking that which the lovers have already found, then the lovers encompass, and in fact constitute, the world. This is an assertion hyperbolic enough to contain its own contradiction, and so to have the effect of instancing the wit and alertness of the speaker, his love-enlivened adroitness at the sort of inventive ratiocination that here is ironic. Wit goes deep in Donne, so deep that he will continue it through his life, in the deeply serious vein of the sermons. The sermons are remarkable for continuing that note, and the "wit" can as easily be seen as a subspecies of hyperbole as vice versa. Deliberately overshooting their mark by shouting, these poems easily fall into the attitude of curiosities or—what is a version of them—puzzles. Or riddles. Yet the riddling aspect is not offered for the delight of solving the puzzle, but rather as a way of arresting and modalizing the attention to dwell upon the strong assertion that the poem makes: I am important because love is important; or, in other poems, because God is important.

The hyperbolic cast is retained in poems of the most various assertions. So certain poems will fit various circumstances. Their rhetoric subserves their assertiveness, and we would be hard put to classify them as illocutionary or perlocutionary. It is in fact their deftness to suspend that distinction. The command "Go and catch a falling star" is a way of saying "Do the impossible," and also of pretending to say it. But the impossibilia that are offered scale down to a human size by the time the poem gets to the common circumstances of trying to guard against envy or of trying to find a method for succeeding while remaining honest. Then the poem returns to hyperbole in a millennial span for the imagined searcher, bringing him back, after about half the poem is spent, to the single point and project, of beginning a love affair not for its own sake, the poem pretends, but in order to find a faithful woman—an impossibility, as it holds forth in the lightness of a despair that vanishes in the evenly measured short- and-long lines of the song.

The tripping of the short lines plays into the long concluding line. The tripping asserts itself as the concluding note, through the caesurae in the last line, "False, ere I come, to two, or three." The evenness of this measure, its failure in the "song" mode to have recourse to roughness, carries past and gathers up the hesitancies in the caesura and lightens the enjambment-emphasis of be / False—a conclusion effective enough to have the singer hold his breath before getting it out—"Yet she / Will be / False." The cynicism of the sense is here subverted by the mastery of the sound, which returns the tone of the poem to an accession into just the Jacobean courtly dominance of showiness and play. The assertion itself is close to the one built into Shakespeare's *Troilus and Cressida*, nor can the poem be far from that play in date. Yet the tone of the poem could hardly differ more. The very clarity of the speaker, and his fictionalized distance from the intimate addressee, the "thee" whom that locution in itself lets down gently, frame the utterance and orient the modal dexterity of its fusions.

"The Good Morrow" makes its own jokes, since it concludes on what turns out, through simple phrasing, to be a complicated version of the famous "die" pun. This sets up an infinite regress between the sexual death which must happen for a consummation of this love and a real death, when the love is felt to be undying. The poem enlists a version of one argument for immortality in Plato's *Phaedo* to underscore this assertion: "Whatever dies was not mixed equally"—a principle that is subverted by the hint that in order to die in the sexual sense they will in fact mix equally. The first "die" can only mean "lose life." And the second "die" must exclusively mean that too. To read either one as also invoking the sexual "die" would make nonsense of their propositions and subvert the high, lucid functioning of Donne's thought process. So the rhetoric of the poem enforces an alertness about the modalizing logical shifts involved at each point in its use of this key locution.

Such intense trains of thought permeate Donne and are almost his signature. They can be exemplified in such comparably challenging deductions elsewhere as "Change is the nursery . . . of eternity," when we might have thought that permanence was the nursery of eternity. Still, here in "The Good Morrow," even in negation, the reference to "mixed equally" and its suggestion of sexual fruition, framed by the two "dies," also rhythmically jibes with an (absent) sense of the sexual "die" in a version of what Christopher Ricks calls an anti-pun. At the same time, the act of love, which Donne consistently emphasizes elsewhere, is not explicitly named here, to such a point that it would be possible to claim that only looking into each other's eyes will fuse the lovers—except, again, for "mixed equally." So read, there is a euphemism equivalent to implied litotes or implied preterition even in that phrase. "Whatever dies, was not mixed equally" translates into two paradoxes, both of them the propositional equivalents of anti-puns, "Whatever [death] dies has not [sexually] died," and "Whatever [sexually] dies, [death] dies"—false paradoxes that the anti-pun mechanisms bring to hover over the boldly declarative lover.

The witty adduction of such underlying paradoxes is here subordinated to the laudation of a love who, again against the normal courtly tradition, is not here wooed but praised because she has been won. Such poems as these, though they are opposed in their assertions, are alike not only in their playfulness but in the mastery their communicative suppleness forces on the attention of the virtual reader, be that person a celebrated lover of the other sex or a disabused novice of the same sex.

As for the sound into which Donne complicates these utterances, we cannot do better than to begin with the deductions of Arnold Stein.

In Stein's scheme, meter functions "(1) almost as an abstract vehicle, (2) as naturalistic imitation, (3) as a contributing metaphor, (4) almost as a complete metaphor."[28] Taken by itself, as Stein applies it to Donne, this scheme is the most sophisticated and finest-tuned discussion of meter known to me. Taking it as a determinant of Donne's utterance, it can be applied to the communicative connection these poems invoke. As Stein says, "The effects may be observed, but this does not render the effects quite detachable. Donne is thinking *in* metered language, and that must mean both *with* and *against* meter, in the creative tension we attribute to art and assume is reconciled in the form which art creates."[29] The interaction between verse design and the instance of the speaking voice has here found ways to modalize, to double back on itself, to vary meter without the bravura of the theatrical verse of the first decade of the seventeenth century (when Donne does make passing reference to the fact that he himself frequented the theater). In a love poem, the speaker, following the long courtly tradition, stands in the position of a wooer; and in the standard gambit of that tradition he has not attained his object. Donne changes the posture, which gives him, modally, the before-and-after status of both a wooer and a gratified lover. Both these postures converge modally in the very vocal undecidability of the line emphasized by Stein from "Elegy 10, the Dream" (remembering that the title is not Donne's), "So, if I dreame I have you, I have you."

> The first "have," reinforced by the meter, is very emphatic, and so creates a pressure that is felt by the second "have." But the second "have" must resist at least part of that pressure; it cannot coincide with the meter, any more than it can avoid the influence of the rhetorical emphasis. . . . The mind informed by such an ear may recognize that a stressed "I" and "you" will mean that out of the dream a real *I* will possess a real *you*, but with far less emphasis on the reality of the possession than on the reality of the identity. . . . The result is a kind of ambiguous hovering that includes (in the pyrrhic-spondee of the last four syllables) both the reality of possession and the reality of identity, and includes them in their dynamic relationship to each other.[30]

Simultaneous possession and non-possession, past and future, reality and fantasy, are encapsulated here, but not held in an undecidability. Finally, we are assured that the speaker indeed has the ear, and very likely the person, of the beloved. All this play of voice amounts to (an expression of) a play of mind and feeling between them, in which fantasy is a defining element. Drawing from other poems, however, the possibility of inconstancy might also function, as it does to break the voice of the framed speaker into an indecidability that is at the same time overridden by his assertiveness. In the love poems, this quickens the speaker, and it also relieves the object of them from the remote inertness that haunts the conventional courtly beloved. As Roy Roussel says of the woman addressed in "The Flea," "she exists as a presence which somehow exceeds and discomposes each formulation."[31]

The epistle, as a form, interestingly trains the voice back into the conversational mode, but as poetry it necessarily transforms it. So the metrical roughnesses are perceived not just as the qualifying grace notes that Arnold Stein has astutely analyzed in the *Songs and Sonets*. In Donne's verse epistles, the roughnesses display and withdraw into severe formality the intimacy implied by conversation. Someone like Henry Wotton or Lord Herbert of Cherbury or the Countess of Bedford is brought close into voiced intimacy while the relationship is hypostatized into the generalizing formalization that the poem addresses, and the more extravagantly when the addressee is a woman. This is a double attitude, allowing, like other double attitudes, for the richness of a reflexive dialectic.

The wit in the epistles is at a still lower voltage and more sequential than in the *Songs and Sonets,* where it characteristically builds into profundities of coherence. The modern sense of "wit" is already present in the breadth of the seventeenth-century usage of the term. As Freud has allowed wit, seen in its conversational mode, the freedom to release cathexes with sprightly rapidity, so the rapid-fire ratiocinations of these epistles display not just their wit but the confidence and daring of applying it to a conversation that is slipped out for the virtual public to peek at while withdrawn by not being published, by being retained within the coterie.

Such wit permits not just rapid-fire sequence but also a marked modalizing obliquity, though a respect for the addressee would rule out any but a shared irony. In the "Epistle to Sir Edward Herbert at Villiers," Villiers being a famous battle, why is no mention made of the battle—even though the main conceit of the poem, man's psyche as a menagerie of beasts, can be easily related to military activity? This conceit is at lower voltage than those we find in "Aire and Angels" or "A Nocturnal upon St. Lucie's Day." It is also grimmer in tone, while containing the grimness in the confident congratulation of the recipient, which amounts also to the self-congratulation of equality and membership, a role unusual for the poet in any society until modern times.

It is Donne's achievement to keep a sense of pressures on his utterance alive, while bringing an utterance to an integrative transfer, to the special communication that a poem can be conceived of being. Donne indicates his awareness of how sensitive he is both to the nature of his utterance and the nature of his bond to his auditor:

> I know what dead carkasses things written are, in respect of things spoken. But in things of this kinde, that soul that inanimates them, receives debts from them: The Spirit of God that dictates them in the speaker or writer, and is present in his tongue or hand, meets himself again (as we meet our selves in a glass) in the eies and eares and hearts of the hearers and readers: and that Spirit, which is ever the same to an equall devotion, makes a writing and a speaking equall means to edification.[32]

The terms of this commonplace, even including its overtones of flattery and strategic self-deprecation, could be translated into the terms of Lacan's system, or of some other. The quasi-Kantian transcendence that Lacan has taught us to see built into the vocal interchange is further structured when that interchange is written down, and then defined, in what are really age-old terms, as at the service of religion: equality is equality before God. But it can also extend to human beings, and beyond Donne's conventional phallocratic posture there is a notable tone of equality even in Donne's love poems that differentiates them from the "worshipful" ones of Petrarch or Sidney or Spenser or even Shakespeare. Surely this approach to equality, along with his frankness, has given these poems the modern air so appealing to the intelligently literate and passionate young in this century. In the *Epistles* and in the *Anniversaries*, the very hyperbole is so unbelievable that, while largely unironic, it carries with it a constant assertion of a make-believe that throws us back on the underlying equality of an artificer capable of asking that these verbal constructions *not* be taken at face value. And Donne, even in his sermons, varies the equality the pastor assumes before his flock, naturally unbending more intimately at St. Dunstan's in the West or Lincoln's Inn than he does at the more majestic St. Paul's or, differently, before the king at Whitehall.

In the *Anniversaries*, the meters are relatively smooth, and the couplets reinforce this, as though the hyperbole announced by its title when applied to a young deceased, "An Anatomy of the World," organizing the universe around Elizabeth Drury, is so extravagant that it carries off of itself the task of unifying the utterance, so that the poem need not exhibit the roughnesses it is controlling. The exaltation of the subject entails the humility of poet and auditor:

> And learns't thus much by our anatomy
> That 'tis in vain to dew or mollify
> It with thy tears, or sweat, or blood: nothing
> Is worth our travail, grief or perishing,
> But those rich joys which did possess her heart,
> Of which she's now partaker, and a part.
> (429–34)

Finally, after all the rhetorical templates and topoi have been surveyed,[33] the *Anniversaries* are original for being outrageous in their extravagance, even if they would seem outrageously to have carried the day. They are far bolder and more preposterous than their analogues in the work of other poets. There is a kind of wishful thinking, therefore, in the modesty and balance of the central claim for poetry with which he concludes the first:

> And you her creatures, whom she works upon
> And have your last, and best concoction

> From her example, and her virtue, if you
> In reverence to her, do think it due,
> That no one should her praises thus rehearse,
> As matter fit for chronicle, not verse,
> Vouchsafe to call to mind, that God did make
> A last, and lasting'st piece, a song. He spake
> To Moses, to deliver unto all,
> That song: because he knew they would let fall
> The Law, the prophets, and the history,
> But keep the song still in their memory.
> Such an opinion (in due measure) made
> Me this great office boldly to invade.
> Nor could incomprehensibleness deter
> Me, from thus trying to emprison her.
> Which, when I saw that a strict grave could do,
> I saw not why verse might not do so too.
> Verse hath a middle nature: heaven keeps souls,
> The grave keeps bodies, verse the fame enrols.
> (455–74)

While Louis Martz is able to diagram these poems and to show that their organization can be made to correspond to the five stages of an Ignatian meditation, still the meditation provides no cue, or clue, for the monstrous disproportion of their compliment.[34] They expand in a disproportion and violation of decorum which modally subverts all the conflation of genres. "How witty's ruin!" Donne says in "The First Anniversary" (99). The statement begins to prove itself by wittily cataloguing the resourcefulness of the destructive forces in nature, and especially with respect to a sexual life and a matrimony over which the young, dead Elizabeth Drury will have preemptively triumphed. "Let thy maker's praise / Honour thy Laura," he says in the "Harbinger to the Progress" of "The Second Anniversary" (36–37), letting a Petrarchan idealization easily into his mix while leaving aside most of the coordinates of such an idealization. In "The First Anniversary," Donne weaves into the hyperbole a fully physical but wholly unerotic connection between the universe and the dead girl, especially in lines 220–49. The very lines used by T. S. Eliot to illustrate his undissociated sensibility occur here in a context where the poet is performing a balancing act so extreme that he calls attention to himself like a high-wire artist: "Her pure and eloquent blood / Spoke in her cheeks and so distinctly wrought / That one might *almost* [my emphasis] say her body thought" (244–46). The body is brought close when it is furthest distanced, and there is no erotic interest, nor can be, for the line between living and dead. And she is no Beatrice; there is no memory of any possible love either, and Donne had never actually seen the girl. The poem, one of the few he published, did have a literary success, and it did solidify its author into close friendship with the powerful Drury family in Drury Lane, to whose property, after traveling abroad as their guest, he moved with his whole family.

"The Second Anniversary" is a modification. In it Donne retreats to the declaration of metaphoric properties, rather than the extravagant metaphors of "The First Anniversary," "in all she did / Some figure of the Golden Times was hid" (69–70). It is as though he can relax and rely on the triumph of the first, in meters that remain smooth. There is already a range of possibilities in Donne's modalization.

"Unitary, therefore, means only that it is *one* person doings lots of things at once, that is, performing very complex actions while defensively and in self-contradiction restricting his or her being consciously aware of what is being done and why."[35] What Roy Schafer here says of the analysand applies to the speaker under pressure whose unitary act is carried through under such varied and complex conditions. This well characterizes the modal conflations that Donne carried off in his poems. And when he speaks of them himself, it tends to be within the set of an address to a patron, or under the piety of the speaker of a sermon:

> I was your prophet in your younger days,
> And now your chaplain, God in you to praise.[36]

This statement is so moderate as to tone down Donne's usual emphasis for what is in effect further flattery, the more that these are the last lines of the poem, when he made a point of giving last lines a special prominence. And still, the function of a chaplain is one that in fact Donne had already elected to exercise in the *Anniversaries*. A muted discourse about poetry set in a context of flattery is offered at greater length to the same addressee:

> Yet neither will I vex your eyes to see
> A sighing ode, nor cross-armed elegy.
> I come not to call pity from your heart,

Like some white-livered dotard that would part
Else from his slippery soul with a faint groan,
And faithfully, (without you smiled) were gone.
I cannot feel the tempest of a frown,
I may be raised by love, but not thrown down.
Though I can pity those sigh twice a day,
I hate that thing whispers itself away.
Yet since all love is fever, who to trees
Doth talk, doth yet in love's cold ague freeze.
'Tis love, but, with such fatal weakness made,
That it destroys itself with its own shade.
Who first looked sad, grieved, pined, and showed his pain,
Was he that first taught women to disdain.[37]

No poet ever made so unprepossessing a claim for poetry, and this self-effacement must itself be attributed to the rhetoric in which the poet is demonstrating that he has been swallowed. His assertion is stronger, but still enchained in the mastery of contradiction, when he addresses questions of utterance in his Sermons:

> How barren a thing is Arithmetique? (and yet Arithmetique will tell you, how many single graines of sand, will fill this hollow Vault to the Firmament) How empty a thing is Rhetorique? (and yet Rhetorique will make absent and remote things present to your understanding) How weak a thing is Poetry? (and yet Poetry is a counterfait Creation, and makes things that are not, as though they were).[38]

But Donne has all along, as one might expect, the poet's keen sense of metrical effect, "Psalms, which is such a form as is both curious, and requires diligence in the making, and then when it is made, can have nothing, no syllable taken from it, nor added to it."[39] And he honors the choice of diction in any act of expression. Speaking of prayer in 1609, he cites the Spanish aphorist Gratian on the proper posture for the person praying, and says "Yea, words which are our subtlest and delicatest outward creates, being composed of thoughts and breath, are so muddy, so thick, that our thoughts themselves are so, because (at first rising) they are ever leavened with passions and affections." This out-Flauberts Flaubert's notion of words that beat a drum to make bears dance when we would have them move the stars. And the reference to a "first rising" suggests the intensification of revision even when the words to be spoken are just vocal, addressed in a prayer to God.⁴⁰ The override in the rhythm carries forward, confidently in the (remembered) confrontation of delivery, all the backwash of qualification. And Donne reverted fairly often to questions of style and composition, as one might expect, as well as to the ontological status of such utterances as his:

> In the words, and by occasion of them [Christ answering a man's question], we consider the Text, the Context, and the Pretext: Not as three equall parts of the Building; but the Context, as the situation and Prospect of the house, the Pretext, as the Accesse and entrance to the house, And then the Text it selfe, as the House it selfe, as the body of the building.⁴¹

> *Invention*, and *Disposition*, and *Art,* and *Eloquence* and *Expression* and *Elocution*, and *reading*, and *writing*, and *printing*, are secondary things, accessory things, auxiliary, subsidiary things; men may account us, and make account of us, as of *Orators* in the pulpit, and of *Authors,* in the shop; but if they account of us as *of Ministers and Stewards*, they give us our due; that's our name to you.⁴²

> Dost thou love learning, as it is sweetned and set to musique by *Poets*? the King of the Poets testifies the same, *Mens agitat molem, et magno se corpore miscet;* that is, a great, an universall spirit, that moves, a generall soule, that inanimates, and agitates every peece of this world. But *Saint Paul* is a more powerfull Orator, then *Cicero*, and he says, *The invisible things of God, are seen by things which are made*; and thereby man is made *inexcuseable: Moses* is an ancienter *Philosopher*, then *Trismegistus;* and his picture of God, is the Creation of the world. *David* is a better *Poet* then *Virgil;* and with *David, Coeli enarrant, the heavens declare the glory of God*; The power of *oratory*, in the force of perswasion, the strength of conclusions in the pressing of *Philosophy*, the harmony of *Poetry* in the sweetness of composition, never met in any man, so fully as in the Prophet *Esay*, nor in the Prophet *Esay* more, then where he says *Levate Oculos, Lift up your eyes, on high, and behold who hath created these things;* behold them, *therefore*, to know they are created, and to know who is their creator.⁴³

When set off from his parishioners, or at least his auditors, Donne puts himself above them as their pastor but also on a level with them as a meditating sin-prone devotee. In the *Epistles*, where the convention puts the writer on a level with the recipient, he reverses it by reverting to the other convention of extravagant compliment; and, especially when a noble woman is the recipient, he sets the recipient on a pedestal of virtue. Often in these poems, as against his practice with the lyric, he writes up, not down or at a level, unlike Horace and the Renaissance epistolary writers in Spanish and Italian. This, it could be said, forces the wit forward in order to span the distance upward between writer and recipient.

There is a yield, in the Sermons too, from a heightening and even a modalization of their tonal register. They are more orotund than, for example, the sermons of Lancelot Andrewes. And, as Gale Carrithers evocatively reminds us, there is also a yield from the architectural surround for preacher and audience, the physical and acoustic space they occupy together. Carrithers well stresses "the fundamentally dialogic nature of his sermons."[44] Theodore Gill points up Donne's marginal notation of "divisio" as showing the rhetorical structure to the audience. "The sermon is first of all an urgent communication."[45]

This hyperbole, in the Sermons, becomes a constant recourse not to exaggeration but to the subtle, and initially literal, interpretation of the Scriptural text held before his audience, to the anaphora of expanding repetition that shades into an amplificatio, and rhythmically to the oft-punctuated but onward-surging swell of the sentences. These sentences bury in prayerful assertion all the subtleties of possible contrast that the incidental and contributory observations are carrying through. The carrying communicative force of this more-than-rhetoric even in Donne's *Epistles* can be illustrated, as traditionally between public utterance and private communication in the speeches and letters of Cicero, by contrasting the Sermons with the prose letters of Donne, which, unlike the letters of, say, Henry James, but like the letters of Marcel Proust, heavily modify the unifying overlay of the more public utterance.

The sermons for which he was famous would on that evidence have found reverberations in his auditors. They exhibit the same attentiveness to the communicative act that operates in its virtual state within the poems when they are addressed to one alone perhaps fictively, and then again when they are addressed to a dead girl he never met with such effectiveness that her parents became his lifelong friends and patrons.

Poems to the beloved and epistles to friends have a built-in addressee, one who comes to the poet not only out of his actual personal life but out of the large rhetorical staples of inherited poetry. Donne, coming at these forms as such a strong personal presence, forces them to undergo turns of definition that dynamize the relationship of speaker to addressee into a new yield of specificity, comprehensive questioning, and a bold openness of field not envisaged by Propertius, Horace, or Petrarch. His near contemporary Shakespeare engages a more elaborate dialectic of personae in the *Sonnets*, as recent commentators have shown us, by multiplying the figures and splitting the sexes.[46] But Shakespeare does not have recourse to Donne's dramatic coiling of inferences about the self, though his inferences about the self's interactions with others reach the dialectical heights that Fineman has helped us to scale. Shakespeare's references to himself tend to be straight, "I am that I am" (121). The play around "will" and the assertions of lyric power feed into that play. When he exhibits his own person, he tends toward a sort of lyric inspection of his incapacity or decline: "That time of year thou mayst in me behold" (73), "Beated and chopt with tanned antiquity" (62), "My nature is subdued / To what it works in, like the dyer's hand" (111).

In the "Holy Sonnets" and in other poems the addressee, implied or actual, is God; and while these poems may conform to the meditative pattern, they also break beyond it in the strenuousness of their affirmation, "Batter my heart, three-personed God"; "At the round earth's imagined corners blow / Your trumpets, angels, and arise, arise / From death, you numberless infinities." The meditation even of the "Sermon Preached on the Death of Sir William Cockayne" moves as quickly through theological speculation as the shorter-breathed sermons of Lancelot Andrewes do with the self-querying of definition. Both sermoners show an energy less than properly quietistic and subdued. But the speculations of the sermoner Donne in this "Holy Sonnet," as in others, has been turned into a direct address that implies and subsumes the scansions of the doctrine put under examination in the matching sermon. Yet the sermon, locked to the public occasion of homily and edification, cannot allow the expansions and turns of the poem. This large capacity of the poem falls into relief if we compare with Donne's last sermon, "Death's Duell," the poem which had the reputation for being the last he ever wrote, "Hymn to God my God, in my Sickness." And it would have that contrastive force even if the poem had actually been written instead during his severe illness of 1623:

> Since I am coming to that holy room,
>   Where, with thy choir of saints for evermore,
> I shall be made thy music; as I come
>   I tune the instrument here at the door,
>   And what I must do then, think here before.
>
> Whilst my physicians by their love are grown
>   Cosmographers, and I their map, who lie
> Flat on this bed, that by them may be shown
>   That this is my south-west discovery
>   *Per fretum febris*, by these straits to die,

Sound, Sense, and Religion in Donne's Poetry 129

I joy, that in these straits, I see my west;
    For, though their currents yield return to none,
What shall my west hurt me? As west and east
    In all flat maps (and I am one) are one,
    So death doth touch the resurrection.

Is the Pacific Sea my home? Or are
    The eastern riches? Is Jerusalem?
Anyan, and Magellan, and Gibraltar,
    All straits, and none but straits, are ways to them,
    Whether where Japhet dwelt, or Cham, or Shem.

We think that Paradise and Calvary,
    Christ's Cross, and Adam's tree, stood in one place;
Look Lord, and find both Adams met in me;
    As the first Adam's sweat surrounds my face,
    May the last Adam's blood my soul embrace.

So, in his purple wrapped receive me Lord,
    By these his thorns give me his other crown;
And as to others' souls I preached thy word,

Be this my text, my sermon to mine own,
Therefore that he may raise the Lord throws down.

This has a smoothness of rhythm more akin to the work of Jonson or Herbert than to what we think of as Donne's characteristic rhythmic complexity. But in that rhythmic smoothness, which must surely here suggest through its own music the gathering calm of a devout man before last things, the application of Donne's logical permutations on the self and its relation to God remain unabated. In the first stanza, the "room" of the afterlife is said shortly to receive a speaker who will be transformed totally into music, an extravagant and theologically unusual assertion. Even the Dante at the end of the *Paradiso* had not gone so far. In the present of the poem, however, the speaker is just doing something that seems more ordinary. "As I come / I tune the instrument here at the door." However, across the split between the totalized music of the imagined near future and the imagined "ordinary" present, the speaker is already performing and modalizing his intensifications. Because what is the instrument here? It is the mind, the spirit, the soul of the speaker. But, in the light of Donne's pervasive insistence on the resurrection of the body, it is also ultimately the whole speaker himself. And it must be taken also as these very metered words of the speaker, a tuning up that reflexively defines itself. All this comes through very quietly but no less intensely than the logical permutations in the earlier "characteristic" "Aire and Angels," or the "Nocturnal upon St. Lucie's Day," or even the "Holy Sonnets."

That the body is in view (but always not only the body), is substantiated in the second stanza, where the speaker, being diagnosed and treated, becomes the whole world of which the doctors are the "Cosmographers." Moreover, it is an earth ready for "discovery," and thus the psychology of the moribund speaker makes his hope coterminous with the mood of Renaissance exploration. This goes far beyond the body-world metaphor of Phineas Fletcher's *The Purple Island*. This speaker's discovery proceeds not through prayer but "through the strait of fever," *per fretum febris*. This situation turns out to set the stage in the third and following stanzas for pressing the fictively geographical facts in the form of what the speaker sees as actual, bold theological inferences. A paradox similar to that in "Goode Friday: Riding Westward" has the west meet the east in the "flat map" he claims to be (as west does meet east in a regular Mercator projection). He then mixes remote places like the Pacific with the Jerusalem which is at once actual, historical, and figurative, going on to the division of the world after the Flood among the three sons of Noah. The fifth stanza moves to a comparable but more ordinary conflation of Adam's place and Christ's; and then "both Adams met in me." In the last stanza, the speaker becomes, because he has enacted them, both (scriptural) text and the sermon on the text, since that was his activity in life, as he declares in line 3, collapsing the whole music with the theological commonplace, so far not mentioned, "Therefore that he may raise the Lord throws down." A modalized verse is summoned to summarize a whole life on the threshold of its final definition.

6. Wisdom and Ethics

I

The finality of a poem, and its mounting of modalities, aims its wisdom at a vision of human behavior, and so, implicitly, at ethics. The reader of a story in a novel, too, or the viewer of one on stage wishes to include the story in some pattern of plausibility and rightness, a system of what is ultimately justice, as well as to be moved into a heightened feeling, to share as well as to understand the states that literature envisages. And the reader of a poem wishes the feeling evoked by the poem to accord with some desirable and justifiable ideal. But, first of all, if questions about justice are asked, they lead on the one hand to the irreducibility of story.[1] On the other hand such questions lead to the outer reaches of the philosophy of jurisprudence.[2] If questions about feelings are asked, they lead to structures of depth response and ego psychology, the whole universe of psychoanalytic readings that have contributed so richly to our understanding of literary works—but not to a resolution about justice, or to an understanding of the relation between justice and feeling. Even Jacques Lacan, who raises questions about the structuring of feelings (desire) in connection with justice, frames such questions but does not resolve them when he brings them to the dead heat of his juxtaposition of Kant and Sade; he plumbs desire (but not exactly justice) when he addresses the *Antigone* of Sophocles.[3]

Kant separates ethics from aesthetics by attributing them to different constellations of mental functions, and he also connects them by building some of the same constituents into their functions. The aesthetic, in its orientation to the goals he conjectures, provides a symbolic analogy to the ethical. For Kant, as for Plato, the beautiful and the good are linked.[4] There is no reason for our following him all the way, since the fullness of modern practice would then have to ground itself on an insufficient and sketchy presentation of feeling. But we can take his act of separation as a caution against too ready an identification of ethics and aesthetics, as well as a caution against separating them completely. Just how and how far the aesthetic draws on the ethical, and builds into the ethical through its framing of wisdom, is as fundamental a question as we can have, and literary theory will ignore this at its peril.[5]

Kafka sets the tone and the question, as we should be asking it; his words provide at once a direction and an indication of the precondition to which the wisdom in literature is an ever-abundant and ever-puzzling answer beyond (and too extremely antithetical to) the *plaisir* of Roland Barthes:

> The answer to this letter seemed more important than any earlier letter to you. . . . I firmly believe one should read only such books as bite and sting. If the book we are reading does not wake us with a punch to the head, why read it? To make us happy, as you write? My God, we'd be happy enough even if we had no books, and books to make us happy we could write ourselves if we had to. But we need books that work on us like an blow that hurts us deeply, like the death of someone we loved better than ourselves; like being driven into the woods, away from all men; like a suicide. A book must be the axe for the frozen sea within. That's what I believe.[6]

This declaration, though extreme, is a supplement as well as a corrective to the generally accurate but one-sided analyses of Barthes and of Wayne Booth.[7] Booth does frame the issues well. In a first move, following Hilary Putnam on the non-neutral value of pleasurable experience even in the reductive case of ice cream, Booth carries through a reduced version of the Kantian antinomy, showing that the "subjective" perception of art still gradually "co-duces" it to ethical questions and does not totally subsume it under the social processes so delicately analyzed by others. In a second move, he insists that the "ethical" is central to art. But here lies the question. Extending his argument about *Huckleberry Finn*, that the full meaning of the novel redeems its incidental racism and sexism, one is forced to face the question in further puzzling forms that oblige us to make the third, and most crucial move, an account (necessarily circular, and necessarily partial) of what goes on in the delicacies of *ethical* moves within an art work.

It will not do to make of *Huckleberry Finn* an entertainment, however skillful. Those who look for a moral in it will be prosecuted according to Twain's famous "notice" "posted" at the beginning of the work—itself sending a shot of hyperbole in the direction of ironic self-incapacitation. But Huck's ethical life does proceed under the aegis of a half-abandoned boy who, in Rousseauist fashion, meets most of his ethical tests in the processive confrontation of life decisions that are harrowing but trivial.

Continuously experiencing cruelty at first hand from his father and others, and at second hand through the way society handles his friend, the black slave Jim, he largely, if not unfailingly, proceeds from a pitch of clarity where cruelty cannot find a hold. For all the wavering toward the end of the novel, and for all the occasionally superficial satire of types along the river, Huck keeps fairly steady at judging presumed ethics negatively as he goes along, and in the process he is forming the final decision "to light out for the Territory," to seek not a tabula rasa but a larger, emptier field where he will be purged of ethically compromising situations and be able to define an unconstraining life. As Lionel Trilling says, the novel has "the truth of honesty . . . and also the truth of moral passion: it deals directly with the virtue and depravity of man's heart."[8]

The novel by its approving tone endorses Huck's decision as it unfolds its wisdom. Its indulgence toward the central character is not a self-indulgence because it is controlling toward hope, in a fashion not completely removed from the air of fairy tale, a set of circumstances that could easily be presented as insurmountably dire. Huck's narrative voice from the very beginning links small acts of judgment, assessment, and induction against the grain of oppressive convention, to the narrative of the ongoing action. Dramatized as having to have his wits about him, Huck constantly exercises those wits, and the ethical acumen, his instinctive rightness, builds up cumulatively in the balance of these judgments, even though the reader will depart from some of them, and after they have been proffered through the direct irony governing some of them. Twain, sometimes ostentatiously, reveals Huck's ignorance; but this limitation, like that of his youth and distressed circumstances, all the more impressively is meant to highlight the soundness of his opinions rather than to throw them under the pall of the sort of obscurity covering some loquacious characters in Shakespeare's early comedies. Most of Huck's judgments ring largely true, even if some of them ring false to Twain or to ourselves; in any case, they are shown as all the narrating Huck has to go on, in default of other advantages. Here the ethical yield is not a series of morals, and not the sort of dialectic we find, for example, in Corneille and Racine, or even in Shakespeare. It partakes of the tone and invests the solider events, while the others, in the light of that vision, can be allowed to fall away from it. All this ethical wisdom does not simply counterbalance or outweigh the automatic racial prejudice in the novel. It goes deeper, establishing on its own terms an ethical domain where the racism, taken as examined (or putatively imagined to be so), could not survive.

This process is very complex, and it does not have to exact full congruence between writer and reader. An air of mystery as well as a universe of epistemological questions hangs over or between their junction, in fact, as J. Hillis Miller effectually says.[9] An artist does not have to (though he can and often does) act, in the rhetoric of his work, like a friend in the ways that Booth perspicuously lays out (*The Company We Keep*, 179–80):

> Our reading friends can vary:
>
> 1. in the sheer *quantity* of invitations they offer us.
>
> 2. in the degreee of *responsibility* they grant to us—what we might call the level of reciprocity or domination between author and reader;
>
> 3. in the degree of *intimacy* in the friendship;
>
> 4. in the *intensity* of engagement that they expect or require—from total concentration to slack, comfortable, slowly ripening acquaintance;
>
> 5. in the *coherence* or consistency of the proffered world;
>
> 6. in the *distance* between their worlds and ours . . . the amount of rude challenge or "otherness" they fling at our current norms;
>
> 7. in the kind, or *range of kinds*, of activities suggested, invited, or demanded—from a reassuring concentration on single-minded issues or formal patterns . . . to a reconstruction and embrace of whole "worlds" that seem to include every topic our "real" worlds include.

Now this census can be made to cover the whole literary experience. But that experience is subtly distorted, and sometimes markedly, if seen under this ranging qualification of friendships. As I understand Booth, there is much to agree with in his presentation. But he does not press the really hard cases. In the light of Kafka's cautionary injunctions, there are senses in which the axe for the frozen sea within is not being wielded by anyone who might be thought of as a friend. Like Booth, I do not think of Norman Mailer as a potential friend, not even in his writing, though his personal life and motives are irrelevant, or at least mediated and bracketed, with relation to the force of *The Executioner's Song*. But unlike Booth, I agree with Joan Didion in highly esteeming that work, because for me it carries a penetrating wisdom about human intrications, beyond the appeal that Mailer's central figure, Gary Gilmore, may have had for Mailer, and beyond what Booth reads (and I believe misreads by oversimplifying) as Mailer's apology for Gilmore. If we take Booth's census not as a list of alternatives but as aspects that could all function in a work, dropping the arbitrary "friend" requirement, then *The Executioner's Song* can be seen to carry out most or even all of Booth's desiderata. Its range of persons constitutes a quantity of invitations to the reader; the very "flat" and disjunct presentation endows him with responsibility; the reader is brought inside Gilmore's family and his love relationships and thereby into intimacy with the voice of the author; it is coherent in its large juxtaposition of "Western Voices" with "Eastern Voices"; it implicitly posits a distance between ourselves and either of these worlds; and the range of activities in it broadens and deepens the reader's sense of its world and his own. All this happens without either the person or the persona of the author having to function as my friend in Booth's sense.

My doctor does not have to be potentially my friend. Aristotle (or for that matter the platitudinous Cicero, the author of *On Friendship*) does not have to be my friend in order to help define even friendship. To continue along these lines, I can construct from Aristotle's work as I read it the sense that as a potential friend he would be a priggish genius; I am not sure this complex of characteristics would be a strong basis for friendship, and I derive this sense from what seems the self-satisfaction, and sometimes the unconscious circularity, of arguments about friendship in *The Nicomachean Ethics*. Nietzsche in many ways goes far deeper when he speculates on the psychological substructure of what amounts to friendship, and we have much evidence about his personal capacity for friendship with such different persons as Richard Wagner and Jakob Burckhardt (not to mention Paul Rée and Lou-Andreas Salome). Yet I carry away from his writings, supplemented by such data, that he would be an abrupt, overbearing, often evasive friend. Nor is he a trustworthy guide. But he is a genuine purveyor of wisdom. I have drawn my illustrations here from philosophers rather than poets to throw into relief the fact that even when we are dealing with ideas, in what is arguably a more direct form than that offered by poets and novelists, the criterion of social intimacy is a complex one that cannot be made completely congruent with our sense of the force, acceptability, and penetration of a writer's discourse.

And then, once we have weighed the ethical bearing of a work, there may be a disparity between the ethical behavior of the writer and his ethical insight—as in Saint Paul's caution, that "when I have preached to others I myself be a castaway" (*adokimos*, 1 Cor 9. 27). Matching this, there is a forever uncertain gap between a reader's reponse to a work and his subsequent behavior. Is a spouse more or less likely to commit adultery after reading *Anna Karenina*? After reading D. H. Lawrence, or Henry Miller, or William Burroughs, or Kathy Acker? How then do the feelings and the inescapable judgmental act of weighing the ethical force of Hamlet's deeds or Anna Karenina's come together in a final response? All the elaborations of the analysis of *mentalités*, themselves puzzling, are preliminary to this question.[10] And the considerations of ego psychology, in whatever form, offer their own supplementary, partially overlapping hermeneutic circle.

"A tale of great moral courage may lead me to a private oath to be more courageous, only to discover next day that I am still a coward," Booth well says.[11] But this principle, if taken seriously, throws us back to the consideration of the wisdom, as well as the rightness, of what is offered in a work of verbal art. The wisdom must count the more as what we are called on to ascertain if the force to which it is supposed to lead may not in fact be brought to bear unequivocally in the life of the reader.

One could turn the well-argued claim of J. Hillis Miller the other way from his quasi-deconstructionist conclusions: "This ethical 'I must' cannot . . . be accounted for by the social and historical forces that impinge upon it. Yet impinge upon it they do." In what way the social and historical forces do impinge upon ethical imperatives, and then on the literary versions of them, remains a central question for literary theory, as does the further, indissociable question, of how the transcendences (or for that matter the evasions) in literature stand with relation to those social and historical forces.[12] Without entering into a critique of Miller's arresting connection of narrative with the law, one could bring to bear upon it the very question posed by his further statement (28), "If the story I tell myself is a fictional narrative, it must be at the same time firmly implanted like a bridge's abutments, on both sides of the chasm, in the law as such, which is no chimera, and in the real world where my choices and actions have real effects." This principle does not necessarily lead to the Derrida-derived assertion, "Narrative can be defined as the indefinite postponement of that ultimate direct confrontation of the law which narrative is nevertheless instituted to make happen as an example worthy of respect" (Miller, *The Ethics of Reading*, 33), since even Kafka's versions, or Beckett's, imply a ground as final as Kant's against which the vacillations would have to be measured, even if at the same time (and to this degree Miller, as I understand him, is in harmony with their implications) that ground can never be attained; it is an ethical *Ding an sich*.

Miller effectually supplements and so parallels R. P. Blackmur in acutely pointing out the unexamined contradictions underlying the feeling to which Kant attributes the possibility of the Categorical Imperative.

Centering on Kant's use of the term *Gefühl* ("feeling") to characterize *Achtung* ("attention" or "respect") Miller's distinctions are finely argued:

> If respect, as Kant affirms, is a feeling, it lacks one of the main characteristics of feelings for Kant, namely that feelings are generated as "inclination" or "fear," a tendency to approach or flee, in response to something external to the self. A feeling is a response to an "influence" (Einfluss) which flows into the mind from without, coercing it and generating its affects. Respect, however, is not a feeling in this sense.... It is self-wrought rather than being a response to something external. It is not a movement toward or away from something external. It is not a movement toward or away from something desired or feared. On the other hand, respect is a response to something that preexists it and exists outside the mind, not the creation of that something. If Kant must avoid at all costs (at the cost of logical coherence) the possibility that *Achtung* is mere reflex reaction of desire or fear, in the other direction he must avoid at all costs the possibility that since respect is "self-wrought" it creates or projects its object, the moral law as such.

There is a fine hermeneutic tact here, though there is also much that can in turn be contested at least as fully as Kant's casual usage: are not all feelings in some sense self-wrought? In any case, respect *is* directed toward an external object, and a psychoanalytic reading could easily find desire or fear, or more probably a dynamic interaction of both, in the substructure under "respect." And one could continue to qualify Miller's statements in the same way that he qualifies Kant's, though without fully undoing his effort to adduce ad hoc distinctions between respect on the one hand and inclination or fear; since if respect, contra Miller, does enlist one or both of these feelings, it does so in a reconstructive, and so different, way. In any case, the play of qualifications around Kant's usage, which Miller's offers, does not make Kant's situation "an abyss," as Miller goes on to claim. The pre-Freudian and pre-Romantic Kant is inescapably sketchy on feeling; he can be imagined as not understanding exactly Faust's claim "Gefühl ist alles" ("Feeling is all"; *Faust*, line 3456).[13] Uncovering such (fairly normal) play in ordinary linguistic usage does not arrest the usage at the potential contradiction because it proceeds, or leaps if you will, across to the assertions. Kant, after all, is asserting, and also stating, the categorical imperative, however intricately his assertion is caught in the language of his phrasing.[14]

Miller, in fact, though more fine-grained in his analyses, has at best not gone beyond the principles of R. P. Blackmur's more robust and positive essay on this very subject (ethics in fiction; the ethics of reading, if you will), "Between the Numen and the Moha, Notes Toward a Theory of Literature." As Blackmur there says:[15] "The novel is ethics in action. Feeling and action. What is felt and what is action—a little under our will, a little apart from our intent—are exactly our behavior" (289). He goes on to specify the terms he sets into gapped relation: "The *Numen* . . . is that power within us, greater than ourselves and other than ourselves, that moves us, sometimes carrying us away, in the end moving us forward unless we drop out, always overwhelming us. So far as it may be felt in literature, it resembles the force of the sublime described by Longinus"; as against: "*Moha*, the uncontrollable behavior which tends to absorb and defile both the chill and the fire of spirit . . . *Moha*, then, is a term for the basic, irremediable, irreplaceable, characteristic, and contemptuous stupidity of man confronted with choice or purpose: the stupidity because of which he goes wrong, without which he could not survive" (293–94).

There is a whole repertory of ways to handle in fiction the relation between feeling and justice. Proust, who theorizes a dialectical universe of feeling, connects it to long-term justice when in effect he rejects snobbery, cruelty, and sexual exploitation. Heinrich von Kleist builds his stories in such a way that feeling is separated from justice, creating a paradox that Miller has "deconstructed": presenting Kleist's work as offering an endless regress, when it could also be described more simply as an incongruence between two systems, both valid, presented as incommensurable. The theology of the church, the systems of law, the structure of family ties, and the bonds of trust between men are all very much in place as inter-nesting systems of justice in *Michael Kohlhaas* and in *Der Findling (The Foundling)*. What breaks them down is the feeling responses of protagonists wronged under the code of justice and also under most if not all conceptions of equity. For the reader, both systems, that of justice or equity and that of feeling, must hold to be understood, and so cannot be deconstructed into a kind of chaos. If the reader does not clearly perceive that Michael Kohlhaas has been wronged initially when his horses are mistreated and replaced, and then by his supposed host's manipulation of governmental and legal machinery to cover up this outrage, then Michael's feelings would be groundless, and there would be no point in telling of his powerfully impelled counter-moves of military injustice. "Two wrongs don't make a right" is a simple basis or underlying moral for the story. But if the feelings could find some commensurate solution, there would be no story. Both the feelings and the interlocking social systems are clear and in a sense beyond question. They are givens, and Kleist has a penchant for setting such stories in the past where the conditions are inevitably given; the past cannot be changed and is remote enough not to be felt as open-ended.

So, too, in *Der Findling*. In that story Piachi, a widowed and recently remarried Roman merchant, takes his son with him to Ragusa. The city is struck with the plague and the son dies, but Piachi, further risking infection, rescues an orphan, Nicolo, takes him home, adopts him, and makes him his heir. The young man, as he grows into adolescence, forms a liaison with the bishop's mistress, and in his new sexual awareness he decides to seduce his young stepmother, Elvira, by dressing in the costume of the likeness she worships in her chamber, the picture of a youth who died while rescuing her from a fire. As a result of this shock, she herself ultimately dies, and Nicolo, sheltered by his connection with the high ecclesiastic's mistress, eventually divests Piachi of all his property. Piachi kills him and, condemned to death himself, steadfastly refuses absolution so that he may join Nicolo in hell and plague him eternally.

Now Piachi's Christian act of rescuing an orphan at the risk of being felled by the plague must be accorded its full sense of mercy. The adoption of the orphan must be felt by the reader as generosity. The grown orphan's act of trying to seduce his benefactor's wife and of despoiling his benefactor of the worldly goods he would have inherited anyway is so outrageous, by values the reader must share to make sense of the story, that Piachi's desire to pursue in hell the betrayer he has murdered becomes understandable. This feeling, at the extreme juncture set up by Kleist, is endlessly incommensurate with the practices of the church for condemned men, and with the justifications that can be constructed (and normally do hold) for situations of strong feeling not quite so extreme.

Miller, in an acute study of this story,[16] takes it at the same time at such a sharp hermeneutic angle that he systematically downgrades the bases in feeling and sensed criteria of justice in its incommensurabilities, centering it oversimply as a version of a "prosopopoeia" or troped personification of the figurative into an (imagined) living person, "the fundamental linguistic act making a given story possible" (13). He further specifies, "Reading is a speech act of a peculiar and definable kind, not an epistemological event to be defined as the passing on of a received and codified knowledge" (94). But, on the contrary, the transfer from writer to reader is just such an epistemological event, a transfer of knowledge or wisdom—except that a world of qualification would be necessary to say in what senses Miller's phrase "received and codified" could be allowed. Accordingly, among the many events of the story, Miller centers especially on Elvira's entrapped mistaking of Nicolo for her early beloved. But unlike the Marquise of O, Elvira is led to no consequential acts other than the immediate rejection of Nicolo, along with her mistake; and his own mistake has been one of calculation: to assume that Elvira will be as susceptible and subjected to her impulses as the bishop's mistress. The central act is his own: he has mistakenly tried to capitalize on a momentary mistake brought about through his calculation; there is no symmetry, or not much, between her error not of affection but of perception and his violation of human trust. Her marital loyalty is not shaken, and Nicolo's unfortunate character remains consistently outrageous. Nor are these values questioned by Kleist, however deeply he questions the manageability of the overall pattern in which these values figure. Precisely, his irony depends on the incommensurability between the justifiable fixity of these values and the unpredictability of enchained events. So Miller is both right in one dimension and wrong in his overall assertion that for Kleist "straightforward causality is suspended or put in question" (127).

Now, adoption is not exactly a "wild card" as Miller calls it (120). It is a deep pattern in many societies. Studies of kinship have demonstrated that often an adoptee is an integral part of a family, though with the deep ambiguities that Miller well expresses, as did Sartre more elaborately before him.[17] It might be noted that Piachi's adoption of Nicolo is much firmer in its enlistment of the structures of the society than is Cathy's father's adoption of the gypsy Heathcliff from the streets of Liverpool in *Wuthering Heights*. And Heathcliff's savage vengeance is a response to the family's refusal to allow the natural outlet of matrimony to the deep love he and Cathy share. No defensible values, but only an obscure and virtually unexpressed prejudice, forbid this marriage.[18]

Miller discusses some phallic details in Kleist's story, but not its underlying Oedipal structure. Nicolo is a sort of reverse Oedipus, since Oedipus, too, is adopted, but it is rather his real parents, not his adopted ones, whose death he brings about, and unconsciously rather than in the trammels of vicious calculation. Further, Oedipus marries Jocasta, while Nicolo fails to violate his adopted mother. He despoils his foster father rather than killing him, incurring thereby no perceptions but simply his own death, in the heavy opacity to which he, like many of Kleist's characters, is subject.

By centering too strictly on prosopopoeia and "reading," Miller forces himself to misdescribe the story. There is a radical foreshortening in his indefensible assertion (attached as it is to a fine hermeneutic instinct and execution), that "it is the reading, not the finding, that does the damage" (121). And further (138), "All the cases of mistaken identity in 'Der Findling' can be read as versions of this mistake in reading." Now Miller is talking about the act of finding and then adopting Nicolo. But this act must be accounted not an "interpretation" but an act of charity—an act that involves a *correct* interpretation of the circumstances of charity. By plotting this angle too far, Miller skews the geometry of the story's structure.[19]

"The unlawful law of human life may be that things happen by sheer unreasonable accident that have disastrous effects in this social world" (117). This is well put. Yes, but all the more heroic, rather than arbitrary or themselves accidental, are the human feelings, love and the trust of love; and the equities of trust that justice and its institutions try to manage. The causal explanations by happenstance, on the one hand, and by theological categories, on the other, are not "incompatible" or "irrational" (119) but rather simply incommensurable. Value will persist, I would read Kleist as saying, in the face of ineradicable incongruities. And, conversely, ineradicable incongruities will persist in the face of the heroic maintenance of the deepest values. The fact is that in Kleist's universe one can at no point conclude that charity is to be eschewed, as an unsympathetic reading of *Wuthering Heights* might deduce about that novel. One cannot calculate one's way through life; that is part of Kleist's assumption. To fail to foresee, like Piachi, is not the same thing as to misread. And just because even miscalculations involve communicative structures, this fact does not ground Miller's assertion (astonishing to me), that "ethics seems for Kleist to be a linguistic rather than a subjective region of human behavior" (123). What astonishes me is not the connection but the exclusion—Miller's "rather than."

Since the treacherous adopted son's avenue to his attempt at sexual violation is the young wife's devotion to a picture of the youth who died to save her from a fire, the system of generosity, in a Christian construction, links with her husband's initial rescue of the orphan. Charity functions as a channel of feeling, itself given as a structure by the Church.

In *The Marquise von O*, the system of justice constitutes all that is brought to bear on the social management of sexuality and marriage, while that of feeling hinges on the hidden, imperious force of sexuality itself. Under the extreme strain of widowhood and war, it takes a delicacy on all sides, itself strained almost to the breaking point, to bring the marquise and her mysteriously conceived child inside the fold of legitimacy and marriage with the count. The last sentence of the story, a statement of wife to husband, given in the objectivity of indirect discourse, weaves the factors of the plot into a contrary-to-fact condition built on a religious metaphor, "He would not have appeared to her then as a devil if he had not on his first appearance come before her as an angel."[20]

Kleist's works, as studies of such confrontations of practices and values, depend, in fact, on the firmness of each side of his antithesis between complicated systems of justice and subtle, powerful structures of feeling. In that light, there is a poignancy to the stories when its characters are faced with such extremities of incommensurateness. Typically, then, they are disasters, but they are also celebrations of human resourcefulness against odds that are too great, even for the lovers who are swept off by unmanageable circumstances in *Earthquake in Chile* and *Betrothal in Santo Domingo*. Those lovers have no problems in their own psyches, but insurmountable problems in the society they inhabit, whereas the problems in the *Marquise von O* derive from psychic troubles that affect just one partner of the couple. The model behavior of the Marquise's suitor-husband is reminiscent of that of Corneille's Cid, except that what he does compensates for the never-mentioned but inescapably deducible rape of the Marquise. He gradually overcomes what seem to be insurmountable problems in the attitudes and feelings of her family as they, in turn, manipulate the system of social codes. Success is possible, then, in this world of Kleist, as in the comparably casuistical world of Shakespeare's *Measure for Measure*, and the success has an ethical dimension, just as the more usual failures do.

Literature has an effect on us. It "grips" us, as Freud says of the *Oedipus Rex* and of plays generally. And it awakes questions of judgment, if it does not entirely soothe us into satisfaction with the foregone or with gratuitous excitement. Its effect draws on our capacity for desire; and its attempt at wisdom raises our assessment of human behavior that we associate with law. Kleist's particular mix, and the different ones in Tolstoy, or Beckett, or Coover, of feeling and justice, must be disentangled for us to account for the full presentation. Some writers will work through the feelings by presenting a set of events opaque to the narrator and to the consciousness as presented. So, on the positive side, Miller's reading of Kleist. So Chekhov's *Ward Six* in Irving Massey's reading, which he argues is inversely but equally impermeable if compared to the schematic but only partially transparent *Saint Julien* of Flaubert. "Concepts code themselves spontaneously into images, but images do not factor themselves out into concepts."[21]

An account, and the unattainable ideal of a full assessment, may lag for a long time, and I am now convinced that in Goethe's *Faust*, for example, we must separate the vision of the figure from his moral vision. On the one hand, there is the wisdom inhering in a commanding embodiment of aspirations that Spengler found could characterize our whole "Faustian" culture. On the other hand, there is the giant evasion built centrally into the work of its protagonist's moral responsibility for the death of his mate.[22] Goethe exonerates Faust in heaven on the grounds that aspiration carries its own validation: "Wer immer strebend sich bemüht, Den können wir erlösen," ("Who, ever striving, exerts himself, / Him can we absolve"; lines 11936–11937). But this excuse simply will not do. To work out the relations of desire and the law is a giant philosophical task, and one can accept Lacan's deep elaboration of identical communicative structures between the two without assenting to his then offering the proposition that the two are "the same."[23] And other depth analyses of the dynamics of projections in the writer, reactions of the reader, or the intersubjective engagements and issuances of both in the psyche of the reader, however useful, would then have to coordinate with how judgment is itself encoded.

The work's concatenation of the aesthetic of feeling and the ethics of judgment would then have to be dialectically referred to questions of ethics. How does Trollope's presentation of fine-grained decisions in a long-term but limited social situation (a plot) result in both testing and embodying an ethical ideal that in some respects it has been brought to by an investigation of the principles behind the code of the gentleman?[24] How do the depth responses of the characters brought forward in Dostoevsky, extravagant and indulgent and contradictory as they come up and as they evoke (or in some cases, put off) the reader, issue in a wisdom that gives further depth to its theologized vision of judgment? How do the actions of Hemingway's characters reveal and propound the code that he is implicitly recommending, and how do the reader's feelings both test and endorse that code? The fairy tale as well as the parable can be shown to enunciate the wisdom of ethical judgments under extreme, but also magical, conditions. How this magic can contribute to a vision of behavior in a life that in many ways is unmagical, and for a judgment that on the face of it seems unable to allow magic, is a deep question that we are only beginning to address.[25] These questions are even more evasive for lyric poetry. But as Heidegger and others have effectually shown us, they are there. It is in the wisdom of such writing that feeling and judgment come into firm, and varied, connection.

II

Much of the consolidation of Pound's depth, and much of his best poetry, came about after his acts of treason in support of the Axis, and his depth has had to be consolidated in the face of the ethical question about the traitor who is also a very great poet, a question brought up again sharply in the recent publication of his most Fascist cantos (72 and 73), which he himself, never having altered the numeration, includes in the whole work, as he did all the years when the space was blank from the last of the Adams cantos (71) to the first of the Pisan cantos (74).

Yet the case of the morally flawed person who is also a great poet does not in the last analysis pose grave problems. The distinction can be solved along the lines of the criteria used to resolve the Donatist heresy: the priest does not himself have to be in a state of grace to dispense valid sacraments. Though Milton's adage about the moral soundness of the poet has some weight and throws a long shadow, one could easily multiply cases beyond those of the recidivist thief François Villon, the pillager and rapist Thomas Malory, the incestuous drug-abuser Georg Trakl, and others, of men of deep turpitude who had attained commanding artistic expression.[26]

More difficult is the case in which the unacceptable views are deeply ingrained in the artistic work itself. The *Cantos* do include praise directly, and by extension throughout (especially if Malatesta is allowed to be a stand-in for Mussolini), for unacceptable political behavior. The intrication of his historical vision, with these unsavory aspects, into the whole scheme of the *Cantos* presents further difficulties for the proper assimilation of his wisdom.[27]

Least integrated in some ways are Cantos 72 and 73, since they are in Italian. These cantos constitute a group by themselves, separate from the other larger groupings within the poem. And since they were suspended in a limbo of separate, obscure publication, they stand somewhat "under erasure," to use Derrida's term, though the qualification of their overall status does not affect their unacceptable moral stance. Canto 72, beginning with an assimilation of Churchill and his "patrons" (or bosses, *padroni*) to Dante's fraudulent monster Geryon, proceeds in Dantesque language to answer the request of a certain Filippo Tomaso that he inhabit Pound's body so as to carry on the Fascist war after his own death. Pound, who here touches on Malatesta and other typical concerns, answers that his body is old and that the ghost should enter a young body so as to breed heroes and enter paradise by dying in battle. Marinetti and other Fascists are invoked. Canto 73, written as though by Cavalcanti and in a version of Cavalcanti's (and Dante's) measures, and with passing reference to the idealized Ixotta of Malatesta, celebrates the heroism of a young Italian woman who had her legs blown off when she deliberately misled a group of Canadian soldiers into a minefield. If it is accepted that the Fascist cause was an evil one, especially in its later manifestation of rabid anti-Semitism and mass deportation in the Salò government, where Pound was intimately active,[28] then we must deal with the considerable aesthetic problem of the presence of these ideals in a context where they meld into the layered historical and lyrical vision of the overall poem.

The problem, of course, cannot be resolved just by setting aside these Italian cantos. It recurs through the poem, even leaving aside the distinct but fairly rare effusions of anti-Semitism in the *Cantos*.[29] The role of Mussolini intricates into its historical perspective, feeding back to the simple, disjunct celebration of warfare and bloodshed for its own sake. In 1909, long before the *Cantos* and long before Mussolini's Fascism, Pound had given vent to such sentiments—giving rise in the reader to a possible ethical perplexity—in "Sestina: Altaforte," a persona poem about Bertram de Born: "Hang it all, all this our South stinks peace! / . . . Hell grant soon we hear again the swords clash!"[30] The montage method of the *Cantos* would allow such ideas to be separable; one would simply excise the vicious passage. But the ongoing connection with the exhibited life of the poet in the poem makes the poem, too, comprehensively and interactively personal; the poet is himself his own hero, and he is certainly very much present throughout. So, too, the infolding of individual instances, as nodes of "light" into the large historical vision, would make the intellectual task of detaching their concerns from the guiding wisdom of the poem a difficult one. This does not make it impossible, and I adduce this large, commanding example so as to offer a case in which blanket acceptance and blanket rejection, the commonest postures, are either indefensible or ill-informed.

So, the beginning of Canto 41 presents Mussolini, "the Boss" (Il Duce) "ad interim 1933" (the canto's last words), before either World War II or the invasion of Ethiopia, let alone the cooperation with Hitler's genocide in the government of Salò. But the date is well after various other acts of

Mussolini's, including the totalitarian harassment and imprisonment of such political opponents as Gramsci. The scene of "the Boss's" response to a presentation copy of the earlier cantos—"è divertente"—introduces a propaganda-like recital of his achievements in draining the Pontine marshes and in outsmarting the "mezzo-yit" financiers who want to profiteer by helping finance his regime. This is set into montage-rhyme with fifteenth-century usurious finance, with Mussolini's early career as an exploited laborer and as a hero in World War I; and then with other financial and military activity—which here the Fascist ideal implicitly measures—in that war and in the ambience of Jefferson (with whom Pound compared Mussolini in his prose writings).[31]

The lyric beginning of the Pisan cantos fuses over an evocation of Mussolini's death as though it were not the violent end of a tyrant but the martyrdom of a statesman worthy of comparison with the death of Christ and of the founder of Manichaeism, Manes:

> The enormous tragedy of the dream in the peasant's bent shoulders
>   Manes! Manes was tanned and stuffed,
>   Thus Ben and la Clara a Milano
>   by the heels at Milano
> That maggots should eat the dead bullock
> DIGONOS, Δίγονος, but the twice-crucified
>   where in history will you find it?
> Yet say this to the Possum: a bang, not a whimper,
>   with a bang not with a whimper,
> To build the city of Dioce whose terraces are the colour of stars.
>   (Canto 74)

The ruminative, recapitulative voice makes large connections between Pound's personal sorrow and the macro-historical progress of the world, taking in its own experience the end of World War II as a permanent end, "not with a bang but a whimper." This quotation from T. S. Eliot, identified by his own nickname for himself, "the Possum," educes an ideal of the laconic that it therefore borrows from the less expansive poem "The Hollow Men," where the preceding phrase, "This is the way the world ends" is a refrain that also finds an echo in Pound's near-refrains. Pound here achieves a near equivalent for Eliot's laconic style, his condensation of image, and his near song, in the conversationally adaptive flow by which he presents the energy-expanding bolts of such centralizing asides. The connections of the *Cantos* work at high pitch in these lines, and Deioces' foundation of Ecbatana in the early Persian empire holds up a vivid ideal in the form of achieved architecture that defines this civilization and frames others, even if the reader parts company with Pound when he effectually takes Mussolini as an analogue to Deioces.

"The enormous tragedy of the dream in the peasant's bent shoulders" has the ring of something permanent. The expression also names a figure very likely visible to Pound, who is probably watching a peasant pass as he stands in Pisa, since the germ of each rumination can often be traced to a random sight—and to a theory of the connectable senses of these random incursions.[32] We do not have to connect the peasant to specific policies of Mussolini, or even to the general agrarian populism of his regime, to let this first line measure the rest, by a pure disjunction that permits the peasant at once to be more fortunate than Manes or Mussolini for all his tragedy, oblivious of prestigious leaders or rulers, and part of a process they try to govern. Angling Dionysus in here as the "twice-born" connects and elides revealingly into other presentations of Dionysus throughout the poem, and the puzzle paused over by restating the romanized "Digonos" in Greek persists beyond the hyperbolic comparison of the legendary Greek god with the dead dictator.

The intensity here is measured not only by the vast leaps from the peasant to Manes to Mussolini to Eliot to Christ-Dionysus to Deioces, but by the assured range of the voice. Manes sets the tone as an exact refrain, and the repetitions emphasize, mull over, wonder, and stall the voice and mind. The voice ranges from the formality of the first lines to the glided assimilation into the colloquialism of "Ben and la Clara." Benito Mussolini becomes "Ben" and so is included in a presumptive affectionate gesture that desacralizes him without performing what the speaker lets us know he considers a desecration. The slightly different colloquialism of "la Clara" moves from the residual second person of nicknaming to the virtual third person of the colloquial objectification of the definite article. This term for Clara Petacci names the mistress by this familiar depersonalization that would be less likely appplied to a wife, but it recontains its archness in the piety that the repetition of "a Milano" underscores as it draws the preposition, but not the name of the city, into the native language of the speaker "at Milano"—a stronger musical turn if the reader conceives of these lines as following upon the two all-Italian cantos (as they do in numerical order).

It would take something like a Heideggerian phrasal interrogation to exhaust the power of "the enormous tragedy of the dream," a phrase that, through "enormous," sets into a deliberate antithesis of near vagueness the sharp image of the slightly stooping peasant.[33] The dream is an ideal, but also it touches on the fact of a subservience to the agricultural cycle; the tragedy of the dream invokes something like "Life is a dream" and Pindar's "A dream of a shadow: man" and redirects it to the end-of-the-world apocalypse that guides and opens the feeling of the speaker in these lines.

The ideographic method here reinforces and fuses each of its integers, heavily structured but at the same time washed over by what has been accorded the sound of a voice pulling into recollection, with the two repetitions of lines 4 and 9 being held between poetic refrain and conversational reiteration. The metrical variations line to line are, as always, far more controlled than the Whitmanian afflatus allows, as the connections are dazzling, and they will hold even after we have disallowed the possibility that Mussolini may retain his status as the consummate martyr. The sounds build up to and after the fully regular alexandrine of line 6, which begins with a repetition that is not quite a refrain, the three syllables of "Digonos" in repetition dividing and pairing in a pattern that is exactly half the pattern of the alexandrine it half constitutes: 3, 3; 6, 6. Line 10 sweeps to nineteen syllables, breaking on the tenth after "Dioce." That word, a dactyl, suggests the cyclic dactyls of a Pindar-like evocation, and the dactylic measure continues as an underlay in "terraces" and "colour of." Each of these words pulls together into an image-ideogram that allows its senses to stretch up to, and in fact beyond, the visual; for what would terraces the color of stars look like exactly? Not just like the "olive tree blown white in the wind" brought in three lines later, though it belongs to the same Paradisal register, the Dantesque structure broken up and as though Cubistically reshuffled. And these visual sketches are not like anything in the artistic representations of Duccio, Giovanni Bellini, or Santa Maria in Trastevere, all of which are mentioned twelve lines later, though they too partake at once of the Paradisal vision, of the sorrowing recapitulative memory, and of the macro-historical connections intensifying this utterance into a wisdom that its connection to the vicious cannot recast into the wholly unacceptable. Such condensations become the wisdom of Pound and resonate in the ways his many commentators have urged, though mostly they avoid the question of how an ethically unacceptable position can be incorporated into a whole that includes ideas. Indeed, Mussolini has asked Pound, as a part of the earlier interview in the thirties, why the poet wants to put his ideas in order; and he has got the answer that it is to make his poem (87; 569 and 103; 626). So by implication the dictator, while complimented by Pound for his curiosity about the *Cantos*, is also relegated by him just to a position in it; of being puzzled at exactly the point where the poet comes through with a solution.

"Muss., wrecked for an error," Pound is still saying very late in the *Cantos* (Canto 106; 795), and it is not clear what error he means. Perhaps it could have been tolerance of the monarchy,[34] which the Republic of Salò, sinister to most if not all readers of good will, would have jettisoned in the ideal. Salò is then idealized by Pound not only in his personal, very active adherence to it, but—as here concerns us—in the *Cantos*: "Salò, Gardone / to dream the Republic" (78; 478). Even before the war Mussolini, it is urged, held a rescuing balance, when he aided Franco to win the Spanish Civil War, "And Muss saved, rem salvavit, / in Spain / il salvabile" (105; 746). The *Cantos* are shot through with such interpretations.

Yet, just as in the opening of the Pisan cantos where the death of Mussolini is embedded and deplored, these unacceptable ideals are juxtaposed, incorporated, and somewhat disjunctively matched, as persistently throughout this poem, to lyric perceptions of high penetration and historical connections of almost unprecedented sweep. So the succinct praise, though itself ambiguous, of Hitler's insight, "Adolf furious from perception" (104; 741), passes like a shadow across vividly mounted nineteenth-century reminiscences and luminously complex Chinese discriminations and condensed points of the poet's most seminal experiences. This happens along with the attribution of real wisdom and courage to various persons in the Axis entourage, where ultimately in some cases the ideal itself cannot be questioned, but only the attribution to the person in question.

In the poem itself, a separation of the ethical from the aesthetic cannot be effected because the poem roots itself, as poems often do, in a complex ethical-historical stance, part of which is unacceptable. Yet on balance the unacceptability of one key part of its ethics does not irreparably vitiate the poem, and the communicated creation must in the last analysis be accorded the same status we accord human beings who may wonderfully carry out social responsibilities while exhibiting deep flaws or unsavory records. These powerful delicacies of historical discrimination and psychic penetration do in fact inform and engage a wisdom in line with the maxims of the Confucius they quote in support, exhortation, and mosaic combination.

The achieved rightness of the fused utterance in this large poem and the wisdom of its fused connections preponderate over the questionable inclusions. It is not simply that the reader prepares a balance sheet of positive and negative elements. On the principle that a detected deep order will prevail over instances of chaos, the rightness and the fusions are messages more far-reaching, and that reach has an ethical dimension for the overall poem, in addition to (but partly derived from) its inclusions of luminous ethical principles: the right use of land, the architectural ordering of a city, the openness to art, the encouragement of intelligence and beauty and love, and even the instances of good governance in certain Chinese emperors and in Thomas Jefferson, according to ideals held up by such as John Quincy Adams, Confucius, and "The Commissioner of the Salt Works," among others.

The sixteen maxims recommended in this seventeenth-century treatise, itself based on a seventh-century list that is in turn a digest of Confucianism, are all ethical. Intricated into Cantos 98 and 99, they constitute a compacted, alert ethical vision that expands on the dialogues of practical ethical lessons, equally alert, that were offered in Canto 13, under the name of Confucius himself. All these give an ethical turn to the whole expanse of Chinese history as it is run through in the long sequence of Cantos 52 through 61 and picked up at other points, passing ideographically through some twenty-seven centuries, starting early with a sense of virtue in *virtù* when it is said of the Shang that "Our Dynasty came in because of a great sensibility" at the beginning of Canto 85, the first of the "Rock Drill" cantos. Notably in that canto there is a persistent undercurrent of justification against what Pound sees as the Allies' unjustifiable handling of the Nazis as though they were wholly evil.[35] But even such historical details are caught up in a keenly integrative set of interpretations, and this undercurrent is overmastered by dozens of deductions from the nubs of political wisdom in Confucian ideograms, beginning with the opening "Ling," by the interconnections among them, and by their application to the key actions through several centuries of Chinese history in re-angled interpretation.

The ethical details in this history are brought into a luminous whole with the landscapes among which these figures move, and which are also included by Pound as part of his personal history in the "Seven Lakes" Canto 49, where the verses set forth eight paintings that were hanging on his walls of scenes along a river in China. Here as elsewhere he links these scenes to a proper tending of fields, a recommendation pulled in from the Japanese transliteration of a Chinese poem about them; and then another early Chinese poem, followed by two aphoristic lines of his own:

Wisdom and Ethics   151

> Sun up; work
> sundown: to rest
> dig well and drink of the water
> dig field; eat of the grain
> Imperial power is? and to us what is it?
>
> The fourth: the dimension of stillness.
> And the power over wild beasts

What gives these syllables their strength and rightness is inseparable from the deep ethical balance they enunciate and envision. The landscapes and the maxims pull together in the further, multiple compacting of ideograms, with the ethical dimension characteristically encoded into their history-derived summary. The lines just quoted echo, and become transformed again and again, as in the opening of Canto 99:

> Till the blue grass turn yellow
>   and the yellow leaves float in air
> and Iong Cheng (Canto 61)
>   of the line of Kang Hi
> by the silk cords of the sunlight
>   non disunia

The raptness of the vision here, and the ethical harmony, is so fully realized it would not matter if the Italian of "non disun[i]a," identified as from the Paradiso of Dante, gave some hint of the bundle of sticks holding together in the fasces as the bundle of silk cords does in the Chinese ideogram *hsien* "be illustrious," mentioned here as summary and radical-refrain and printed six times through the *Cantos*, first of all as the first ideogram offered in the Pisan cantos (74; 429).[36] The quotation of such a term, *hsien*, carries with it the intensity that poetry forges into its expression, the external sign of which is the labor Pound put into the phrasings he wrought. It carries with it not only the ethical ideal of coherent illustriousness but the coding of that ideal to a whole civilization in its historical evolutions, the Chinese, and to the wisdom and idealism of the formulator, Confucius, as well as tying into the ideogrammatic method adopted by this poet. And there is a spatial component too: China remains an antipodes, and a revelatory counterpart, itself illustrious, brought to the light of the metered phrasings that catch it like a net, as elsewhere in the *Cantos* where Pound is especially noteworthy for gnomic phrasings wrought into a metrical as well as a verbal finality, here a recursion to the semantically marked variation of the commonest English meter, iambic pentameter:

> The ant's a centaur in his dragon world,
> Pull down thy vanity, it is not man
> Made courage, or made order, or made grace.
> Pull down thy vanity, I say pull down.
> Learn of the green world what can by thy place
> In scaled invention or true artistry,
> Pull down thy vanity,
> Paquin, pull down!
> The green casque has outdone your elegance.
>
> (81; 521)

The first visual image, centaur against dragon, allows a nonce metaphor to frame the much repeated injunction, which continues on for a run longer than what I have quoted. The injunction to something like a religious humility is intricated into the sorrowing voice of the prisoner near the fields who sees the ant magnified at twilight, and also into the historical pattern along lines partially set by Confucius. The sense of the poem expands the gnomic, which it also relies on and in one sense ideogrammatizes: the memorable gnomic utterance is not just rendered into poetry but fixed as an equivalent to the intense words of the "poem containing history" in ways that turn it toward the general possibility of history, not just that of China but also of a Belle Epoque France, in the (assimilated) figure of Paquin, the Parisian couturier whose creations are outdone in elegance by a natural castoff, the husk from which a wasp has just been born, the "green casque" more beautiful than man-made ones. This phrase echoes and partly reverses the somewhat earlier metaphor where sunset becomes a superb couturier in the disjunct (and therefore somewhat ideogrammatized) conclusion to Canto 80 five pages back: "sunset grand couturier."

Entering the pattern of the gnomic, and going beyond it, are the political-psychological-social-artistic virtues before which man should be humbled, "It is not man / Made courage, or made order, or made grace." These three powerful terms can be extended throughout the *Cantos* and also into history, if we imagine the exercise of defining courage and order and grace, separately and together, by the instances throughout the poem of each of the three. All this offers not only codified wisdom, but combinatory wisdom, of which a vision of history is only one of the constituent components. And all such questions brightly extend the gnomic run that began just ten lines before:

> What thou lovest well remains,
> $\qquad\qquad\qquad$ the rest is dross
> What thou lov'st well shall not be reft from thee
> What thou lov'st well is thy true heritage

What is meant by love, and what is meant by heritage, are deep notions for which the large context of the *Cantos* provides abundant answers—answers connected to other gnomic utterances and refrains, such as "nothing counts save the quality of the affection" (77; 466), or what refers at once to the patterning of the poem, the ordering of experience, the quality of a kind of affection, the registering of an exact visual perception, and a recommendation for a mood in the face of mortality:

> Hast 'ou seen the rose in the steel dust
> $\qquad\qquad\qquad$ (or swansdown ever?)
> so light is the urging, so ordered the dark petals of iron
> we who have passed over Lethe.
> $\qquad\qquad\qquad\qquad$ (74; 449)

This concludes the canto, and connects with its beginning, and amplifies it, and reverberates out of "the enormous tragedy of the dream in the peasant's bent shoulders." It does so in ways that cannot be written off as perversity or mere verbal dexterity, or even just artistic and constructive power, though all these are contributory. It ultimately exemplifies, splendidly, the wisdom that can reside in poetry.

III

However despairing the position of Beckett may be, to the point that a just man, however much he entered the writer's vision, still could not share the *ignava ratio* of his deducible position, his utterance, just by its existence, has not quite hit the bottom of despair, which would result in silence or suicide, as Blanchot has remarked of gloomy writing generally. As a mood, the work of Beckett strikes a note and also purifies, a mood that had already found less penetrating expression in Victorian times in the poems of William Ernest Henley and in James Thomson's *City of Dreadful Night*. The note had already been purified, but also complicated, by Hopkins in poems like "Carrion Comfort" and a sonnet:

> No worst, there is none. Pitched past pitch of grief,
> More pangs will, schooled at forepangs, wilder wring.
> Comforter, where, where is your comforting?
> Mary, mother of us, where is your relief?
> My cries heave, herds-long; huddle in a main, a chief
> Woe, world-sorrow; on an age-old anvil wince and sing—

Hopkins of course never lets go of his whole theological system, and moves to characteristic reassurance as he continues the poem. And the self-transcendence in his expression is already coded into the uttered sounds of his sprung rhythm. But the mood comes close to the one Beckett brings to still a further pitch of what amounts to grief, and the ethical question lies in how we are to accept this position without such assurances. It is as though *Worstward Ho* were an amplification of these lines.

Beckett's language throughout his work, sometimes explicitly, enacts the paradoxes of the conclusion to *The Unnamable*, "You must go on, perhaps it's done already, perhaps they have said me already, perhaps they have carried me to the threshold of my story, before the door that opens on my story, that would surprise me, if it opens, it will be I, it will be the silence, where I am, I don't know, I'll never know, in the silence you don't know, you must go on, I can't go on, I'll go on." These clauses are characteristically short, like the blunt utterances of *Waiting for Godot* or the curt narrative integers of *Comment c'est*. They resonate, allegorize, and deepen around the exact namings and the insoluble complications. A modality is retained by the modulation between the resonating adequacy of the clauses, emphasized by shortness and simplicity, and the elusive disjunctions of the events, trivial, vanishing, and set at an angle beyond even defamiliarization. Defamiliarization here loses the coordinates by which we could define it. Yet Beckett, in the overriding unity of his tone and in the virtual identity of the sense behind the events in his fiction, purifies it to the vanishing point. To adapt an explanation by Hugh Kenner, the Pythagorean *alogon* or "unnamable," the square root of 2, is matched by the equivalent surd of words. Taken by themselves the words are as sound as the number 2; they are, for example, not subjected to the surrealism that was dominant in Paris throughout the entire period of Beckett's maturation. What tries to square these word integers (or, putting it the other way, what they try to square) are the events that remain incommensurable all the while they are being named.[37] Or as Beckett—strangely!—reads Proust:

> The point of departure of the Proustian exposition is not the crystalline agglomeration but its kernel—the crystallized. The most trivial experience—he says in effect—is encrusted with elements that logically are not related to it and have consequently been rejected by our intelligence.[38]

If this were so, we would have to say, then Proust's novel is a Beckett novel; but this is the cue Beckett gives us here by so totally rewriting the author's experience.

In stretching his words and his utterance, Beckett achieves a pitiless but wise evocation of Being, and the inclusion of nothingness into it evidences a wakefulness of such intensity that it amounts to the wisdom of testimony. It can be said that a whole world comes into being by facing nothingness squarely, almost as though Beckett were glossing Heidegger. Here is Arsene, the not-yet-named servant of Mr. Knott in *Watt*:

> And all the sounds, meaning nothing. Then at night rest in the quiet house, there are no roads, no streets any more, you lie down by a window opening on refuge, the little sounds come that demand nothing, explain nothing, propound nothing, and the short necessary night is soon ended, and the sky blue again all over the secret places where nobody ever comes, the secret places never the same, but always simple and indifferent, always mere places, sites of a stirring beyond coming and going, of a being so light and free that it is as the being of nothing.

This lays bare the nothing in the secret places with something like the "undisclosing," the *Unverborgenheit* of Heidegger. If a coherent, rather than a randomized plot, were to gather Arsene up into the household to which he is here being introduced, it would interfere with the perception here offered, which could have been uttered by almost any of Beckett's characters—and which offers, in the depths of its namings and the energies of its summaries, something akin to the sprung rhythm of Hopkins.

Neither absurd nor not absurd, the wisdom of Beckett transcends the specific recommendations that can be drawn from it, and resonates from beyond whatever confusion of voices, logical sequences, and emotional stoppages he has deployed. Its own exiguous abundance, and the startling abundance of commentary on Beckett, testifies to this wisdom. As Adorno says in framing Beckett's cognitive act:

> The truth of the new, as that which is not yet entrenched, has its locus in the intention-free. That sets it into contradiction with reflection, the motor of the new, and raises it to the second power. Truth is the opposite of the ordinary philosophical conception of it, such as Schiller's doctrine of the "sentimental," which amounts to loading art works down with intentionality. A second reflection takes hold of the *modus operandi*, the language of the art work in its widest sense, but it aims at blindness. The watchword "absurd," insufficient as always, betokens that Beckett's refusal to interpret his images, connected with extreme consciousness of techniques, of the implications of the contents of his linguistic materials, is no merely subjective aversion: with the increase of reflection, and through its stepped-up power, the content darkens of itself.[39]

In the rock-bottom language that all but dispenses with the rhetorical resources of both Proust's amplifying-philosophical reflection and Joyce's polyglot etyms and cycled vast recombinations, Beckett has not parted company wholly with the wisdom of these two masters on whom he had early written, but rather has taken them over, redefined them, purged them of any other reflection than the endgame of reflection and any other recombination than the spiritual torpor and distress they can be inverted to come to. As Maurice Blanchot says, preserving the integral gesture of this language in his description, "Indeed he has entered the circle in which he obscurely turns, drawn on by the wandering word, one not deprived of sense but of center."[40] The lack of center subverts the sense, but the sense overcomes its lack of center by laying it out and clearing its decks for the reader in the way that its wisdom can be taken without being overwhelmed by the hopelessness, an *ignava ratio* that the clarity of its power can be taken to induce us beyond. Or otherwise we would be well justified in following what is in effect the ancient lead of Plato and jettisoning it as vitiating the spirit of the citizens of an ideal Republic. Take the beginning of *Ill Seen Ill Said*:

> From where she lies she sees Venus rise. On. From where she lies when the skies are clear she sees Venus rise followed by the sun. Then she rails at the source of all life. On. At evening when the skies are clear she savors the star's revenge. At the other window. Right upright on her old chair she watches for the radiant one. Her old deal spindle-backed kitchen chair. It emerges from out the last rays and sinking ever brighter is engulfed in its turn. On. She sits on erect and rigid in the deepening gloom. Such helplessness to move

Wisdom and Ethics 157

she cannot help. Heading on foot for a particular point she often freezes on the way. Unable till long after to move on not knowing whither or for what purpose. Down on her knees especially she finds it hard not to remain so forever. Hand resting on hand on some convenient support. Such as the foot of her bed. And on them her head. There then she sits as though turned stone face to the night. Save for the white of her hair and faintly bluish white of face and hands all is black. For an eye having no need of light to see. All this in the present as had she the misfortune to be still of this world.

Denotation and connotation converge in the words, one by one, with or without allegory. "On" denotes the movement on a particular path, the path of a planet on the heavens, and also the path of the possible speaker in life; indeed, the word can be taken as a command, of the author to her, or of the author to himself. As he centralizes all these denotations, he is connoting all the progressions of life, and beyond.[41] This is a step further, or a step beyond, the centralization of what could be called the Heideggerian resonances in *Comment c'est* anywhere, as for example in the run nine sections from the end of part 2:

> jamais fait pour personne ce que moi pour lui animer non sûr oui jamais senti contre la sienne une autre chair non heureux non malheureux non s'il me sent contre lui non seulement quand je le martyrise oui

> never did for anyone what I for him animate no sure yes never felt another flesh against his no happy no unhappy no if he feels me against him no only when I torment him yes

The echo of the end of *Ulysses* is redirected outward to a larger connotation that includes past, present, and future, in the text and in the references, as the denotations converge into ever-expanding connotations and back. In the light of what is going on here, the small differences and accentuations between the English and the French words cancel out, since the denotations and the connotations come to the same thing, and the rhythms need only remain exact and intense, whatever the particular weight they may have in either version. Concurrently the allegorical structures, so largely and schematically present in *Comment c'est*, have disappeared from the very beginning of *Ill Seen Ill Said*, leaving just the generalizing structures. In either text, the Hamm of *Endgame* has fused with his parents, and there is no difference between tower room and ashcan. The starry heavens give rise to a reinforcement of a resentful reaction, "revenge." The decrepitude of the human body, not heavily delineated here, is drawn on for its philosophical challenge in such a way as to silence the possible answers in the induced full-alertness that might, as counter finally to such work, produce them.

Ventriloquizing his voice into an adopted language, in the manner of Joseph Conrad or Vladimir Nabokov, Beckett has turned his circumstances of language into a stereophonic possibility that would reinforce the strong lodging of the words, in whichever language, toward the sense of wisdom-evocation. *How It Is* is a translation of *Comment c'est, Murphy* in French of the *Murphy* in English. Translation can go either way, once the book is there, and the language of origin comes to seem an accident. They are alike in their access not only to wisdom but to their own wisdom, and the properties of each individual language as an expressive tool fall into secondary importance just because they have been enlisted for primary use.[42]

Beckett is self-ventriloquized, then, to the simplicity of his words. These remain the anchoring, resonating constant, whether the persons stand merely in the natural aging body of *Ill Seen Ill Said*, buried to the neck in a pile of sand (*Happy Days*) or stuck atop a giant pot before a restaurant (*The Unnamable*) or enclosed in urns (*Play*) or caught in a desert almost without resources (*Waiting for Godot*) or stacked in the constraining structures of *The Lost Ones* or contained blind in an imprisoning tower (*Endgame*). However fully and curtailingly allegorical these situations may be, the language contains as well as expresses them; it is never senseless, far more syntactically fluent than the diction-implosions of *Finnegans Wake*. They are signs for something as well as signs of something, and their references bite hard to their heavy referents.[43] They guide the allegory that opens them up but also falls back from them as less than they.

The speaker and Watt (III, p. 186) conjoin disgust and degraded religious awe when they feed a live rat

> to its mother, its father, its brother, its sister, or to some less fortunate relative. It was on this occasion, we agreed, after an exchange of views, that we came nearest to God.

This adult form of what is usually thought of as childish cruelty to animals, here taken to an extreme, is coupled in the narrative with a religious experience. The irony is not simply resumptive here, in Gary Handwerk's already complex sense.[44] It deconstructs the emotions in an act of what amounts to rejection, to the end of an illusionless acceptance.

The novel functions like a psychoanalysis, as Wolfgang Iser says of it.[45] It both immobilizes the reader and wakens him; immobilizes, because when deep-seated sadism is rendered as so casual and connected with such presumably exalted sentiments he can find no exit, even in assuming a skeptical or pessimistic view of religion, which the casualness of the association here forbids as it seems to endorse. Nor can the reader put the two motives here brought into a single complex experience into the endless regress of Derrida's *Glas*, where the texts of Genet glorifying a sadomasochistically tinged homosexuality are juxtaposed to texts of Hegel on the philosophy of law. In Beckett's work, the text wakens the reader by forcing him into such speculations, while providing no exit or terminus for his wakefulness, even the minimal reassurance of Derrida's endless regress. The wisdom here lies in the intolerability, but also in the discontinuity of this "small" experience as presented.

The text must depend on, but does not exactly ironize, the reader's disgust for rats, rooted psychoanalytically in the sorts of considerations that Freud himself raises in his analysis of the Rat Man. All that preliminary substructure is sealed off as well as evoked when the reader confronts characters who, with seeming ease, have first allowed these rats to play all over their own bodies, breaking a physical taboo, before they evoke the juridical taboo, transferred to the animal kingdom by the use of the human kinship terms here, against fratricide, parricide, and matricide. The feeling of the reader, forced into conjunction with the comparably shocking adduction of the arousal of a religious feeling in the characters, must arrest itself for an issueless ethical speculation; and the connection between feeling and justice is pushed "beyond its limits" to take up in the new wakefulness for which the text has prepared it, a post-analytic state that has broached the possibility of deconstructing the superego—so as to reconstitute it in the far-echoing resonances of the text.

Is the behavior presented in these novels and plays repetitive-compulsive? Not in the same sense that the calculations and tiresome repetitions (which question tiresomeness and repetition) are so in the same novel. The reader is forced into the wisdom inherent in the acknowledgment that no systematic account can be offered that can link—or sever—one of this kind of event in its relation to another kind, other than in the pure and purified flow of the narrative. The same is true with the preoccupation with physical objects, stones or whatever, that will crop up through the same inexplicability.

> Bloody well you know what bucket! cried Mr. Gorman, not however an impatient man as a rule. The muck bloody bucket, blast your bloody—. He paused. The day was Saturday. Your bloody eyes, he said.
> Watt distinguished fragments of a part:
> ...... *von Klippe zu Klippe geworfen*
> *Endlos ins* ...... *hinab.*
> Mr. Gorman and Mr. Nolan advanced together, stooping, the bucket, heavy with slime, held between them.[46]

There is a long breakdown in the language here when broken phrases from the conclusion of a sublime lyric by Hölderlin are set in a context of the flattest narrative and of dialogue that within itself breaks down into curses which, through overuse, have themselves broken down into mere phatic markers: "muck" and "bloody" framing the trivial, somewhat disgusting, shared task in which lexically, but not pragmatically, the "muck" of the expostulation is a near synonym for the slime they are transporting. But they share only a liquid component with the cliff waterfall of Hölderlin's metaphor, here not fully quoted:

> Es schwinden, es fallen
> Die leidenden Menschen
>   Blindlings von einer
>   Stunde zur anderen,
>   Wie Wasser von Klippe
>   Zu Klippe geworfen,
>   Jahrlang ins Ungewisse hinab.

> There vanish, there fall
> Suffering men
>   Blindly from one
>   Hour to another
>   Like water from cliff-ledge
>   To cliff-ledge thrown
>   Yearlong down into the uncertain.

The "Ungewisse," of course, is the domain Beckett has entered, a domain Hölderlin merely names. He does not call it *das Unbekannte*, the unknown. His men are bright water dashed off a cliff, where Beckett's here are measured by slogging in inconceivable contrast to that loftiness. The radiance of hope that clings to the seemingly despairing "Hyperions Schicksalslied" comes out in this wholly randomized and partial quotation, both distracting from and commenting on the bogged-down interchanges recounted. The variant of "Endlos" is given for "Jahrlang"; the process is more than year-long. And the uncertain, the "Ungewisse," is made even more uncertain by being elided from the quotation, "Jahrlang ins Ungewisse hinab." The disjunctions of *Comment c'est* are in one sense greater by comparison, but in another sense more harmonious. And again, the wisdom of Beckett lies in his presenting us with a text about which it is possible for us to make such assertions.

Only finally, after all the penultimate positions that a man of good will would have to reject, and just because it has radically based its rhetoric on what amounts to a rejection of ethics, does the result of wisdom in the experience of the work become ethical.

Notes

Preface

1. I owe awareness of these to Daniel Ingalls, who outlined them in a lecture at Brown University, April 12, 1989. Among many other formulations, he gave an account of *alākāra*, the science of ornament or rhetoric. This applies to literature even more fully than does Western rhetoric, since Indian rhetoric is not oratorical. Advice was given to kings in private. Further terms are "elaboration," *utprekēsa*, "fancy" rather than simile. "Sweetness," "clarity," "strength" are named qualities, as is *dhvani*, "pure suggestion," which Ingalls compares to the sublime of Longinus. *Rāsa*, "juice, taste, flavor," gets into features of play, the comic, the tragic, the heroic, and other "genres." It cannot be direct. All this was formulated by Anānda by about 780.
2. Personal communication.
3. Christopher Ricks, "John Gower: Metamorphosis in Other Words," in *The Force of Poetry* (New York: Oxford, 1987), 1–33.

Chapter 1: The Canon of Poetry and the Wisdom of Poetry

1. As recent theorists in the Lacanian and other traditions keep demonstrating, questions about the speaking self, the persona, the ego, the individual, identity, and the like are so vast that they can be made coterminous with the whole domain of epistemology. So, for example, Manfred Frank distinguishes (1) the "individual not a subject" as a question from (2) "individuality not identity," and (3) the individual as incommensurably ineffable. He reclassifies the first under the paradigms of speech and the symptomatology entailed by the historically determined concepts of semantics; the second as psychogenesis and the social history of the individual; and the third as art in the conjunction of speech and communication, or the functional orientation involving the construction and deconstruction of representation and individual expression (Manfred Frank, "Introduction," in *Individualität*, ed. Manfred Frank and Anselm Haverkamp [Munich: Fink, 1988], 11–12). All this refines the modern project of bracketing, attenuating, bypassing, and de-essentializing the "subject," from Heidegger on. But the term "subject" is still a useful one, and some form of what the term addresses is inescapable when discussing the experience of a text. What else but a version of "subject" does Derrida mean by "signature"? For a defense of the viability of the conception of

the subject in the full current of discourse about the "decentered subject" on the part of Derrida, Foucault, Lyotard, and Paul Smith, see Charles Altieri, "Reconstituting Subjects," in *Canons and Consequences* (Evanston, IL: Northwestern University Press, 1990), 193–224. Peter Baker in *The Ethical Turn: Postmodern Theories of the Subject* (manuscript), masterfully explores the explanatory power and ethical force of Derrida's *différance* and *traces* as they question and realign the mechanisms of relating to exteriority, in the light of the partially comparable theories of Foucault, Lyotard, Habermas, Deleuze, Lacan, Merleau-Ponty, Levinas, and Kristeva, among others.

2. A particularly telling example is discussed by John Baker in "Towards a Poetics of Showing: Heidegger, Poetic Language, and the Reduction" (manuscript study). Baker, on the question of engaged subjectivities, introduces another whole set of terms by applying Husserl's conception of a phenomenological reduction to Heidegger's use of poetry and Hölderlin's practice, as evidenced in the hymn "Der Rhein."

> "Ein Rätsel ist Reinentsprungenes. Auch / Der Gesang kaum darf es enthüllen" [A riddle is of pure origin. / The song itself may hardly disclose it]. In Hölderlin's hymn the Rhine carries with it wherever it flows the secret of its origin. In this way the river preserves in its flow its point of origin. The river thus unites instant and duration. But the import of these lines does not consist uniquely in the use of the river as a historico-mythological topos. For the river is also a figure for poetry and the poet, and is so in such a way that there can be no reduction of the one to ground and the other to its figuring . . . Hölderlin's image presses so hard on the metaphorical relation of ground and figure as to make it disappear. . . . This disappearance [is] a species of reduction. If river and poem constitute a double order of signification, in which the one is the sign of the other, they also point in their mutual signification to the inexpressible nature of their own origin. This inexpressible is a third element to which they reduce. This third element, however, is not a concept but a phenomenon.

3. Thomas McFarland, *Shapes of Culture* (Iowa City: University of Iowa Press, 1987), 46–81. In McFarland's typology, transcendent meaning is a third kind, distinguished from experienced meaning and meaning by analogy. Of course, in quasi-Hegelian fashion, transcendent meaning embraces and synthesizes the other two kinds. It is a term Merleau-Ponty used in a slightly different context.

4. T. S. Eliot "The Social Function of Poetry," in *On Poetry and Poets* (London: Faber, 1957), 15–25.

5. Ezra Pound, "How to Read," in *The Literary Essays of Ezra Pound* (New York: New Directions, 1968 [1931]), 24–28. Albert Cook, "Thought, Image, and Story: The Slippery Procedures of Literature," in *Figural Choice in Poetry and Art* (Hanover, NH: University Press of New England, 1985), 1–6.

6. William Butler Yeats, "The Symbolism of Poetry," in *Essays and Introductions* (New York: Macmillan, 1961), 153–64.

7. Hans Blumenberg, *Work on Myth*, translated by Robert M. Wallace (Cambridge, MA: MIT Press, 1985), 175–76:

Die menschliche Frontaloptik bedingt, dass wir Wesen mit "viel Rücken" sind und leben müssen unter der Bedingung, dass immer ein Grossteil der Wirklichkeit uns im Rücken liegt und von uns hinter uns gelassen werden muss.

Hans Blumenberg, *Arbeit am Mythos* (Frankfurt am Main: Suhrkamp, 1979), 193–94.

8. For a discussion of how images transcend such analyses, see Albert Cook, *Figural Choice in Poetry and Art*.

9. Robert Greer Cohn, *Modes of Art* (Stanford, CA: Anma Libri, 1975), 136. Cohn's trenchant formulation, of course, derives not only from a broad base for French *Symbolisme* but from a central and powerful Romantic tradition, itself based on the theological use of the term and reticulated by the strongest thinkers of the time into philosophical definition and poetic use. For an account of this strong tradition in the context of a refutation of those who would downplay or "demystify" symbol, and for an indication of De Quincey's interesting term "involute" as a characterization of its combinatory properties, see Thomas McFarland, "Involute and Symbol in the Romantic Image," in *Coleridge, Keats, and the Imagination: Romanticism and Adam's Dream*, ed. J. Robert Barth, S.J., and John L. Maloney (Columbia: University of Missouri Press, 1990), 29–57.

10. The possibility has been raised of applying this phrase to Aristotle, though Vergil is immediately spoken to, because some commentators resist assigning so comprehensive a designation to a poet, and even with the pun *mar/Maro*. On *theologus* as it pertains to both poet and theologian, see Ernst Robert Curtius, *European Literature in the Latin Middle Ages* (New York: Harper, 1963), 222–25.

11. Immanuel Kant, *Kritik der Urteilskraft*, I, 1, 21, Immanuel Kant, *The Critique of Judgement*, translated by James Creed Meredith (Oxford: Oxford University Press, 1952), 83:

Erkenntnisse und Urteile müssen sich, samt der Überzeugung, die sie begleitet, allgemein mitteilen lassen; denn sonst käme ihnen keine Übereinstimmung mit dem Objekt zu; sie wären insgesamt ein bloss subjektives Spiel der Vorstellungskräfte, gerade so wie es der Skeptizism verlangt. Sollen sich aber Erkenntnisse mitteilen lassen, so muss sich auch der Gemütszustand, d. i. die Stimmung der Erkenntniskräfte zu einer Erkenntnis überhaupt, und zwar diejenige Proportion, welche sich für eine Vorstellung (wodurch uns ein Gegenstand gegeben wird) gebührt, um daraus Erkenntnis zu machen, allgemein mitteilen lassen; weil ohne diese, als subjektive Bedingung des Erkennens, das Erkenntnis als Wirkung nicht entspringen könnte.

12. Theodor Adorno is willing, indeed, to expand the Kantian system into what amounts to a resolution of the antinomy: "Kant möchte, analog zur Vernunftkritik, ästhetische Objektivität aus dem Subjekt begründen, nicht jene durch dieses ersetzen. Implizit ist ihm das Einheitsmoment des Objektiven und Subjek-

tiven die Vernunft, ein subjektives Vermögen und gleichwohl, kraft seiner Attribute von Notwendigkeit und Allgemeinheit, Urbild aller Objektivität" ("Kant was able, in analogy to his critique of reason, to base his aesthetic objectivity on the subject, not to replace the former with the latter. Reason is for him implicit as the moment of unity between objective and subjective, a subjective capacity and at the same time, with the aid of its attributes of necessity and generality, a primal image of all objectivity"). Theodor W. Adorno, *Ästhetische Theorie*, Gesammelte Schriften, Band 7 (Frankfurt am Main: Suhrkamp, 1970), 245.

13. Cary Nelson, *Repression and Recovery: Modern American Poetry and the Politics of Cultural Memory, 1910–1945* (Madison: University of Wisconsin Press, 1989), 129.

14. For the details of Blake's occasions, see David Erdman, *Blake: Prophet Against Empire* (Princeton, NJ: Princeton University Press, 1977).

15. The same limitation governs poems like Tennyson's *Ode on the Death of Wellington* and Alcaeus's effusion on the death of Myrtilus. Horace, and the Roman poets generally, present the more complex case, also normal at other times and places including the Renaissance; this is the case when the personal interfaces the political. Such composites, by that very fact, aim beyond a specific public occasion.

16. Theodor Adorno, *Ästhetische Theorie*, 19. "Kunst ist die gesellschaftliche Antithesis zur Gesellschaft, nicht unmittelbar aus dieser zu deduzieren."

17. "Kunstwerke sind Nachbilder des empirisch Lebendigen, soweit sie diesem zukommen lassen, was ihnen draussen verweigert wird, und dadurch von dem befreien, wozu ihre dinghaft-auswendige Erfahrung sie zurichtet" (ibid., 14).

18. "Der Wahrheitsgehalt der Kunstwerke ist fusioniert mit ihrem kritischen" (ibid., 59).

19. "Der Geist von Werken kann die Unwahrheit sein. Denn der Wahrheitsgehalt postuliert als seine Substanz ein Wirkliches, und kein Geist ist ein Wirkliches unmittelbar" (ibid., 136). As he goes on, working in the German opposition of *Natur* and *Geist*,

> Denn als solche Negation des naturbeherrschenden tritt der Geist der Kunstwerke nicht als Geist auf. Er zündet in dem ihm Entgegengesetzten, in der Stofflichkeit. Keineswegs ist er am gegenwärtigsten in den geistigsten Kunstwerken. Ihr Rettendes hat Kunst an dem Akt, mit dem der Geist in ihr sich wegwirft. . . . Damit partizipiert Kunst am realen geschichtlichen Zug, dem Gesetz von Aufklärung gemäss, dass was einmal Realität dünkte, kraft der Selbstbesinnung des Genius in die Imagination einwandert und in ihr überdauert, indem es der eigenen Unwirklichkeit bewusst wird. Die geschichtliche Bahn von Kunst als Vergeistigung ist eine der Kritik am Mythos sowohl wie eine zu seiner Rettung: wessen die Imagination eingedenkt, das wird in seiner Möglichkeit von dieser bekräftigt. Solche Doppelbewegung des Geistes in der Kunst beschreibt eher deren im Begriff liegende Urgeschichte als die empirische. (Ibid., 180.)

For as such a negation of the nature-dominant, the spirit of art works does not emerge as spirit. It kindles in that which is opposed to it, in materiality.

In no way is it the element most present in the most spiritual art works. Art saves itself in the act with which the spirit in itself throws itself away. . . . Art participates in the real course of history, in accordance with the law of enlightenment, that what once seemed reality, with the help of the self-awareness of genius, migrates into the imagination and persists there, while it is conscious of its own unreality. The historical path of art as inspiriting is one connected with the criticism of myth as well as one connected to its salvation: what the imagination is mindful of will be mastered in the possibility of it. Such a double movement of spirit in art describes more its primal history residing in the concept than it does the empirical.

20.

Dies Verhältnis von Erkenntnistheorie und Kunst ist umzukehren. Jene vermag durch kritische Selbstreflexion den solipsistischen Bann zu zerstören, während der subjektive Bezugspunkt von Kunst real nach wie vor das ist, was in der Realität der Solipsismus bloss fingierte. Kunst ist die geschichtsphilosophische Wahrheit des an sich unwahren Solipsismus. In ihr kann nicht willentlich der Stand überschritten werden, den Philosophie zu Unrecht hypostasiert hat. Der ästhetische Schein ist, was ausserästhetisch der Solipsismus mit der Wahrheit verwechselt. (Ibid., 70)

21. "Ästhetische Verhaltensweise ist die Fähigkeit, mehr an den Dingen wahrzunehmen, als sie sind; der Blick, unter dem, was ist, in Bild sich verwandelt. Während diese Verhaltensweise mühelos vom Daseienden als inadäquat dementiert werden kann, wird es erfahrbar doch einzig in ihr" (ibid., 488).

22. "Ästhetisches Verhalten aber ist weder Mimesis unmittelbar noch die verdrängte sondern der Prozess, den sie entbindet und in dem sie modifiziert sich erhält" (ibid., 489).

23. "Das Kunstwerk, das den Gehalt von sich aus zu besitzen glaubt, ist durch Rationalismus schlecht naiv: das dürfte die geschichtlich absehbare Grenze Brechts sein" (ibid., 47).

24. "Der bis heute von der allerdings ihrerseits misslungenen Bildung nicht beeinträchtigte Hang, Kunst ausser- oder vorästhetisch wahrzunehmen, ist nicht nur barbarischer Rückstand oder Not des Bewusstseins Regredierender. Etwas in der Kunst kommt ihm entgegen. Wird sie strikt ästhetisch wahrgenommen, so wird sie ästhetisch nicht recht wahrgenommen" (ibid., 17).

25. "Axiomatisch ist für eine umorientierte Ästhetik die vom späten Nietzsche gegen die traditionelle Philosophie entwickelte Erkenntnis, dass auch das Gewordene wahr sein kann. Die traditionelle, von ihm demolierte Ansicht wäre auf den Kopf zu stellen: Wahrheit ist einzig als Gewordenes" (ibid., 12).

26. I, 1, 22, *Analysis of the Beautiful*; Meredith, pages 84–85:

Die Notwendigkeit der allgemeinen Beistimmung, die in einem Geschmacksurteil gedacht wird, ist eine subjektive Notwendigkeit, die unter der Voraussetzung eines Gemeinsinns als objektiv vorgestellt wird. Also ist der Gemeinsinn, von dessen Urteil ich mein Geschmacksurteil hier als ein Beispiel angebe, und weswegen ich ihm *exemplarische* Gültigkeit beilege, eine blosse idealische Norm, unter deren Voraussetzung man ein Urteil, welches mit ihr zusammenstimmte, und das in demselben ausgedrückte Wohlgefallen an einem Objekt für jedermann mit Recht zur Regel machen könnte: weil zwar das Prinzip nur subjektiv, dennoch aber für subjektiv-allgemein (eine jedermann notwendige Idee) angenommen, was die Einhelligkeit verschiedener Urteilenden betrifft, gleich einem objektiven, allgemeine Beistimmung fordern könnte; wenn man nur sicher wäre, darunter richtig subsumiert zu haben.

27. Fish's relativization by rough-sketching interpretive communities, for example, in *Is There a Text in This Class?* (Cambridge, MA: Harvard University Press, 1980), is refuted, or at least qualified, on its own ground without recourse to bracketing, or appeal to the fundament of wisdom in the apperception of a poem, by Robert Scholes, "Who Cares about the Text," in *Textual Power* (New Haven, CT: Yale University Press, 1985), 149–65. Scholes shows several weaknesses in Fish's account, which could theoretically be fortified by fuller descriptions, though a fundamental failure to distinguish between understanding and belief, and between some steadiness in a text and the variability of the interpreter, could not be obviated if the limits Fish claims for his notion of the "interpretive community" were given finality. In his later work (*Doing What Comes Naturally* [Durham, NC: Duke University Press, 1989]), Fish essentially posits a normative set of conditions for both interpretation and its interlocking contextual-community constraints. One can diverge too much from the literal, he argues, or too little; one can pay too much attention to the constraints of the interpretive community or too little. This is not exactly a relativism. It is an assertive, well-meant description, which shares some of Heidegger's assumed procedure in spite of itself in so far as it sets itself the task of applying a template of descriptions to aspects of the actual conditions. It can be faulted not on its own ground, but for what it leaves out, which is just about all that carries a poem (of Herbert or Milton, for example) through to the depth Fish would effectually deny by ignoring it, or by pretending that what he analyzes precludes it from existing.

28. Barbara Herrnstein Smith, *Contingencies of Value* (Cambridge, MA: Harvard University Press, 1988). Smith describes the social conditions and tries to bring them to bear in such a way that they undo the Kantian antinomy—which she does not at all address, not even in her chapter on Kant. Her "contingent," in fact, simply offers a context for Kant's "subjectivity." And it can be seen as begging the question, since it broaches the very interconnectedness that itself mirrors the contingency of the constituents. She brackets, as she must, the universal inhering in a sense of wisdom for poetry.

Charles Altieri (in *Canons and Consequences* [Evanston, IL: Northwestern University Press, 1990]) offers counter-arguments to both Smith and Fish from within a descriptive area that assesses antifoundational conclusions by characterizing "cultural embeddings" toward a position I understand as close to my own. As he says of Fish, using Wittgenstein's arguments to endorse "going on,"

> Fish sets up an absolute opposition between categories like literalness, with fixed and hence dependable criteria, and categories that depend only on will

or convention. This brings him very close to assumptions like Bertrand Russell's, and that in turn explains why Derrida is attractive to Fish, since Derrida's "scandal" depends on ironically subverting Russellian demands for *propre sens*. Yet neither Russell's form of philosophy nor its skeptical inversions can handle cultural institutions like the law because they have no way of dealing with levels of embedding and the practical, not analytic, judgment they require. . . . Fish bases his radical relativism on the demand that any opposing position produce a fixed definition or proper sense for concepts like "normal" or "literal." . . . Normalcy is not the kind of concept that involves necessary and sufficient conditions, and hence it cannot be deemed "arbitrary" in particular cases by relying only on isolated counter-examples. . . . So judging normalcy involves not definitive descriptions of states of affairs that can be falsified, but the probabilistic evaluation of which situation types best combine for understanding appropriate contexts and embedded values. Thus, it will not do to make Fish's leap from the correct assumption that coherence is relative to the problematic one that all the terms that establish coherence are equally relative.

29. Jürgen Habermas, "Bewusstmachende oder rettende Kritik—Die Aktualität Walter Benjamins (1972)," in *Kultur und Kritik: Verstreute Aufsätze* (Frankfurt am Main: Suhrkamp, 1973), 302–44. If, as Habermas urges, Adorno is in implicit conflict with Benjamin, allowing in his analyses a "universal" canon while discussing relativities of collective subjectivism and so in some modified way validating the aura that Benjamin would deny to modern works, then Adorno's adherence to expressed preferences within a framework of canonicities, for all the dialectic of social interaction he brings to bear upon the works he discusses, could be reconciled, in spite of his arguments against Heidegger, with Heidegger's hermeneutic and depth-conceptual characterization of the work of art seen as bringing about an act of saying, a stability that gives it the permanence for which canonicity is only another, differently angled, name. In this connection Adorno's criticism, too, stands under a false sublation of art, which does, to be sure, destroy the aura, but liquidates the art work's correspondence to truth at the same time as its masterly organization.

30. "Ist das Phänomen des Verstehens angemessen definiert, wenn ich sage: Verstehen heisst, Missverstehen vermeiden? Liegt nicht in Wahrheit allem Missverstehen etwas wie ein 'tragendes Einverständnis' voraus?" Hans-Georg Gadamer, "Die Universalität des hermeneutischen Problems," in *Kleine Schriften I* (Tübingen: Mohr, 1967), 104, as cited by Habermas.

31. "Und die Metakommunikation kann sich nur der Sprache bedienen, über die zugleich als Objekt gesprochen wird: denn jede natürliche Sprache ist ihre eigene Metasprache. Darauf beruht jene Reflexivität, die es, entgegen der Typenregel, erlaubt, dass der semantische Gehalt sprachlicher Äusserungen neben der manifesten Mitteilung zugleich eine indirekte Mitteilung über deren Applikation enthält. Das gilt beispielsweise für den metaphorischen Sprachgebrauch" ("And metacommunication can only enlist the language about which at the same time it is spoken as an object, for every natural language is its own metalanguage. On this

principle rests that reflexivity which permits, against the rules of typification, that the semantic content of a linguistic utterance, beside its manifest communication, contains at the same time an indirect communication about its application. This is valid, for example, in the linguistic use of metaphor"). Jürgen Habermas, "Der Universalitätsanspruch der Hermeneutik (1970)," in *Kultur und Kritik: Verstreute Aufsätze*, 266. As Adorno says elsewhere, "Kunst wird dabei zum blossen Exponenten der Gesellschaft, nicht zum Ferment ihrer Veränderung, und so jene Entwicklung gerade des bürgerlichen Bewusstseins approbiert, welche alle geistigen Gebilde zur blossen Funktion, einem nur für anderes Seienden, schliesslich zum Bedarfsartikel herabsetzt" ("Art becomes thus [in a simply sociologized analysis] a mere exponent of society, not the ferment for its transformation, and thus it directly approves that development of bourgeois consciousness that finally degrades all spiritual formations to a mere function, one as existent only for another, into an article of use"). Theodor W. Adorno, *Philosophie der neuen Musik* (Frankfurt am Main / Berlin: Ullstein, 1958), 29.

32. The process, of course, is always an elaborate one. See, among many studies of this question for scriptural canonization, Isidor Frank, *Der Sinn der Kanonbildung* (Freiburg: Herder, 1971).

33. Once again, a process that engages much of what philosophy engages would be required, as Heidegger among others exemplifies, to account for what such wisdom is and how it is transmitted. One bold construction, in the context of modern critical and ethical theory, is offered by Charles Altieri ("An Idea and Ideal of a Literary Canon," *Critical Inquiry*, X:1 [September 1983]), 37–60. Admitting, effectually with Heidegger, the circularity of his account, Altieri presents three features that characterize the wisdom marking works as canonical: they "institutionalize idealisation," they "project . . . beyond the specific interpretive community," and they establish the "dialectic" for an "alternative society" to "shape possible selves." This would carry us far, and while it would not help to define in some cases practically (Emily Dickinson? Pound?), it could be made to do so ideally.

34. For a positive study of Longfellow's poetry in context, see Newton Arvin, *Longfellow: His Life and Work* (Boston: Little, Brown, 1963). Of course, my summary remarks here are only at best notes for a program toward countering Arvin's assessments. Kitsch is indeed hard, or even impossible to define, and discussions about it tend to get trammeled in finding the givens of social expression that enter into "popular" works, and "high" ones too, nearly inextricable. So, for example, the illustrious literary critics, social critics, and philosophers who entered into dialogue about kitsch at Saratoga recently (the proceedings are printed in *Salmagundi*, 85–86 [Winter–Spring 1990]) soon got into inextricable tangles as they tried to attain discriminations and definitions in this area. As Adorno says, "Kitsch ist ein idiosynkratischer Begriff, so verbindlich, wie er nicht sich definieren lässt" ("Kitsch is an idiosyncratic concept, as obligatory as it is indefinable"). *Ästhetische Theorie*, 60. But as he further says, "Der Kitsch ist jenes Gefüge von Invarianten, das die philosophische Lüge ihren feierlichen Entwürfen zuschreibt" ("Kitsch is that structure of invariants that the philosophical lie ascribes to its celebratory schemes"). *Minima Moralia* (Frankfurt: Suhrkamp, 1951), 194.

35. Here, as throughout when I give individual assessments of poems, I am assuming judgments without grounding them in a full critical discussion. But my justification for doing so resides in the fact that the entire machinery of literary criticism as it bears on judgments is still subject to the general questions I am discussing here. That is, evolving a judgment through a careful weighing of the attributes of the poem, *Hiawatha* in this instance, were I to go through the process of evolving such a judgment, would not release it from the antinomy between subjective and universal.

The relativism of assessments of poems provides countless illustrations. So Baudelaire overvalued not only some poems of Poe (if it be conceded that a poem can be overvalued) but also on one occasion even of Longfellow. Baudelaire's "Le Calumet de Paix" ("The Pipe of Peace") recasts the American poet in hexameters:

Or Gitche Manito, le Maître de la Vie,
Le Puissant, descendit dans la verte prairie,
Dans l'immense prairie aux coteaux montueux;
Et lè, sur les rochers de la Rouge Carrière,
Dominant tout l'espace et baigné de lumière,
Il se tenait debout, vaste et majestueux.

I believe almost any modern reader of this translation-imitation of Longfellow would take it as a parody from what seems to be the tone of this first stanza, but Baudelaire took it seriously enough to include it in the third edition of *Les Fleurs du mal*. Such egregious assessments are often cross-cultural, as in what I believe to be the overestimation of Byron's poetry by Pushkin and Goethe.

36. See Hans Egon Holthusen, "Über den sauren Kitsch," in *Ja und Nein* (Munich: R. Piper, 1954).

37. One could extend the parallel between Longfellow and Whitman, as Leslie Fiedler does ("A Review of *Leaves of Grass* and *Hiawatha* as of 1855," *American Poetry Review*, 2:2 [March–April 1973], 45–46). In addition to juxtaposing the two poems with thematic similarities and differences, Fiedler points out that Longfellow in his novel *Kavanagh* has a character call for a national epic poem that vaguely matches what would become *Leaves of Grass*.

38. Mark Van Doren, *American Poets 1630–1930* (Boston: Little Brown, 1932), 134–43. The anthology, of course, illustrates the variability of taste as it contributes to a canon in other ways, too. Longfellow here gets 33 pages to Whitman's 35, where Emily Dickinson gets slightly fewer (21) than William Cullen Bryant (23). Stevens gets 6 pages to Conrad Aiken's 16, and Williams gets 6 to John Gould Fletcher's 15; here Williams is no more prominent than the now forgotten poets James Rorty and William Rose Benét.

39. William Labov and David Fanshel, *Therapeutic Discourse* (New York: Academic Press, 1977).

40. Erving Goffman, *Forms of Talk* (Philadelphia: University of Pennsylvania Press, 1981), especially 128–50. I have further discussed how Goffman's constraints work for poetry in general, and particularly for prophetic poetry, in "Prophecy and

the Preconditions of Poetry," in *Soundings* (Detroit: Wayne State University Press, 1991), 44–56.

41. "Von Anbeginn erfuhr ich . . . das Werk nicht als eine blosse Erkenntnistheorie, als Analyse der Bedingungen wissenschaftlich gültiger Urteile, sondern als eine Art chiffrierter Schrift, aus der der geschichtliche Stand des Geistes herauszulesen war, mit der vagen Erwartung, dass dabei etwas von der Wahrheit selber zu gewinnen sei." Theodor Adorno, *Noten zur Literatur III* (Frankfurt am Main: Suhrkamp, 1965), 83–84.

42. "Sogar vermeintlich extrem individuelle Reaktionsweisen sind vermittelt durch die Objektivität, auf die sie ansprechen, and müssten dieser Vermittlung um ihres eigenen Wahrheitsgehalts willen innewerden" (ibid., 91).

43. As Gadamer says of the hermeneutic circle in terms that would apply to Heidegger's usage and Dilthey's as well as to his own, "The hermeneutic circle says that in the domain of understanding there can be absolutely no derivation of one [the structure of a logical concept] from the other [the theory of scientific proof], so that here the logical fallacy of circularity does not represent a mistake in procedure, but rather the most appropriate description of the structure of understanding" (Diane P. Michelfelder and Richard E. Palmer, eds. *Dialogue and Deconstruction: The Gadamer-Derrida Encounter* [Albany: State University of New York Press, 1989], 22).

44. Adorno has some strictures about fading: "Vielleicht sogar herrscht eine Relation zwischen der Qualität und einem Prozess des Absterbens. Manchen Kunstwerken wohnt die Kraft inne, die gesellschaftliche Schranke zu durchbrechen, die sie erreichten. Während die Schriften Kafkas durch die eklatante empirische Unmöglichkeit des Erzählten das Einverständnis der Romanleser verletzten, wurden sie eben vermöge solcher Verletzung allen verständlich" ("Perhaps indeed a relation obtains between quality and a process of withering away. The force resides in many art works to break through the social limits they attained. In the writings of Kafka through the striking impossibility of what is narrated, having injured the agreement of the reader, everything becomes comprehensible just through this very injury"). Adorno, *Ästhetische Theorie*, 291.

45. Hugh Kenner, *The Pound Era* (Berkeley: University of California Press, 1971), 420.

46. I here quote from *The Cantos* (New York: New Directions, 10th printing, 1986).

47. Christopher Ricks, *The Force of Poetry* (Oxford: Oxford University Press, 1987), 426–32.

48. "Über die affirmative Antwort sind wir uns einig, nicht einig darüber, wie dieser vorgängige Konsensus zu bestimmen ist" (Habermas, 294).

49. "Gadamer . . . sieht keinen Gegensatz zwischen Autorität und Vernunft. Die Autorität der Überlieferung setzt sich nicht blind durch, sondern durch die reflektierte Anerkennung derer, die, in einer Tradition stehend, diese verstehen und durch Applikation fortbilden" (ibid., 298).

50. In this connection, expansive discussions are undertaken by Gaston Bachelard, *L'Eau et les rêves*, (Paris: José Corti, 1963); and Frederic Will, "The Argument of Water," in *Thresholds & Testimonies* (Detroit: Wayne State University

Press, 1988), 43–92. Echoic reminders of these connections occur at several points of the whole poem, of course, most specifically in Canto 96 (10th printing, 658), "PANTA 'REI, said Du Bellay translating, / the base shall we say"; and more succinctly for the "all flows" quotation but otherwise more expansively:

> So that Dante's view is quite natural:
>   this light
>   as a river
> in Kung; in Ocellus, Coke, Agassiz
>
> ῥεῖ, the flowing
> this persistent awareness
>   (Canto 107; p. 762)

The connections with Dante's river of light in Paradise (possibly *Par.* 10, 40–43, but elsewhere, too) are lined up to Confucius; to an obscure Pythagorean, a legendary pupil of the fifth century B.C. who supposedly wrote a treatise on the universe and said "to build light"; to the Renaissance jurist whom Pound singles out in the later cantos; and to the nineteenth-century speculative geologist.

51. Samuel Levin, *Metaphoric Worlds* (New Haven, CT: Yale University Press, 1988).

52. Longinus, 17.2, as quoted by Neil Hertz, "A Reading of Longinus," in *The End of the Line* (New York: Columbia University Press, 1985), 17. For further modern application of Longinus's deductions about the sublime, see Albert Cook, *Dimensions of the Sign in Art* (Hanover, NH: University Press of New England, 1989), introduction. An especially penetrating discussion of the Kantian sublime(s) as it (they) function in English Romantic poetry is provided by Thomas Weiskel, *The Romantic Sublime: Studies in the Structure and Psychology of Transcendence* (Baltimore, MD: The Johns Hopkins University Press, 1976).

53. "Dabei handelt es sich um verhaltenssteuernde Symbole, und nicht bloss um Zeichen, denn die Symbole haben echte Bedeutungsfunktion; sie stellen Interaktionserfahrungen dar. Im übrigen fehlen aber dieser Schicht der Paläosymbole alle Eigenschaften der normalen Rede" (Habermas, 286).

54. "Paläosymbole sind nicht in ein grammatisches Regelsystem eingefügt. Sie sind keine geordneten Elemente und treten nicht in Zusammenhängen auf, die grammatisch transformiert werden können. Man hat deshalb die funktionsweise dieser vorsprachlichen Symbole mit der von Analogrechnern im Unterschied zu der von Digitalrechnern verglichen" (ibid., 286).

Of course, the whole work of Lévi-Strauss heavily qualifies, and even largely negates, this deduction. For the calibrations of difference between the base of such symbols and linguistic expression see Albert Cook, *Myth and Language* (Bloomington: Indiana University Press, 1980).

55. "Was Geschichte ist an den Werken, ist nicht gemacht, und Geschichte erst befreit es von blosser Setzung oder Herstellung: der Wahrheitsgehalt ist nicht ausser der Geschichte sondern deren Kristallisation in den Werken" (Theodor W. Adorno, *Ästhetische Theorie*, 200).

174 Notes to Chapter 2

56. "Wertfreie Ästhetik ist Nonsens. Kunstwerke verstehen heisst . . . des Moments ihrer Logizität innewerden und ihres Gegenteils, auch ihrer Brüche und dessen, was sie bedeuten" (ibid., 391).

Chapter 2: "Most Take All": The Good and the Beautiful in Herbert's Temple

1. Suzanne Langer, *Mind: an Essay on Human Feeling* (Baltimore, MD: Johns Hopkins University Press, 1967).
2. For the intricacies of the interaction between Bradley and Eliot, see Richard Wollheim, *On Art and the Mind* (Cambridge, MA: Harvard University Press, 1974).
3. The implications for aesthetic judgement of this identification between the beautiful and the good by Kant bears on much recent discussion about the connection between ethics and aesthetics. See Paul Crowther, *The Kantian Sublime: From Morality to Art* (Oxford: Oxford University Press, 1989).
4. Helen Vendler, *The Poetry of George Herbert* (Cambridge, MA: Harvard University Press, 1975), 82.
5. Stanley Fish, *The Living Temple: George Herbert and Catechizing* (Berkeley: University of California Press, 1978).
6. All quotations are from F. E. Hutchinson, ed., *The Works of George Herbert* (Oxford: Clarendon Press, 1945).
7. Louis Martz, *The Poetry of Meditation* (New Haven, CT: Yale University Press, 1954).
8. William Empson, *Seven Types of Ambiguity* (London: Chatto & Windus, 1949 [1930]), 226–233.
9. So in "The Holy Scriptures" the sacred writ is seen as comprehensive enough, and its correspondence to the world rich enough, for them to be called in the space of one sonnet successively a medicinal honey, health, eternity, "a masse of strange delights," a mirror, a well, "heav'n's Lidger," and "joyes handsell."
10. Chana Bloch, *Spelling the Word* (Berkeley: University of California Press, 1985), 98–112. The congruence of this poem with the widespread Lutheran-derived emphasis on salvation by faith alone is well, if somewhat too exclusively, delineated by Richard Strier (*Love Known: Theology and Experience in Herbert's Poetry* [Chicago: University of Chicago Press, 1983]). As Strier says (73–74), "In 'Love (III)' Herbert dramatizes his awareness that the doctrine of faith alone can be undermined by assertions of merit and cooperation, but by assertions of unworthiness as well. 'Love (III)' shows that at the deepest level the two forms of assertion are the same."
11. As Richard Strier says (op. cit., 74), "The courtesy-contest situation of 'Love (III),' the guest-host framework, allows Herbert to dramatize with great precision the steps by which self-denial becomes self-assertion."
12. For this reason the presentation of Herbert in Stanley Fish's *Self-Consuming Artifacts* (Berkeley: University of California Press, 1974), which treats of the paradoxes as self-canceling, while offering some acute local readings, entirely misses the mark by describing as negative the speaker's positive aim of union with

God. "If God is all, the claims of other entities to a separate existence, including the claims of the speakers and readers of these poems, must be relinquished" (*Self-Consuming Artifacts*, 156). Such a notion would astonish both Herbert and his readers; it is arrived at by providing something like a psychoanalytic interpretation, often by exaggerating or inventing ambiguities in the text, whereby a secret hostility to God underlies the devotion and a secret pride the humility of the poet. Herbert, of course, presents such hostility and pride as a problem, and if we do not take his assertions, initial and final, at face value, we negate the perlocutionary thrust and testimentary communication of the poems. It is as though some perverse psychoanalyst, looking at a happy, fruitful, fulfilled, and companionate marriage, were to inspect its moments of stress and pronounce it stalled for being riddled by those ambivalences that Freud has in fact found in any human love whatever. In Fish's misguided words, "The stated wish to praise God, then, is a thinly disguised accusation of him" (160). But for the poem at hand, "The Temper (I)," his interpretation involves arresting the thrust of its "complaint" and totally discounting the progressions from it. This arbitrary inversion of values on Fish's part entails an oversimplification of Herbert's subtle manipulation of "plain sense" which Fish claims to be discussing. "By thus enrolling himself in the ranks of plain-style poets, Herbert indicates indicates a willingness to give up a large part of those very resources with which he had proposed . . . to glorify his God" (195). But this is to oversimplify the poet's idealization of simplicity and to deprive him of the very resources that Herbert's *literary* sense is managing toward. This would also illegitimize the poet's very satisfaction with his expression (though in ultimate modesty Herbert submitted his work to the arbitration of Nicholas Farrer in the deathbed command to test the poems before having them published). Fish would effectually deprive Herbert of a satisfaction that all poets must feel at some point about the attainment of their works. It is not overweening pride but a worthy satisfaction at a difficult expression brought to term that properly identifies the poet's attitude. Fish's attention, often revelatory in its subtleties of definition, by refusing to share the poet's communicative act, perversely misdefines it.

13. I borrow this point from Annabel Patterson, "The Structure of George Herbert's *Temple*," in *Essential Articles for the Study of George Herbert's Poetry*, ed. John R. Roberts (Hamden, CT: Archon Books, 1979), 352–53.

14. Joseph H. Summers, "Herbert's Form" (in ibid., 87–104 [100]). Summers (103) stresses the intricacy brought to order in the overmastering metrical regularity of "The Collar":

> Although readers accustomed to Renaissance poetry might feel uncomfortable with the disorder of the first thirty-two lines, they could hardly divine the stanzaic norm which is the measure for that disorder until it is established, simultaneously with the submission of the rebel, in the final quatrain: 10(a) 4(b) 8(a) 6(b). That pattern of line lengths and rhyme does not occur until the final four lines; before those lines the elements of the pattern are arranged so as to form almost the mathematical ultimate in lack of periodicity. If we consider that the first thirty-two lines represent eight quatrains, we discover six different patterns of rhyme (the only repeated one is the unformed a b c d)

and seven patterns of line lengths. "The Collar" is a narrative in the past tense. The message for the present concerns the necessity of order.

And more generally: "*The Temple* is almost a casebook of examples showing how 'Order' gives 'all things their set forms and hours.' It reflects Herbert's belief that form was that principle by which the spiritual created existence out of chaos, and Herbert assumed that that process could be rationally apprehended."

15. Barbara Leah Harman, *Costly Monuments* (Cambridge, MA: Harvard University Press, 1982), 63.

16. Arnold Stein, "George Herbert: The Art of Plainness," in *Essential Articles for the Study of George Herbert's Poetry*, 160–80 (165).

17. "The titles to esteem which verse is not are first detailed; then it is declared that verse nevertheless is the *quiddity* of them all, in the very real sense that Herbert in his poetry comes nearest to God and most partakes of the creative power that sustains all these excellences." John Middleton Murry, as quoted in *The Poetry of George Herbert*, ed. F. E. Hutchinson (Oxford: Clarendon Press, 1941), 500.

18. There is the difficulty that in the second reading, if it were allowed to stand alone, there would be a logical inconsistency, since, according to that reading, the poet would have to be allowed as taking all anyway but doing so in a fuller fashion if he is with God. But the beginning of the poem, ruling out functions for poetry, would then be in contradiction to this corollary; it would rule out the possibility that you could have something without God, which the smoother reading of the phrase by implication allows. I owe the indication of this second reading to Bill Mensel. For a parallel to my reading, in which italics are used to set a final phrase into quotation marks but also to double it, compare the ending of "The Cross":

> And yet since these thy contradictions
> Are properly a crosse felt by thy Sonne,
> With but foure words, my words, *Thy will be done*.

19. See the discussion in Albert Cook, *Myth and Language* (Bloomington: Indiana University Press, 1980), "The Large Phases of Myth," especially 57–59: "Beyond such allegorization [as the Renaissance made of classical gods], they subject the conflation of classical god with the feeling of love to the delicate, dissecting irony of poetic artifice, as though to say that the relations within the love-sphere are as delightfully formal as the very manner in which the poem at hand can attribute the name of a deity disbelieved by the poet to the idea of love and the force of love."

20. Richard Todd, *The Opacity of Signs: Acts of Interpretation in George Herbert's* The Temple (Columbia: University of Missouri Press, 1986), 2.

21. William H. Palka elaborately connects the regularity and mastery of Herbert's meter to an underlying congruence with the theories of Saint Augustine's *De Musica* (*St. Augustine's Meter and George Herbert's Will* [Kent, OH: Kent State University Press, 1987]): "Herbert rejected the Elizabethan emphasis on the me-

diation between the human order and the natural order and tried to restore an Augustinian emphasis on mediation between the human and the divine" (57–58). "Three principles govern Herbert's meter: (1) a high degree of syllabic regularity; (2) a relatively strict and narrow allowance for substitutions of non-iambic feet; and (3) inventive use of varying line lengths to create proportional stanzaic forms" (69). In other poems, the order of the meter allows a shift of tempo, often, even into dimeter, without a shift of tone.

Albert Hayes finds seven major types of stanza patterns in Herbert's poems, a wide variety that can be taken to correspond to the rhetoric of the constantly self-reordering persona: (1) Harmonic stanzas, (2) Approximately harmonic stanzas (where divergence of metrical pairing is allowed), (3) Isometrical stanzas, (4) Approximately contrapuntal stanzas, (5) Contrapuntal stanzas (allowing no rhymed lines to be syllabically identical), (6) Off-balance stanzas (one line shorter than the rest), and (7) Irregular stanzas (a large and miscellaneous group). (Albert McHarg Hayes, "Counterpoint in Herbert," *Essential Articles for the Study of George Herbert's Poetry*, 290–94.)

22. For a discussion of these see Albert Cook, "Between Prose and Poetry: The Speech and Silence of the Proverb," in *Myth and Language*, 211–24.

23. See Arnold Stein, *The House of Death: Messages from the English Renaissance* (Baltimore, MD: Johns Hopkins University Press, 1986).

24. Politics is absent from the explicit content of his poetry, but not, of course—which would be anthropologically impossible—from the assumed attitudes and gestures underlying the social patterns he takes for granted. So, as Mark C. Schoenfeldt well says (*Prayer and Power: George Herbert and Renaissance Courtship* [Chicago: University of Chicago Press, 1991], 8), "Herbert's profound insight in *The Temple* and *The Country Parson* into courtliness does not always insulate him from implication in its practices." Schoenfeldt goes on, in the best traditions of the "new historicism" (or simply "new history") to trace those implications in the underlying congruences between Herbert's posture toward God and the behavior of "courtesy" toward king and court. He spells out these implications in passage after passage, and with such sensitive detail that there is some danger in misreading the primary thrust of the poems, which remains primarily devotional and resolutely non-political (even though secondarily in a social context no posture or set of gestures is without political attitudes and implications). To slight Herbert's main devotional assertions is to slight not only the manifest content of the poems but the capital gesture of his withdrawal from high and successful social action.

25. Annabel M. Patterson, *Pastoral and Ideology: Virgil to Valéry* (Berkeley: University of California Press, 1987).

26. On the interactions in this poem see Harry Berger, *Second World and Green World: Studies in Renaissance Fiction-Making* (Berkeley: University of California Press, 1988), 269–75.

27. Marion White Singleton, *God's Courtier: Configuring a Different Grace in George Herbert's* Temple (Cambridge: Cambridge University Press, 1987).

28. Donald Davie, *Purity of Diction in English Verse* (London: Routledge & Kegan Paul, 1967 [1952]), 70–82.

29. See Albert Cook, *Thresholds* (Madison: University of Wisconsin Press, 1985), "Emily Dickinson's White Exploits."

30. Barbara Herrnstein Smith, *On the Margins of Discourse* (Chicago: University of Chicago Press, 1978).

31. Harold Bloom, *Ruin the Sacred Truths* (Cambridge, MA: Harvard University Press, 1989), 137.

32. Joel Fineman, *Shakespeare's Perjured Eye: The Invention of Poetic Subjectivity in the Sonnets* (Berkeley: University of California Press, 1986), 8. However, as a control on Fineman's splendid analyses, it should be noted that the universality he posits for deictics would really entail an equivalent complexity in any other structure that uses them complexly, so that the kind of usage he discusses would not be, without further qualification, exclusively a Renaissance phenomenon, as Lee Patterson and Marshall and Jane Brown have pointed out (personal communications). The "I" of Dante is equivalently complex, and some version of this complexity can be mapped for the lyrics of the troubadors, for Chaucer's role in the *Canterbury Tales*, and even for Sappho. See note 1, Chapter 1.

33. One could further use Fineman (*Shakespeare's Perjured Eye*) as an instrument to match and distinguish Herbert's dialectic in the light of Shakespeare's, where "The young man sonnets regularly halve and double what are taken to be traditional dual unities, and they do so in order then to place the poet at the intersection of the four terms thus produced, between both the two halves of the four *and* between the division of each half. No doubt this represents a peculiarly double and divided place for the poet, and a particularly limited place as well." Herbert provides a mechanism for transcending this limitation, which brings him more directly, as it were, toward the sublime than Shakespeare in the sonnets. This means that the strategies of the two poets are different, without that difference entailing a difference in value either way.

Chapter 3: Heidegger and the Wisdom of Poetry

1. These thinkers will serve as a sample of the extensive and profound discourse on poetry in our time that in some way addresses its essence: Maurice Blanchot, *La Part du feu* (Paris: Gallimard, 1949); R. P. Blackmur, *Form and Value in Modern Poetry* (New York: Anchor, 1957); Jacques Maritain, *Creative Intuition in Art and Poetry* (New York: Bollingen, 1953); Leone Vivante, *English Poetry and Its Contribution to the Knowledge of a Creative Principle*, with a preface by T. S. Eliot (London: Faber & Faber, 1950).

2. I am here following, to some degree, Gerald L. Bruns, *Heidegger's Estrangements* (New Haven, CT: Yale University Press, 1989). I emphasize, however, not the estrangement, the rift, and the occlusion that are dominant in Heidegger's late thinking, on which Bruns well insists, but that which leads to recuperative wisdom. Bruns's formulation sets the balance: "The work is earthly as well as worldly, *phusis* as well as *logos*, darkening as well as lightening, and in this wise it

withholds itself, closes itself up, withdraws into its materials (the poem hiding itself in its words)" (152).

3. See Paul de Man, "Heidegger's Exegeses of Hölderlin," in *Blindness and Insight* (London: Methuen, 1983 [1953]), 246–66. As I have pointed out elsewhere at some length (Albert Cook, *Thresholds*, 265–66), de Man insists on misreading the exuberant phrase "Worte wie Blumen entstehen" against the grain of its poem as a sort of negative based on de Man's (allegedly Hölderlin's) attention to separation in the dead metaphor of the prefix *ent-*. Since Being in Heidegger's system is contradictorily present and absent, de Man can easily underline the contradictions, and in fact he spends the first nine pages of his essay giving a fairly accurate summary of Heidegger on the question of Being. But then, as a bare assertion, he takes the leap of claiming, with no evidence, and against the very readings he adduces, that *"Hölderlin says exactly the opposite of what Heidegger makes him say"* (italics de Man's). *No further evidence is offered for this arresting claim.* And much of de Man's own qualifying summary belies it—as does his immediately following statement: "Such an assertion is paradoxical only in appearance. At the level of thought it is difficult to distinguish between a proposition and that which constitutes its opposite. In fact, to state the opposite is still to talk of the same thing, though in an opposite sense, and it is already a major achievement to have, in a dialogue of this sort, the two interlocutors manage to speak of the same thing." Just so, and if this principle is allowed, it cannot then be dismissed by saying Heidegger's comments on Hölderlin at once "surpass other studies" but at the same time "reverse his thought"—an assertion, again, he says it would take too long to demonstrate. Indeed! See also Gerald Bruns, *Heidegger's Estrangements*, 115. As Walter A. Davis says, apropos of the related procedures of Derrida, "The liberation of *différance* is an essential moment in that process, but it is in danger of remaining an abstract and merely antithetical one unless it becomes a moment in a larger dialectical effort.

"I have no desire to minimize the difficulties of such a rapprochement. All the key words of deconstruction have *double contradictory meanings* [italics Davis's] which resist sublation. Reflection, for Derrida, identifies aporias that can't be resolved, while deferral supplants Heideggerian finitude in an arrested dialectic which recovers repressed political and sexual energies but remains unable to constitute them. The hermeneutic circle of Derrida's thought refuses engagement in favor of charting intellectual binds that condemn us, in effect, to the solipsism of the linguistic moment" (Walter A. Davis, *Inwardness and Existence: Subjectivity in/ and Hegel, Heidegger, Marx, and Freud* [Madison: University of Wisconsin Press, 1989], 348).

4. Jacques Derrida, *Signéponge* (New York: Columbia University Press, 1984); *Schibboleth* (Paris: Galilée, 1986); *L'Esprit* (Paris: Galilée, 1987). For further discussion, see Herman Rapaport, *Derrida and Heidegger: Reflections on Time and Language* (Lincoln: University of Nebraska Press, 1989).

5. "Aus Einem Gespräch über die Sprache," in *Unterwegs zur Sprache* (Pfüllingen: Neske, 1957), 83–156. The passages in question run in the dialogue thus ("F" is for the "Asker," Heidegger himself—who is thus not an answerer. "J" is the

Japanese who comes to ask key cross-cultural questions after having studied with a Japanese ex-student of Heidegger, both closing and opening the circle):

F Benötigen Sie Begriffe?
J Vermutlich ja; denn seit der Begegnung mit dem europäischen Denken kommt ein Unvermögen unserer Sprache an den Tag.
F Inwiefern?
J Es fehlt ihr die begrenzende Kraft, Gegenstände in der eindeutigen Zuordnung zueinander als wechselweise über-und untergeordnete vorzustellen. (86–87)

F Vielleicht ist es der Grundmangel des Buches "Sein und Zeit," dass ich mich zu früh zu weit vorgewagt habe.
J Dies lässt sich von Ihren Gedanken über die Sprache kaum behaupten. (93)
F Ich habe einen früheren Standpunkt verlassen, nicht um dagegen einen anderen einzutauschen, sondern weil auch der vormalige Standort nur ein Aufenthalt war in einem Unterwegs. (98–99)

F Schliesslich betonte ich, das Hermeneutische meine, als Beiwort zu "Phänomenologie" gebraucht, nicht wie üblich die Methodenlehre des Auslegens, sondern dieses selbst.
J Dann verlor sich unser Gespräch ins Unbestimmte.
F Zum Glück. (120)

F Do you need concepts?
J It would seem so; for since the encounter with European thinking an incapacity in our language comes to light.
F To what extent?
J It lacks the limiting power to represent objects in a univocal order with respect to one another as hierarchized into comprehensive categories and subcategories.

F Perhaps it is the basic lack of the book *Sein und Zeit* that I have ventured too far too soon.
J One could scarcely assert that of your thoughts on language.

F I have abandoned an earlier standpoint not in order to exchange it for another but because the foregoing position was only a sojourn on a progressing voyage. What remains in thinking is the way.

F Finally, I asserted, Hermeneutics means, when it is used as an epithet for "phenomenology," not as usually the method of exposition, but exposition itself.
J Then our conversation would lose itself in the undefined.
F Happily.

    6. *Unterwegs zur Sprache*, 99. "Das Bleibende im Denken ist der Weg. Und Denkwege bergen in sich das Geheimnisvolle, dass wir sie vorwärts und rückwärts gehen können, dass sogar der Weg zurück uns erst vorwärts führt."

7. *Vorträge und Aufsätze* (Pfüllingen: Neske, 1954), 138. "Das dichtend Gesagte und das denkend Gesagte sind niemals das gleiche. Aber das eine und das andere kann in verschiedenen Weisen dasselbe sagen. Dies glückt allerdings nur dann, wenn die Kluft zwischen Dichten und Denken rein und entschieden klafft."

8. *Unterwegs zur Sprache*, 157–216.

9. *Erläuterungen zu Hölderlins Dichtung* (Frankfurt am Main: Klostermann, 1971 [1944]), 33–48. Heidegger calls them the five guiding expressions (*die fünf Leitworte*): "1. Dichten: Diss unschuldigste aller Geschäfte. 2. Darum ist der Güter Gefährlichstes, die Sprache dem Menschen gegeben . . . damit er zeuge was er sei . . . 3. Viel hat erfahren der Mensch / Der Himmlischen viele genannt, / seit ein Gespräch wir sind / Und hören können voneinander. 4. Was bleibet aber, stiften die Dichter. 5. Voll Verdienst, doch dichterisch wohnet / Der Mensch auf dieser Erde."

10. Ibid, 49–152. This remains his practice through the solid middle of his career, in the still longer disquisitions about Hölderlin conducted in his seminars: Martin Heidegger, *Gesamtausgabe* (Frankfurt: Klostermann); Vol. 39, *Hölderlin's Hymnen* Germanien *und* Der Rhein (1980 [1934–1935]); Vol. 52, *Hölderlins Hymne* Andenken (1982 [1941–1942]); Vol. 53, *Hölderlins Hymne* Der Ister (1984 [1942]).

11. See Albert Cook, "The Transformation of 'Point': Amplitude in Wordsworth, Whitman, and Rimbaud," *Studies in Romanticism* (Summer 1991), 169–88.

12. See Herman Rapaport, *Heidegger and Derrida: Reflections on Time and Language*, 246–64 and passim.

13. "Le poème, par la parole, fait que ce qui est infondé devient fondement, que l'abîme du jour devient le jour qui fait surgir et qui construit. *Das Heilige sei mein Wort*, il fait en sorte que le Sacré soit parole et que la parole soit sacré." "La Parole 'sacrée' de Hölderlin," in *La Part du feu* (Paris: Gallimard, 1949), 118–36 (131).

14. Derrida, in *L'Esprit*, works out Heidegger's complexes of relation to terms like *Geist*, *geistlich*, and *geistig*, in his general writings and in his interpretations especially of Trakl.

15. "Tous deux, dans leur implication réciproque et à cause de la réciprocité de leur absence, sont déjà portés l'un vers l'autre et par ce mouvement dépassent leur solitude et leur sommeil" (*La Part du feu*, 124–25). See also Heidegger, *Erläuterungen*, 57–58.

16. "Schon blühen ihre Blumen, die ernsten Veilchen / Im Abendgrund," from "In Heilbrunn," in *Offenbarung und Untergang, Die Dichtungen* (Salzburg: Müller, 1938), 187.

17. *An Introduction to Metaphysics* (New York: Anchor, 1961), 75:

"Über allen Gipfeln / ist Ruh"; das "ist" lässt sich gar nicht umschreiben und ist doch nur dieses "ist"!, hingesagt in jene wenigen Verse, die Goethe mit Bleistift an den Fensterpfosten eines Bretterhäuschens auf dem Kickelhahn bei Ilmenau geschrieben (vgl. den Brief an Zelter vom 4. 9. 1831). Seltsam, dass wir hier mit der Umschreiben schwanken, zögern, um sie dann schliesslich ganz zu lassen, nicht weil das Verstehen zu verwikkelt und zu schwierig wäre, sondern weil der Vers so einfach gesagt ist, noch einfacher und einziger als jedes sonst geläufige "ist," das sich uns unbesehen fortgesetz ins alltägliche Sagen und Reden einmischt.

Einführung in die Metaphysik, Gesamtausgabe 40 (Frankfurt am Main: Klostermann, 1983 [1953]), 96.

Goethe had written the poem there fifty years before, in 1780, and replies to a letter dwelling on Faust and on Hegel from the composer who set it to music. He reaches past the fame "to all the world" and considers the double bearing of transience and permanence—"das Dauernde, das Verschwundene." This is also, of course, a topic of Heidegger's poetics, but he passes over it in favor of the ontological implications of the poem. It should be noted that Goethe does not here mention Alcman.

A possible qualification to Heidegger's reading—a frequent possibility in comparing, and nevertheless also supplementing his work by the thought of the contemporary who often contests it—may be seen in Adorno's interpretation of "ist" in Trakl: "Noch die bei Trakl omnipräsente Copula 'ist' entfremdet im Kunstwerk sich ihrem begrifflichen Sinn; sie drückt kein Existentialurteil aus sondern dessen verblasstes, qualitativ bis zur Negation verändertes Nachbild; dass etwas sei, ist darin weniger und mehr, führt mit sich, dass es nicht sei. Wo Brecht oder Carlos Williams im Gedicht das Poetische sabotieren und es dem Bericht über blosse Empirie annähern, wird es keineswegs zu einem solchen: indem sie polemisch den erhoben lyrischen Ton verschmähen, nehmen die empirischen Sätze bei ihrem Transport in die ästhetische Monade durch den Kontrast zu dieser ein Verschiedenes an. Das Gesangsfeindliche des Tons und die Verfremdung der erbeuteten Fakten sind zwei Seiten desselben Sachverhalts" ("The omnipresent copula 'ist' in Trakl alienates itself from its conceptual sense; it expresses no existential judgment [Heidegger might disagree and we might join him!] but an after-image of it, paled and transformed to the point of negation [a keen perception easily assimilable to Heidegger's *Nicht-sein*]; that something is in it less and more entails that it is not. Where Brecht and Carlos Williams sabotage the poetic and approach a report on the flatly empirical, it in no way becomes one [with such a poet as Trakl]; while they polemically disdain the elevated lyrical tone, the empirical sentences [propositions] take on something different by their transport into the aesthetic monad through the contrast to it. That which is hostile to song in the tone and the alienation of the captured facts are two sides to the same content"). *Ästhetische Theorie, Gesammelte Schriften*, Band 7 (Frankfurt am Main: Suhrkamp, 1970), 187.

18. "Nietzsche's Wort 'Gott ist tot,'" in *Holzwege* (Frankfurt: Klostermann, 1950), 193–247.

19.

"Gott ist"; d.h. *wirklich gegenwärtig*. "Die Erde ist"; d.h. wir erfahren und meinen sie als *ständig vorhanden*; "Der Vortrag ist im Hörsaal"; *er findet statt*. . . . "Der Bauer ist aufs Feld"; d.h. *er hat seinen Aufenthalt aufs Feld verlegt, er hält sich dort auf.* . . . "Über allen Gipfeln / ist Ruh":.d.h. ??? Heisst das "ist" in den Versen: Ruhe befindet sich, ist vorhanden findet statt, hält sich auf? All das will hier nicht passen. Und doch ist es dasselbe einfache "ist". Oder meint der Vers: Über allen Gipfeln *herrscht Ruh*, so wie in einer Schulklasse Ruhe herrscht? Auch nicht! Oder vielleicht: Über allen Gipfeln liegt Ruh oder waltet Ruh? Solches schon eher, aber diese Umschreibung trifft auch nicht.

20. Insistence on the dimensions of the deconstructive possibilities in Heidegger's readings of Hölderlin, initially broached by Maurice Blanchot in *La Part du feu*, we owe to Paul de Man, even though he himself demonstrably misreads Hölderlin, and Heidegger too. See note 3, above.

21. Fragment 5 (Page) of Alcman, only discovered in 1957, is taken as cosmogonic by a late Aristotelian commentator, and with qualifications by G. S. Kirk, J. E. Raven, and M. Schofield (*The Pre-Socratic Philosophers* [Cambridge: Cambridge University Press, 1983], 47–50). Glenn Most sees complications in this reading, too. (Glenn Most, "Alcman's 'Cosmogonic Fragment' [Fgt 5 Page, 81 Calame]," *Classical Quarterly*, XXXVII:1 [1987], 1–9). He sees it to be from a book of *partheneia*, which argues against its being cosmogonic, as does the absence of any testimonia in this direction from antiquity. In many passages, Most shows, *physis* implies allegory in scholia. Peleus (metamorphosis) and Thetis (*tithemi*) figure in the passage, as foundational; they are easily assimilable to allegory. Yet both Most and Kirk-Raven-Schofield exhibit the unwarranted assumption, which Heidegger would never have made, and surely not about pre-Socratic verses, that cosmogony and allegory are mutually exclusive. So there may indeed be a concealed cosmogony incorporated into the poetry of a fragment that ends "The way (*poros*) and the limit (*tekmor*) to the beginning and end." The cosmological incorporation of the sea into such a framework would license our reading the "sleep" fragment in question as including such possible speculation. For a discussion of Alcman in general along these lines see Albert Cook, "The Possible Intersections of Cosmology, Religion, and Abstract Thought in the Lyric Fragments of Alcman," *Hellas* (Winter 1992).

22. Hans Robert Jauss, *Literaturgeschichte als Provokation* (Frankfurt: Suhrkamp, 1970), 144–207.

23. See Vincent Scully, *The Earth, the Temple, and the Gods* (New York: Praeger, 1969 [1962]).

24. "Der Aufbau und die grössern Zusammenhänge des Gedichts werden im Hinblick auf das zentrale Wort erfasst." Beda Allemann, *Hölderlin und Heidegger* (Zurich: Atlantis, 1954), 115.

25. "Die Sprache ist als die Welt-bewëgende Sage das Verhältnis aller Verhältnisse. Sie verhält, unterhält, reicht und bereichert das Gegen-einander-über der Weltgegenden, hält und hütet sie, indem sie selber—die Sage—an sich hält." Heidegger, *Unterwegs zur Sprache*, 215.

26. "Dieses Verhältnis aber ist nicht eine Beziehung zwischen dem Ding auf der einen und dem Wort auf der anderen Seite. Das Wort selber ist das Verhältnis,

das jeweils in sich das Ding so einbehält, dass es ein Ding 'ist.'" "Das Wesen der Sprache," *Unterwegs zur Sprache*, 170.

27. "Die Sage ist keineswegs der nachgetragene sprachliche Ausdruck der Erscheinenden, vielmehr beruht alles Scheinen und Verscheinen in der zeigenden Sage. Sie befreit Anwesendes in sein jeweiliges Anwesen, entfreit Abwesendes in sein jeweiliges Abwesen." *Unterwegs zur Sprache*, 257.

28. "Das Wort Unter-Schied wird jetzt dem gewöhnlichen und gewohnten Gebrauch entzogen. Was das Wort 'der Unter-Schied' jetzt nennt, ist nicht ein Gattungsbegriff für vielerlei Arten von Unterschieden. Der jetzt genannte Unter-Schied ist nur als dieser Eine."

"Der Unter-Schied für Welt und Ding *ereignet* Dinge in das Gebärden von Welt, *ereignet* Welt in das Gönnen von dingen." . . .

"Der Unter-Schied ist weder Distinktion noch Relation. Der Unter-Schied ist im höchsten Fall Dimension für Welt und ding." *Unterwegs zur Sprache*, 25. And further, "Die Mitte von Zweien nennt unsere Sprache das Zwischen. die lateinische Sprache sagt: inter. Dem entspricht das deutsche 'unter.' Die Innigkeit von Welt und Ding ist keine Verschmelzung. Innigkeit waltet nur, wo das Innige, Welt und Ding, rein sich scheidet und geschieden bleibt. In der Mitte der Zwei, im Zwischen von Welt und Ding, in ihrem inter, in diesem Unter- waltet der Schied" [ibid., 24] ("The middle of two things our language calls the between. The Latin language says *inter*. To this corresponds the German 'unter.' The inwardness of world and thing is no fusion. Inwardness holds sway only where the inner, world and thing, cleanly separates itself and remains separated. In the middle of the two, in between world and thing, in their inter, in this Unter, the separation holds sway").

29. "Schliesslich ist das vom Menschen betätigte Ausdrücken stets ein Vorstellen und Darstellen des Wirklichen und Unwirklichen." *Unterwegs zur Sprache*, 14.

30. "Die Sprache ist in ihrem Wesen weder Ausdruck, noch eine Betätigung des Menschen. Die Sprache spricht. Wir suchen jetzt das Sprechen der Sprache im Gedicht" (ibid., 19).

31. "Rein Gesprochenes ist jenes, worin die Vollendung des Sprechens, die dem Gesprochenen eignet, ihrerseits eine anfangende ist. Rein Gesprochenes ist das Gedicht. Wir müssen diesen Satz zunächst als nackte Behauptung stehen lassen" (ibid., 16).

32. "Die Sprache des Gedichtes ist ein mehrfältiges aussprechen. Die Sprache erweist sich unbestreitbar als Ausdruck. Das jetzt Erwiesene steht aber gegen den Satz: Die Sprache spricht, gesetzt, dass Sprechen im Wesen nicht ein Ausdrücken ist" (ibid., 19).

33. "Zum ersten und vor allem ist Sprechen ein Ausdrücken" (ibid., 14).

34. "Wir wollen das Wesen der Sprache nicht auf einen Begriff bringen, damit dieser eine überall nutzbare Ansicht über die Sprache liefere, die alles Vorstellen beruhigt" (ibid., 12).

35. "Vernunft ist Sprache, *logos* . . . ich warte noch immer auf einen apokalyptischen Engel mit einem Schlüssel zu diesem Abgrund" (ibid., 13).

36. Albert Cook, *Figural Choice in Poetry and Art* (Hanover, NH: University

Press of New England, 1985), especially Chapter 1, "Thought, Image and Story: The Slippery Procedures of Literature."
37. Georg Trakl, *Die Dichtungen* (Salzburg: Otto Müller Verlag, 1938), 124.
38. *Unterwegs zur Sprache*, 14.
39. I have been applying the terms evoked for art in *Der Ursprung des Kunstwerkes*.
40. *Unterwegs zur Sprache*, 22. In one sense, the quartet is a reformulation, or a reinscription in broader terms of the situational characterization of the human situation in *Sein und Zeit*:

> Die genannten Dinge versammeln, also gerufen, bei sich Himmel und Erde, die Sterblichen und die Göttlichen. Die Vier sind ein ursprünglich-einiges Zueinander. Die Dinge lassen das Geviert der Vier bei sich verweilen. Dieses versammelnde Verweilenlassen ist das Dingen der Dinge. Wir nennen das im Dingen der Dinge verweilte einige Geviert von Himmel und Erde, Sterblichen und Göttlichen: die Welt. Im Nennen sind die genannten Dinge in ihr Dingen gerufen. Dingend ent-falten sie Welt, in der die Dinge weilen und so je die weiligen sind. (*Unterwegs zur Sprache*, 22.)

The named things gather together to themselves, thus invoked, heaven and earth, mortals and the godly. The four are an original-unitary relation. The things let the quartet of the four dwell with each other. This gathering allowance to dwell is the thinging of things. We call the dwelling unitary quartet of heaven and earth, mortal and the godly, the world. In the naming are the named things invoked to their thinging. Thinging, they unfold the world in which things linger and thus are in each case that which lingers.

41. See note 4, above.
42. Gerald Bruns, *Heidegger's Estrangements*, 64.
43. "Das Nennen verteilt nicht Titel, verwendet nicht Wörter, sondern ruft ins Wort. Das Nennen ruft. Das Rufen bringt sein Gerufenes näher." *Unterwegs zur Sprache*, 21.
44. "Der Dichter ruft in den vertrauten Erscheinungen das Fremde als jenes, worein das Unsichtbare sich schicket, um das zu bleiben, was es ist: unbekannt. '. . . dichterisch wohnet der Mensch.'" *Vorträge und Aufsätze*, 200.
45. Otto Bollnow, *Rilke* (Stuttgart: Kohlhammer, 1951); Jean-Pierre Richard, *L'Univers imaginaire de Mallarmé* (Paris: Seuil, 1961).
46. "Nichts ist klar; aber alles bedeutend." *Unterwegs zur Sprache*, 167.
47. *Blaues Wild, blaue Seele, blauen Glocken, blaues Lächeln, Bläue der Nacht, blauer Augenblick, heilige Bläue, blaue Frühling*, are examples one might give. As Heidegger's freedom in assigning sense to colors implies, they do not code to simple significations but vest a dense immediacy in ranges of senses. See Albert Cook, "The Dimensions of Color," in *Dimensions of the Sign in Art* (Hanover, NH: University Press of New England, 1989), 39–61.
48. "Wozu Dichter?" in *Holzwege*, 248–95.
49. Rainer Maria Rilke, *Sämtliche Werke, II* (Munich: Insel, 1956), 179–80.

50. Interestingly, Rilke's fellow Czech, Milan Kundera, has stayed in the same key but inverted the speculations in *The Unbearable Lightness of Being*.

51. Martin Heidegger, *Poetry, Language, Thought*, translated by Albert Hofstadter (New York: Harper and Row; Colophon edition, 1975), 53.

> Und dennoch: über das Seiende hinaus, aber nicht von ihm weg sondern vor ihm her, geschieht noch ein Anderes. Inmitten des Seienden im Ganzen west eine offene Stelle. Eine Lichtung ist. Sie ist, vom Seienden her gedacht, seiender als das Seiende. Diese offene Mitte ist daher nicht vom Seienden umschlossen, sondern die lichtende Mitte selbst umkreist wie das Nichts, das wir kaum kennen, alles Seiende.

Martin Heidegger, *Der Ursprung des Kunstwerkes* (Stuttgart: Philipp Reclam Jun., 1960; 1977). One may measure the difference of Rilke's spiritual, almost bodily "Mitte" from Heidegger's philosophical one as defined by Mark Taylor: "Heidegger's *Mitte* is not the Hegelian mean (*Mitte*) that mediates identity and difference by securing the *identity* of identity and difference. The delivery *of* difference is also the delivery *from* every form of all-inclusive identity that negates, reduces, absorbs, or swallows up otherness. As 'the threshold' of identity and difference, *dif-ference* is neither identical nor different. This distinctive *Unter-Schied* is what Heidegger labels 'the same [*das Selbe*],' 'Then identical always moves toward the absence of difference, so that everything may be reduced to a common denominator. The same, by contrast, is belonging together of what differs, through a gathering by way of the difference. We can say "the same" only if we think difference.' (*PLT*, 218). The 'sameness' (*Selbigkeit*) with which Heidegger tries to pass beyond Western philosophy 'approaches (*herkommt*) from further back than the kind of identity defined by metaphysics in terms of Being as a characteristic of Being' (*ID*, 28). By taking a 'step back' (*Schritt zurück*) from the ontotheological tradition, Heidegger attempts 'to return to' (*zurückgeben*) that which is 'prior' to thought." Mark C. Taylor, *Altarity* (Chicago: University of Chicago Press, 1987).

52. Rainer Maria Rilke, *Duino Elegies and the Sonnets to Orpheus*, translated by A. Poulin, Jr. (Boston: Houghton Mifflin Co., 1977), I, 19; 120–21.

53. Not all short poems have this feature. Heidegger's own in *Aus der Erfahrung des Denkens* do not, though they are short. Indeed, these doctrinal poems fail, like the poems of Nietzsche, to attain the difference, and so also to attain the likeness, between poetry and philosophy. They fall short of *Sagen* as they implicitly praise *Sage*. For the tradition of Album verse, see Zdenko Skreb, *Das Epigram in Deutschen Musenalmanachen und Taschenbüchern um 1800* (Vienna: Verlag der Österreichischen Akademie der Wissenschaften, 1977).

54. Rilke, *Sämtliche Werke*, II, 261.

55. *Holzwege*, 254.

56. I owe the force of this affirmation to the ongoing work on Hölderlin, Trakl, and Heidegger by John Baker.

57. "Für Hamann besteht dieser Abgrund darin, dass die Vernunft Sprache ist. Hamann kommt auf die Sprache zurück bei dem Versuch, zu sagen, was die Vernunft sei. Der Blick auf diese fällt in die Tiefe eines Abgrundes. Besteht dieser

nur darin, dass die Vernunft in der Sprache beruht, oder ist gar die Sprache selbst der Abgrund? Vom Abgrund sprechen wir dort, wo es vom Grund weggeht und uns ein Grund fehlt, insofern wir nach dem Grunde suchen und darauf ausgehen, auf einen Grund zu kommen." *Unterwegs zur Sprache*, 13.

58. "Das Fragen nicht die eigentliche Gebärde des Denkens ist, sondern— das Hören der Zusage dessen, was in die Frage kommen soll." *Unterwegs zur Sprache*, 175.

59. "Wir hätten die Dichtung zu einer Belegstelle für das Denken herabgesetzt und das Denken zu leicht genommen und auch schon vergessen, worauf er ankommt, nämlich eine Erfahrung mit der Sprache zu machen." *Unterwegs zur Sprache*, 166.

60. "Der Gegensatz zum rein Gesprochenen, zum Gedicht, ist nicht die Prosa. Reine Prosa ist nie 'prosaisch.' Sie ist so dichterisch und darum so selten wie die Poesie." *Unterwegs zur Sprache*, 31.

Chapter 4: Finalities of Utterance and Modalities of Expression

1. John Baker, "Towards a Poetics of Showing: Heidegger, Poetic Language, and the Reduction" (manuscript study).
2. See Samuel R. Levin, "Wordsworth and the Kantian Sublime," in *Metaphoric Worlds: Conceptions of a Romantic Nature* (New Haven, CT: Yale University Press, 1988), 206–38. In a discussion of metaphor, Levin provides some essential characterizations of Kant's beautiful and sublime, adding to the mathematical sublime and the dynamic sublime his own category that in some ways combines their effects, the "conceptual sublime:"

> The imagination, controlled and guided by the rational idea, works upon these intuitions to the effect that a field of associated representations is produced. The field constitutes the body of the aesthetic idea. Its termini are the rational idea and an intuition figuring an aesthetic attribute. Between these termini there moves a shifting mass of impressions, associations, relations, and insights, which the imagination has engendered in its effort to provide substantial form for the rational idea.

3. See Albert Cook, "Heraclitus and the Conditions of Utterance," in *Myth and Language* (Bloomington: Indiana University Press, 1980), 69–107. Heidegger, again, does not broach this question in his writings about Heraclitus but simply probes aphorisms or parts of aphorisms for clarifications of his own quasi-system.
4. This is the case in Jacques Derrida, "La Métaphore Blanche," *Marges* (Paris: Minuit, 1972). Walter A. Davis well stipulates the limits of Derrida's theory, both for poetry and in general, "Finding the unguarded textual moment that convicts every thinker of falling into the dream of 'self-presence' remains the Derridean operation. But traces and margins disrupt texts only where no process of mediation is in progress. Play disrupts order only when order is conceived of in severely

logical terms. Fiction and metaphor unravel truth and the literal only when language and reality are conceived of along positivistic or Cartesian lines." Walter A. Davis, *Inwardness and Existence: Subjectivity in/and Hegel, Heidegger, Marx, and Freud* (Madison: University of Wisconsin Press, 1989), 347.

5. George Lakoff and Mark Turner, *More Than Cool Reason: A Field Guide to Poetic Metaphor* (Chicago: University of Chicago Press, 1989), 70. Earlier, in addition to those submerged propositions listed, they had found in Sonnet 73 PEOPLE ARE PLANTS, NIGHT IS A COVER, STATES ARE LOCATIONS, and DEATH IS REST (30).

6. On this question, see Albert Cook, *Figural Choice in Poetry and Art* (Hanover, NH: University Press of New England, 1985), especially "The Range of Image," 8–34.

7. See "Metaphor: Literature's Access to Myth," in *Myth and Language*, 248–59.

8. There is the further, very large issue, of a hierarchy among the wisdoms provided by poets. The practical critic makes such dispositions all the time, not only as to the presence or absence of (what amounts to) wisdom, but as to the comprehensiveness, force, and depth of the wisdom involved. Grounding it is another matter, and it would require at least another whole book even to lay out the relevant considerations bearing on this question. Here the comparison of Daniel and Tibullus is easy, since both are love poets writing fairly simply within an easily defined love tradition, the Hellenistic and the Renaissance respectively (with the bearing of the former on the latter a really subsidiary question). More difficult, even if one accords with them, is the sort of judgment that, for example, William Elford Rogers makes in *The Three Genres and the Interpretation of Lyric* (Princeton, NJ: Princeton University Press, 1983), when he assesses "the subject matter itself" of "Tintern Abbey" "more important" than that of a typical poem by Herrick (173).

9. Ibid., 48–58.

10. For a discussion that mounts many issues on this relation between poetry and belief, see Henry David Aiken, "The Aesthetic Relevance of Belief," *Journal of Aesthetics and Art Criticism*, IX:4 (June 1951), 301–15.

11. A book in progress by John Baker poses the subtleties of this problem, while resisting the simpler formulations that will sometimes satisfy the interpreter who wishes tidy solutions.

12. "Mit den Kategorien haben auch Materialien ihre apriorische Selbstverständlichkeit verloren, so die Worte der Dichtung. Der Zerfall der Materialien ist der Triumph ihres Füranderesseins." *Ästhetische Theorie*, 31.

13. "Kunst geht auf Wahrheit, ist sie nicht unmittelbar; insofern ist Wahrheit ihr Gehalt. Erkenntnis ist sie durch ihr Verhältnis zur Wahrheit; Kunst selbst erkennt sie, indem sie an ihr hervortritt. Weder jedoch ist sie als Erkenntnis diskursiv noch ihre Wahrheit die Widerspiegelung eines Objekt" (ibid., 419).

14. *The Collected Poems of John Wheelwright*, ed. Alvin H. Rosenfeld (New York: New Directions, 1971), 79.

15. See Albert Cook, "Emily Dickinson's White Exploits," in *Thresholds* (Madison: University of Wisconsin Press, 1985), 179–202.

16. "The Vision of the Empire," from *Taliessin Through Logres* (London: Oxford University Press, 1938), 6.

17. The quotation is from Uther, Arthur's father, and Aurelie is his brother. This elaborate sequence is expounded masterfully by Christine Brooke-Rose, "'Lay me by Aurelie': An Examination of Pound's Use of Historical and Semi-Historical Sources," in *New Approaches to Ezra Pound*, ed. Eva Hesse (London: Faber & Faber, 1969), 242–79.

18. For the many figures and events from the Byzantine Empire and its dependencies worked into the poem at this point, see James J. Wilhelm, *The Later Cantos of Ezra Pound* (New York: Walker and Company, 1977).

19. A book-length account of this process for Canto 4 is offered by Christine Froula, *To Write Paradise: Style and Error in Pound's* Cantos (New Haven, CT: Yale University Press, 1984).

20. I am deriving my information here from Curtis Bradford, "Yeats's Byzantium Poems: A Study of Their Development," *PMLA*, LXXV:1 (March 1960), 110–25.

21. Only at this point did Yeats establish the important ordering principle of a particular rhyme scheme for "Byzantium": AABBCDDC.

Chapter 5: Sound, Sense, and Religion in the Dialogized Context of Donne's Poetry

1. For a discussion of such complexities, see Salim Kemal, *Kant and Fine Art* (Oxford: Clarendon, 1986). As he says, "Kant seeks to justify the necessity of aesthetic judgments by arguing that the pursuit of beauty through understanding, criticizing and evaluating fine art is a morally important activity. This is because actual judgments are governed by the ideal of the *sensus communis*, and as an ideal for fine art the latter is dependent on Kant's expanded notion of the *summum bonum*" (159).

2. Cleanth Brooks, *The Well-Wrought Urn* (London: Dobson, 1949), 3–20.

3. For how this wittiness leads to kinds of hyperbole, see Angus Fletcher, *Colors of the Mind* (Cambridge, MA: Harvard University Press, 1991), 52–67.

4. A. Leigh De Neef, *Traherne in Dialogue* (Durham: Duke University Press, 1988). My quotations are from Thomas Traherne, *Centuries, Poems, and Thanksgivings*, ed. H. M. Margoliouth, 2 vols. (Oxford: Clarendon Press, 1958).

5. *Traherne in Dialogue*, 40. As De Neef also says, "Most Renaissance religious poetry draws man into relation with God by proposing metaphoric correspondences. For the modern reader, it is the very awareness of those metaphors *as metaphors*—as hypotheses about the unknown and the unknowable on the basis of the presumably known—that makes the imagined relations intellectually or even emotionally credible, which is to say, plausible. But Traherne patently eschews this strategy by insisting upon a relation that is radical in its literalness: the soul is divine, not by metaphoric hypothesis, but by logical demonstration of its essence and its acts, its necessary capacity. This is not to say that Traherne's poetry is nonmetaphoric, but rather that its claims do not allow the comforting *alterité* of metaphor as such. That Traherne is himself conscious of this maneuver might be seen in the amazement with which he experiences his own thoughts and in

the astonishment his poetry constantly incites in the reader confronting those thoughts" (26).

6. Sermon preached at Whitehall, February 29, 1627; from *The Sermons of John Donne*, ed. George Potter and Evelyn Simpson (Berkeley: University of California Press, 1953–1962). This edition will be cited from here on.

7. "This fact requires some critical adjustment, for what in most other seventeenth-century contexts we would applaud as the detailed imagery of concrete things is, in Traherne, merely the surface substance, the ontic matter concealing the thing's true phenomenological and ontological being. And in these terms, it is precisely that 'clothing' of deceptive and concealing specificity that Traherne's poetry tries to remove"; "Since things must 'be absent somewhat' (*CM* [*Centuries of Meditation*] II.20) in order to appear at all, it is necessary to understand from the start the spatial and temporal difference within which things are grounded" (De Neef, 74); "Like Herbert, but even more insistently, Traherne points directly at this avoidance of typical poetic imagery. Such imagery, he tells us, merely veils the 'Naked Things' themselves:

> Their Worth they then do best reveal
> When we all Metaphors remove,
>   For metaphores conceal
>   And only Vapours prove.
> ('The Person,' ll. 23–26)"
>
>   (De Neef, 75)

"Discussing the creation Traherne invokes a familiar Renaissance principle to argue that 'All Things were already full' and to reiterate that God is 'he to whom nothing proper to himself could be added' (*CM*, IV:75). If we recall Derrida's notion that the supplement is always added to a plenitude, we will not be surprised by Traherne's next thought. Although God is already full, the particular supplement now added is man himself, last created even as he is always already inscribed within the creative act. Man is, Traherne cites, the '*Creaturarum Internuncius . . . Naturae Interpres. Stabilis Aevi et fluxi Temporis Interstitium, et . . . Mundi Copula*' (*CM*, IV:74). Supplement of the copula, to adopt a Derridean phrase, man is messenger, interval, interpreter; the added link which binds each to each and each to all; he who brings the spatial and temporal coordinates of meaning and worth to ford the abyss of nonmeaning and infinite, eternal emptiness" (De Neef, 200).

8. Thomas Traherne, *Centuries*, 1.100. De Neef (56–58) convincingly analyzes these and the ensuing definitions as an adaptation of and equivalent for an extrapolation of Aristotle's eight categories of "the different senses by which one thing is said to be in another" (Aristotle's *Physics*, 1.3). Donne is never philosophical with this comprehensiveness or integrative coherence.

9. *Traherne in Dialogue*, 73.

10. Poems from *Christian Ethicks*, IV (Traherne's prose theological treatise), lines 31–32.

11. From *Thanksgivings for the Body*, lines 100–123, in *Poems and Thanksgivings*, I, 216–17.

12. From *The Works of Henry Vaughan*, ed. L. C. Martin (Oxford: Clarendon Press, 1963 [1914]), 483–84.

13. Austin Warren, *Richard Crashaw: a Study in Baroque Sensibility* (Ann Arbor: University of Michigan Press, 1957 [1939]); Wylie Sypher, *Four Stages of Renaissance Style* (New York: Doubleday, 1957).

14. T. S. Eliot, in his essay "The Metaphysical Poets," connects the slowness of these lines with their solemnity. It is my enterprise to weigh what that solemnity comes to in the signification of Crashaw's unitary poetic act.

15. It should be remembered that the Lacanian system as an analysis of human interactions is theologically neutral. It is applied with powerful results to religious poetry by De Neef, and to such theological questions as angelology by Stuart Schneiderman in *An Angel Passes: How the Sexes Became Undivided* (New York: New York University Press, 1988).

16. All quotations are from the text of John Donne, *The Complete English Poems*, ed. A. J. Smith (Harmondsworth, England/New York, U.S.A.: Penguin Books, 1971; reprinted with corrections, 1973–80).

17. See Stanley Fish, *Self-Consuming Artifacts* (Berkeley: University of California Press, 1972). The work of Fish, applied to Donne's sermons and to Herbert's poems more than to Donne's, is still a model of possible inferences (and misleading exclusions) in this area. A recent study of comparable persuasion, enlisting Fish along with Heidegger, Nietzsche, de Man, Barthes, and others, is Thomas Docherty, *John Donne, Undone* (London: Methuen, 1986). Finally, however, it is fair to say that such efforts can be referred back to Donne's likely view of them, in view of his conception of the theological centering of his utterance, especially in sermons: "All knowledge that begins not, and ends not with his glory, is but a giddy, but a vertiginous circle, but an elaborate and exquisite ignorance" (Sermon Preached at Whitehall, March 4, 1624; Volume 6.11.227).

18. Stephen Orgel, *The Illusion of Power: Political Theatre in the English Renaissance* (Berkeley: University of California Press, 1975); Jonathan Goldberg, *James I and the Politics of Literature* (Baltimore, MD: Johns Hopkins University Press, 1983); Frank Whigham, *Ambition and Privilege: The Social Tropes of Elizabethan Courtesy Theory* (Berkeley: University of California Press, 1984).

19. One does not have to introduce a set of depth-psychological analyses to perceive and to connect the force of such intrications in Donne's life. His steadiest source of income for twenty years, until long after he had become Dean of St. Paul's and passed his fiftieth birthday and himself stopped it, was an allowance from his father-in-law, Sir George More, who had caused Donne's initial destitution by urging his first patron to fire him on the heels of his secret marriage to Ann More. The More family perpetuated the reverberations of Donne's own family's long and deep connection with the Roman Catholic church, since it revered their and Donne's common forebear, the great Catholic martyr of the previous century, Sir Thomas More. More's own religion, like Donne's, was of course interwoven with the political shifts of the time. Donne's resolutely Roman Catholic mother, until her death in 1631 two months before his, resided under his very roof at the deanery of St. Paul's.

20. Letter to Sir Robert Ker, April 1627; Edmund Gosse, *The Life and Letters of John Donne* (London: Heinemann, 1899), II, 245.

21. Erving Goffman, *Forms of Talk* (Philadelphia: University of Pennsylvania Press, 1981), especially 128–50.

22. Sermon Preached at Lincoln's Inn, Volume 3.3.110.

23. Arnold Stein, "Structures of Sound in Donne's Verse," *Kenyon Review*, 12 (1951), 21–36; 256–78.

24. Stein, in *John Donne's Lyrics* (Minneapolis: University of Minnesota Press, 1962), discusses "the wit . . . [that] lies in the sustained imaginative power and imaginative consciousness we experience in the poem" (69), and he goes on to describe mutations of epigrammatic reversal, binary form, and ternary reversal (101–41). For how the pressure on such paradoxical assertion results in a subversion of rhetorical staples and in a sharp focusing of images, see Albert Cook, "Image Intensification and Dialogic Posture in Donne's Eighth Elegy," in *The Reach of Poetry* (forthcoming).

25. Of course, Empson and Rosamund Tuve are among the many who have commented superbly on these qualities of Donne's poetry. And how supple such attention can be is shown by writing about related poets as well; for example in Christopher Ricks, "Andrew Marvell: 'Its Own Resemblance,'" in *The Force of Poetry* (Oxford: Clarendon Press, 1987), 34–59. Binarity and the equivocation between paradox and antithesis are extended into their psychological, ontological, and epistemological sources and rhetorical constructs by Rosalie Colie, *Paradoxia Epidemica* (Princeton, NJ: Princeton University Press, 1966).

26. Lope de Vega, *Castigo sin Venganza*, 261–90.

27. "The whole frame of the Poem is a beating out of a piece of gold, but the last clause is as the impression of the stamp, and that is it that makes it currant." Sermon preached upon the Penitential Psalms, Spring, 1626, Volume 6.1.41. This, interestingly, defines a poem as going into circulation when it is ready. The minting metaphor well characterizes the finality built into the poem and exhibited by it.

28. Arnold Stein, "Structures of Sound," 22.

29. Stein, *John Donne's Lyrics*, 29.

30. Stein, *John Donne's Lyrics*, 42–43. The range, from high design to high instance, as revealed in the musical settings we have for Donne's lyrics, is indicated by John Hollander, "Donne and the Limits of Lyric," *Vision and Resonance* (New Haven, CT: Yale University Press, 1985), 44–58: "Donne's rhythmic modulation of language is such that even the most musicianly attention to word stress . . . will frequently not suffice to accentuate correctly the textual syntax" (49); "Many of Donne's major lyrics involve a constant process of dialectic between modalities, conducted by an ingenuity masked as a reality principle, juggling hyperbole and abuse, insisting that the truest tenderness is the most feigning, that the most faithful caresses are those of wit and will combined" (58). This is very fine; in accord with this, I believe, I am arguing that the suppleness of Donne's communicative set is managed so as to encompass what really is a very deep reality principle that governs all the feigning.

31. Roy Roussel, *The Conversation of the Sexes* (New York: Oxford, 1986), 13.

32. Dedicatory letter "to the right honourable the Countess of Montgomery" to a sermon preached in 1618 or 1619, Volume 2.8.179.

33. For Donne's conflation of the epideictic and other traditions, see Barbara

Lewalski, *Donne's Anniversaries, and the Poetry of Praise* (Princeton, NJ: Princeton University Press, 1973).

34. Louis Martz, *The Poetry of Meditation*, 220–48. Other problems of confining the structure of these poems just to the meditative tradition are discussed by Stanley Archer, "Meditation and the Structure of Donne's Sonnets," in *John Donne's Poetry*, ed. A. L. Clements (New York: Norton, 1966), 237–45.

35. Roy Schafer, *The Analytic Attitude* (New York: Basic Books, 1983), 64.

36. "First Epistle to the Countess of Huntingdon," lines 69–70.

37. "Second Epistle to the Countess of Huntingdon," lines 21–36.

38. Preached upon Easter Day at St. Paul's, 1622, IV, 87.

39. Sermon preached at Lincoln's Inn, spring or summer 1618, I, 50.

40. Letter to Sir Henry Goodyer, from Edmund Gosse, *The Life and Letters of John Donne* (New York: Dodd, Mead, 1899), I, 228.

41. Sermon preached at Whitehall, March 4, 1624, 6.11.224.

42. Sermon preached at St. Dunstans, April 25, 1624, 6.4.103.

43. Sermon Preached at Hanworth, August 25, 1622, 4.6.167.

44. Gale Carrithers, *Donne at Sermons* (Albany: State University of New York Press, 1972).

45. Theodore Gill, *The Sermons of John Donne* (New York: Meridian, 1958), 66.

46. Joel Fineman, *Shakespeare's Perjured Eye: The Invention of Poetic Subjectivity in the Sonnets* (Berkeley: University of California Press, 1986).

Chapter 6: Wisdom and Ethics

1. For the irreducibility of story, see Albert Cook, *Figural Choice in Poetry and Art* (Hanover, NH: University Press of New England, 1985); Albert Cook, *History/Writing* (Cambridge: Cambridge University Press, 1988); Roy Schafer, *The Analytic Attitude* (New York: Basic Books, 1983).

2. Derrida, most explicitly in recent writing on Kafka but also in the range of questions posed by *Glas* (Paris: Galilée, 1974) has recourse to law to explain literature, and to literature to explain law. See "Préjugés, *devant la loi*," in *La Faculté de juger* (Paris: Minuit, 1985), 87–140; 122.

> Voilà le procès, le jugement, processus et *Urteil*, la division originaire de la loi. La loi est interdite. Mais cette auto-interdiction contradictoire laisse l'homme s'auto-déterminer "librement," bien que cette liberté s'annule comme auto-interdiction d'entrer dans la loi. Devant la loi l'homme est sujet de la loi, comparaissant devant elle. Certes. Mais *devant* elle parce qu'il ne peut y entrer, il est aussi *hors la loi*.

> Here is trial, judgment, process and *Urteil*, the originary division of the law. The law is forbidden. But this contradictory self-interdiction lets man determine himself "freely," although this liberty annuls itself as a self-interdiction against entering into the law. Before the law man is subject to the law, ap-

pearing before it. To be sure. But *before* it because he cannot enter it; he is also *outside the law*.

All this analysis of Kafka could be applied appositely to Kleist, and of course generally.

An interesting case is that of a literary critic, Stanley Fish, who has received the social endorsement of having his skills as a critic recognized through his appointment as a professor of law—through his skill at examining words, it must be said, and not directly for his handling of story.

3. Jacques Lacan, "Kant avec Sade," in *Écrits* (Paris: Seuil, 1966), 765–92; "L'Essence de la tragédie: Un commentaire de *l'Antigone* de Sophocle," in *Séminaire VII, L'Éthique de la psychanalyse* (Paris: Seuil, 1986), 285–336.

4. This assertion gathers force toward the end of *The Critique of Judgment*, though it is framed explicitly in Section 59, "Von der Schönheit als Symbol der Sittlichkeit" ("About Beauty as a Symbol of Moral Virtue"). As always in his terminological reticulations, Kant is at pains to specify exactly how the term "symbol" here integrates into his system: "Alle Hypotypose (Darstellung, subiectio sub aspectum) als Versinnlichung, ist zwiefach: entweder *schematisch*, da einem Begriffe, den der Verstand fasst, die korrespondierende Anchauung a priori gegeben wird; oder *symbolisch*, da einem Begriffe, den nur die Vernunft denken und dem keine sinnliche Anschauung angemessen sein kann, eine solche untergelegt wird, mit welcher das Verfahren der Urteilskraft demjenigen, was sie im Schematisieren beobachtet, bloss analogisch ist" ("Every hypotyposis [Representation, *subiectio sub aspectum*] as a sense-materialization is twofold: either *schematic*, when to a concept, that the understanding grasps, the corresponding perception is given a priori; or *symbolic*, when to a concept—that only the reason can think of and to which no sense perception can be matched—such a perception is attributed, by which the procedure of the faculty of judgment is purely analogical to that which it observes in the schematization").

5. J. Hillis Miller (*Versions of Pygmalion* [Cambridge: Harvard University Press, 1990], 16, 97–99, 125–37) presses—I would argue too far—Kant's discrepancies and ambiguities between the aesthetic and the ethical, and within the ethical itself. I shall here be taking general cues from the most challenging modern discussion I know of these questions, Irving Massey's *Find You the Virtue: Ethics, Image, and Desire in Literature* (Fairfax, VA.: George Mason University Press, 1987). For an account of his handling of the way literature manages desire and image in facing actual or possible violence, see my review of his book in *The Kenyon Review*, X:4 (Fall 1988), 121–24.

6. Letter, 27 Jan. 1904, to Felix Pollack, in *Briefe*, 27–28:

weil die Antwort auf diesen Brief wichtiger schien als jeder andere frühere Brief an Dich . . . Ich glaube man sollte überhaupt nur solche Bücher lesen, die einen beissen und stechen. Wenn das Buch, das wir lesen, uns nicht mit einem Faustschlag auf den Schädel weckt, wozu lesen wir dann das Buch? Damit es uns glücklich macht, wie Du schreibst? Mein Gott, glücklich wären wir eben auch, wenn wir keine Bücher hätten, und solche Bücher, die uns glücklich machen, könnten wir zur Not selber schreiben. Wir brauchen aber die Bücher, die auf uns wirken wie ein Unglück, das uns sehr schmerzt, wie der Tod eines, den wir lieber hatten als uns, wie wenn wir in Wälder verstossen würden, von allen Menschen weg, wie ein Selbstmord, ein Buch muss die Axt sein für das gefrorene Meer in uns. Das glaube ich.

7. Wayne Booth, *The Company We Keep: An Ethics of Fiction* (Berkeley: University of California Press, 1988).

8. Lionel Trilling, *The Liberal Imagination* (New York: Anchor, 1953 [1950]), 109. For an assessment of the historical siting of the larger narrative conventions employed by Twain in this novel, with relation to the social factors involved in canonization, see Jonathan Arac, "Nationalism, Hypercanonization, and *Huckleberry Finn*," *Boundary 2*, 19:1 (1992), 14–33.

9. This premise, as well as others, governs *Versions of Pygmalion*.

10. Apposite here is James Kincaid's set of puzzling questions over how to assess social effects and presuppositions in times relatively near our own, the Victorian:

> The Victorian power model fumes and fusses at the speech and at the silence—and we do not better. What *about* silence and its origins? [Kincaid is interrogating, among others, Foucault.] Why does not a certain discourse exist, at least in a recognizable form: How do we understand an absence? Does it indicate repression, ignorance, activity, acceptance, indifference, or what?

James R. Kincaid, "What the Victorians Knew about Sex," edited by Robert Viscusi, *Browning Institute Studies*, XVI (1988), 91–99 (97).

11. Booth, 277.

12. J. Hillis Miller, *The Ethics of Reading* (New York: Columbia University Press, 1987), 9.

13. For a study of the dimensions of feeling as structured by thought in major Romantic works, see Albert Cook, *Thresholds* (Madison: University of Wisconsin Press, 1985).

14. For further critique of Miller, see Robert Scholes, *Protocols of Reading* (New Haven, CT: Yale University Press, 1989), 145–55. As for Kant's "feeling," however sketchy he may be in the light of twentieth-century usage, he does build the term intricately into his system, in a way that echoes and employs the equivalence of the word to the Greek *aesthesis*, the root term for esthetics. As Ralf Meerbote says ("Reflection on Beauty," in *Essays in Kant's Aesthetics*, ed. Ted Cohen and Paul Guyer [Chicago: University of Chicago Press, 1982], 55–86):

> Kant, for better or worse, postulates a rather large number of capacities or abilities the joint exercise of which he deems necessary for subsumption, judgment, and cognition.... His wide interpretation [of judgment] demands

at one and the same time that more careful attention be paid to his conditions of subsumption under determinate concepts *and* to his conditions of use of nondeterminate concepts as exemplified in aesthetics. (61, 65)

Connections across a wide range of philosophical questions in the use of the terms "aesthetic," "feeling," and "Empfindung," for Kant, as well as for Schiller and Peirce, are made by Jeffrey Barnouw ("'Aesthetic' for Schiller and Peirce: A Neglected Origin of Pragmatism," *Journal of the History of Ideas* [1988], 607–32).

15. R. P. Blackmur, *The Lion and the Honeycomb: Essays in Solicitude and Critique* (New York: Harcourt, Brace, 1955), 289–309.

16. *Versions of Pygmalion*, 82–140.

17. Jean-Paul Sartre, *Saint Genet* (Paris: Gallimard, 1951). Sartre erects virtually an entire ethico-metaphysical system on the circumstance that Jean Genet was an adopted child.

18. For a discussion of the evasions and ambiguities governing this novel, see Albert Cook, *Thresholds*, 11–13.

19. As he gets himself farther out on this limb, Miller effectually calls death itself a trope: "Death is perhaps the most radical name, though still one figurative name among others, for the intermittences that break the continuity of human life all along the line. Of those blank spaces nothing can be known directly. They can be named only in trope. . . . Prosopopoeia is a way of compensating for the ultimate loss of death" (125). Here Proust, as it were, joins Heidegger: the *intermittences* inform the *Sein zum Tod* in an act of strong perception on Miller's part that he impoverishingly weds to an oversimplification.

20. "Er würde ihr damals nicht wie ein Teufel erschienen sein, wenn er ihr nicht, bei seiner ersten Erscheinung, wie ein Engel vorgekommen wäre."

21. Massey, op. cit., 76.

22. I am indebted here to discussions of this question with Michael Roemer.

23. "Kant avec Sade," 782. "Le désir, ce qui s'appelle le désir suffit à faire que la vie n'ait pas de sens à faire un lâche. Et quand la loi est vraiment là, le désir ne tient pas, mais c'est pour la raison que la loi et le désir refoulé sont une seule et même chose, c'est même ce que Freud a découvert" ("Desire which calls itself desire suffices to make it that life has no sense in making a coward. And when the law is truly there, desire does not hold, but that is for the reason that the law and repressed desire are one and the same thing; that's exactly what Freud discovered"). But all desire is not repressed desire, even if the superego on which the law is based is itself an expression of (but again not identical with) repressed desire. The delicacy and power of Lacan's analyses are such that it would take considerable further discussion to assess the limits to their implied assertion of total comprehensiveness. In *Séminaire VII* (99), he does, however, make clear that it is in their structures that desire and law are identical: "Dans ce *Tu ne mentiras point*, comme loi, est incluse la possibilité du mensonge comme désir le plus fondamental" ("In this 'Thou shalt not lie' as a law is included the possibility of lying as the most fundamental desire").

24. I am here borrowing, and slightly shifting, the emphasis of Shirley Robin Letwin, *The Gentleman in Trollope: Individuality and Social Conduct* (Cambridge: Harvard University Press, 1982).

25. See Irving Massey, op. cit.; Albert Cook, "Parable," in *Myth and Language* (Bloomington: Indiana University Press, 1980), 234–47; Martin Andic, "Simone Weil on Fairy Tales," *Cahiers Simone Weil*, XV:1 (1992), 61–91.

26. To these could be added the case of Christopher Marlowe, a possible murderer and probable secret agent—as against the demonstrable hermeneutic thrust of plays like *Doctor Faustus*, though some recent commentators have oversimply assumed that the ethos deducible from the action of the man must also be retrievable in the ethos of the plays. See Albert Cook, "Some Observations on Shakespeare and the Incommensurability of Interpretive Strategies," in *Soundings* (Detroit, MI: Wayne University Press, 1991). Still different would be the case of thinkers who have joined odious movements based to some degree on thought, or who have participated in questionable politics. Seneca would seem to be one example of the latter in antiquity, and Francis Bacon in the Renaissance, while in our time we have for the former the case of Heidegger himself, even if we do not share the unexamined (and untenable) assumption that every idea borrowed from the mainstream of German culture by the Nazis is thereby contaminated. Still, leaving aside his indefensible earlier actions and his inexcusable postwar silence, some of the passing remarks in Heidegger's lectures of 1942–1944 can be taken in context as having Nazi overtones, while reduced from that specificity in the general tenor of his ideas, where the contaminating connection would have to be bracketed out if one were to accept them, as I am doing. The case of the Belgian-American critic Paul de Man is still a different one, since his later ideas show no traces of Nazism except in an attenuated and interesting form: their implicit nihilism could be said to exhibit a rarified version of the standard transition from National Socialism to agnostic anarchism often found in ex-Nazi German intellectuals of the decades immediately after World War II. De Man's early career raises simply moral, not intellectual, questions of an elective, opportunistic, possibly convinced, but certainly in some ways extreme Nazi who somewhat voluntarily expressed notions even some Nazis would not express: the notorious recommendation that Jews could without loss be shipped off to some remote part of the globe (the recommendation that was on the table of the German High Command at the moment of de Man's article, written before "The Final Solution"). In his wartime writings can also be found, among other notions, lengthy extravagant praise for the editor of the official SS literary journal *Das innere Reich*, as well as another article offering a blanket condemnation of supposedly degenerate French writers along with praise for the shining exceptions to this rule (a list of "good" French writers, just about all of them rabid Nazis). Such views were not expressed so vehemently at the time, for example, by the quasi-Nazi German officer and writer Ernst Jünger, whom de Man himself also praises. All this activity, however, took place in a relatively short period—the whole question is mitigated and complicated by the fact that in most of his American career, so far as one can tell, de Man was not only superbly effective in his public and published performances but seems also to have been the model of benignity and care.

27. For some assessment of Pound's historical vision as such, see Albert Cook, *History/Writing* (Cambridge: Cambridge University Press, 1988), 24–27. Michael André Bernstein, in a book that abounds in acute analyses of Pound's procedures (*The Tale of the Tribe: Ezra Pound and the Modern Verse Epic* [Princeton, NJ: Prince-

ton University Press, 1980]), goes farther and presses the pessimistic statements from the Pisan cantos on as Pound's admission of failure both in the practical political sphere and in the project of unifying a personal lyric and a historic vision. At very least, even if one would qualify Bernstein's view (as I would), he offers evidence of a mitigating consciousness in Pound, a sort of pre-confession.

28. E. Fuller Torrey, *The Roots of Treason* (New York: McGraw-Hill, 1984), especially 121–76.

29. In Pound's life, these effusions were consistent and even more virulent than in the poem. For abundant evidence, see Torrey, passim.

30. This notion is inscribed into the *Cantos*: "Bellum canto perenne" ("I sing perpetual war"), at the conclusion of Canto 86 (568). On the other hand, Pound shows even Fascists holding up economic discrimination over combat willingness. "'Ten men,' said Ubaldo, 'who will charge a nest of machine guns / for one who will put his name on a chit'" (89; 597 and 93; 628). I cite *The Cantos of Ezra Pound* (New York: New Directions, 1986).

31. For an assessment of Mussolini's response as it gears with and implies the aesthetic presuppositions of the *Cantos*, see Peter Baker, "Pound's Cantos and the Myth of Transparency," in *Obdurate Brilliance: Exteriority and the Modern Long Poem* (Gainesville: University of Florida Press, 1991).

32. It only extends Pound's possible reference to trace an echo here to a very famous poem of his boyhood, Edwin Markham's "Man with the Hoe": "Bowed by the weight of centuries, he leans / Upon his hoe and gazes on the ground, / The emptiness of ages in his face, / And on his back the burden of the world." This is itself an ekphrasis of Millet's painting so entitled.

33. A connection between Pound's use of poetic language and Heidegger's theory is made by Jean-Michel Rabaté, *Language, Sexuality and Ideology in Ezra Pound's Cantos* (Albany: State University of New York Press, 1986).

34. This is the interpretation of Carroll E. Terrell, *A Companion to the Cantos of Ezra Pound* (Berkeley: University of California Press, I, 1984 [1980]; II, 1984), ad loc. I follow Terrell generally for the detail of my account.

35. Here Pound is following Russell Grenfell's *Unconditional Hatred* (Greenwich, CT: Devin-Adair, 1953) and its view of the alleged falsifications involved in the demand for unconditional surrender. It is noteworthy that Pound stays with such exaggerations, and not with the moderating claims of those like George Kennan who urged after the war that mere collaboration with Nazis should not disqualify capable people from being utilized in postwar governments.

36. Along these lines, this ideogram is a quotation from Confucius's *Unwobbling Pivot*, and some unfortunate credence to a possible Fascist intimation here would be added by the fact that Pound himself makes the connection between that work and the Fascist cause explicit, when his first published translation of the work appeared in Venice during the war, and the first word, "Pivot" is rendered as "Asse" ("Axis"), "*L'Asse che non vacilla*" ("the Axis that does not waver").

37. Hugh Kenner, *Samuel Beckett* (New York: Grove Press, 1961), 32–33.

38. Samuel Beckett, *Proust* (New York: Grove, n.d. [original date, 1931]), 55.

39. "Die Wahrheit des Neuen, als des nicht bereits Besetzten, hat ihren Ort im Intentionslosen. Das setzt sie in Widerspruch zur Reflexion, den Motor des

Neuen, und potenziert sie zur zweiten. Sie ist das Gegenteil ihres philosophisch üblichen Begriffs, etwa der Schillerschen Lehre vom Sentimentalischen, die darauf hinausläuft, Kunstwerke mit Intentionen aufzuladen. Zweite Reflexion ergreift die Verfahrungsweise, die Sprache des Kunstwerks im weitesten Verstand, aber sie zielt auf Blindheit. Die Parole des Absurden, wie immer unzulänglich, bekundet das. Becketts Weigerung, seine Gebilde zu interpretieren, verbunden mit äusserstem Bewusstsein der Techniken, der Implikationen der Stoffe, des sprachlichen Materials, ist keine bloss subjektive Aversion: mit dem Ansteigen der Reflexion, und durch ihre gesteigerte Kraft, verdunkelt sich der Gehalt an sich." Adorno, *Ästhetische Theorie*, 47.

40. "Ou bien est-il entré dans un cercle où il tourne obscurément, entraîné par la parole errante, non pas privée de sens mais privée de centre." Maurice Blanchot, *Le Livre à venir* (Paris: Gallimard, 1959), 256.

41. For a discussion of this feature of Beckett's language, see Albert Cook, *Prisms* (Bloomington: Indiana University Press, 1967), 50–52.

42. For an acute practicum on Beckett's phenomenal powers of rhythm and diction in working between his two languages, see Hugh Kenner, "Beckett Translating Beckett," in *Historical Fictions* (San Francisco: North Point, 1990), 184–202.

43. I am here using the post-Peircean terminology of Max Bense, *Die Theorie Kafkas* (Köln: Kiepenheuer & Witsch, 1952).

44. Gary Handwerk, *Irony & Ethics in Narrative* (New Haven, CT: Yale University Press, 1985), 172–94.

45. Wolfgang Iser, *The Act of Reading* (Baltimore: Johns Hopkins University Press, 1978), 222–25. And what Iser elsewhere says of Molloy could also be applied to the reader, "Dieser Friede lässt sich aber nicht sichern durch das, was man weiss, sondern durch ein Wissen, das weiss, dass alles Wissbare nichts ist" ("This peace cannot be secured through what is known but only through a knowing that knows that everything knowable is nothing"). *Der Implizite Leser* (Munich: Fink, 1972), 402.

46. Samuel Beckett, *Watt* (New York: Grove, 1959), 239.

Works Cited

Adorno, Theodor W. *Asthetische Theorie, Gesammelte Schriften.* Band 7. Frankfurt am Main: Suhrkamp, 1970.
———. *Minima Moralia.* Frankfurt am Main: Suhrkamp, 1951.
———. *Noten zur Literatur III.* Frankfurt am Main: Suhrkamp, 1965.
———. *Philosophie der neuen Musik.* Frankfurt am Main and Berlin: Ullstein, 1958.
Aiken, Henry David. "The Aesthetic Relevance of Belief." *Journal of Aesthetics and Art Criticism,* 9, no. 4 (June 1951): 301–15.
Allemann, Beda. *Holderlin und Heidegger.* Zurich: Atlantis, 1954.
Altieri, Charles. "An Idea and Ideal of a Literary Canon." *Critical Inquiry,* X:1 (September 1983): 37–60.
———. *Canons and Consequences.* Evanston, IL: Northwestern University Press, 1990.
Andic, Martin. "Simone Weil on Fairy Tales." *Cahiers Simone Weil,* 15, no. 1 (1992): 61–91.
Arac, Jonathan. "Nationalism, Hypercanonization, and *Huckleberry Finn.*" *Boundary 2,* 19, no. 1 (1992): 14–33.
Archer, Stanley. "Meditation and the Structure of Donne's Sonnets." In *John Donne's Poetry,* ed. A. L. Clements, 237–45. New York: Norton, 1966.
Arvin, Newton. *Longfellow: His Life and Work.* Boston: Little, Brown, 1963.
Bachelard, Gaston. *L'Eau et les rêves.* Paris: Jose Corti, 1963.
Baker, John. "Towards a Poetics of Showing: Heidegger, Poetic Language, and the Reduction" (manuscript study).
Baker, Peter. *The Ethical Turn: Postmodern Theories of the Subject* (manuscript study).
———. "Pound's Cantos and the Myth of Transparency." In *Obdurate Brilliance: Exteriority and the Modern Long Poem,* 76–93. Gainesville: University of Florida Press, 1991.
Barnouw, Jeffrey. "'Aesthetic' for Schiller and Peirce: A Neglected Origin of Pragmatism." *Journal of the History of Ideas,* 49, no. 4 (1988): 607–32.
Beckett, Samuel. *Proust.* New York: Grove, n.d. (original date, 1931).
Bense, Max. *Die Theorie Kafkas.* Cologne: Kiepenheuer & Witsch, 1952.
Berger, Harry. *Second World and Green World: Studies in Renaissance Fiction-Making.* Berkeley: University of California Press, 1988.
Bernstein, Michael André. *The Tale of the Tribe: Ezra Pound and the Modern Verse Epic.* Princeton, NJ: Princeton University Press, 1980.
Blackmur, R. P. *Form and Value in Modern Poetry.* New York: Anchor, 1957.

———. *The Lion and the Honeycomb: Essays in Solicitude and Critique*. New York: Harcourt, Brace, 1955.
Blanchot, Maurice. *Le Livre à venir*. Paris: Gallimard, 1959.
———. *La Part du feu*. Paris: Gallimard, 1949.
Bloch, Chana. *Spelling the Word*. Berkeley: University of California Press, 1985.
Bloom, Harold. *Ruin the Sacred Truths*. Cambridge, MA: Harvard University Press, 1989.
Blumenberg, Hans. *Arbeit am Mythos*. Frankfurt am Main: Suhrkamp, 1979. Trans. Robert M. Wallace, as *Work on Myth*. Cambridge, MA: MIT Press, 1985.
Bollnow, Otto. *Rilke*. Stuttgart: Kohlhammer, 1951.
Booth, Wayne. *The Company We Keep: An Ethics of Fiction*. Berkeley: University of California Press, 1988.
Bradford, Curtis. "Yeats's Byzantium Poems: A Study of Their Development." *PMLA*, 75, no. 1 (March 1960): 110–25.
Brooke-Rose, Christine. "'Lay me by Aurelie': An Examination of Pound's Use of Historical and Semi-Historical Sources." In *New Approaches to Ezra Pound*, ed. Eva Hesse, 242–79. London: Faber & Faber, 1969.
Brooks, Cleanth. *The Well-Wrought Urn*. London: Dobson, 1949.
Bruns, Gerald L. *Heidegger's Estrangements*. New Haven, CT: Yale University Press, 1989.
Carrithers, Gale. *Donne at Sermons*. Albany, NY: State University of New York Press, 1972.
Cohn, Robert Greer. *Modes of Art*. Saratoga, CA: Anma Libri, 1975.
Colie, Rosalie. *Paradoxia Epidemica*. Princeton, NJ: Princeton University Press, 1966.
Cook, Albert. *Dimensions of the Sign in Art*. Hanover, NH: University Press of New England, 1989.
———. *Figural Choice in Poetry and Art*. Hanover, NH: University Press of New England, 1985.
———. *History/Writing*. Cambridge: Cambridge University Press, 1988.
———. "Image Intensification and Dialogic Posture in Donne's Eighth Elegy." In *The Reach of Poetry*. Forthcoming.
———. *Myth and Language*. Bloomington: Indiana University Press, 1980.
———. "The Possible Intersections of Cosmology, Religion, and Abstract Thought in the Lyric Fragments of Alcman." *Hellas* (Winter 1992).
———. *Prisms*. Bloomington: Indiana University Press, 1967.
———. "Prophecy and the Preconditions of Poetry." In *Soundings: On Shakespeare, Modern Poetry, Plato, and Other Subjects*, 44–56. Detroit, MI: Wayne State University Press, 1991.
———. Review of Irving Massey, *Find You the Virtue*. *The Kenyon Review*, X:4 (Fall 1988): 121–24.
———. *Thresholds*. Madison: University of Wisconsin Press, 1985.
———. "The Transformation of 'Point': Amplitude in Wordsworth, Whitman, and Rimbaud." *Studies in Romanticism*, 30 (Summer 1991): 169–88.
Crowther, Paul. *The Kantian Sublime: From Morality to Art*. Oxford: Oxford University Press, 1989.

Curtius, Ernst Robert. *European Literature in the Latin Middle Ages*. New York: Harper, 1963.
Davie, Donald. *Purity of Diction in English Verse*. London: Routledge & Kegan Paul, 1967 [1952].
Davis, Walter A. *Inwardness and Existence: Subjectivity in/and Hegel, Heidegger, Marx, and Freud*. Madison: University of Wisconsin Press, 1989.
de Man, Paul. "Heidegger's Exegeses of Holderlin." In *Blindness and Insight*, 246–66. London: Methuen, 1983 [1953].
De Neef, A. Leigh. *Traherne in Dialogue*. Durham, NC: Duke University Press, 1988.
Derrida, Jacques. *L'Esprit*. Paris: Galilée, 1987.
———. *Glas*. Paris: Galilée, 1974.
———. "La Metaphore blanche." In *Marges*. Paris: Minuit, 1972.
———. "Préjugés, devant la loi." In *La Faculté de juger*, 87–140. Paris: Minuit, 1985.
———. *Schibboleth*. Paris: Galilée, 1986.
———. *Signéponge*. New York: Columbia University Press, 1984.
Docherty, Thomas. *John Donne, Undone*. London: Methuen, 1986.
Donne, John. *The Complete English Poems*. Ed. A. J. Smith. Harmondsworth, UK, and New York, USA: Penguin Books, 1971; reprinted with corrections, 1973 through 1980.
———. *The Sermons of John Donne*. Ed. George Potter and Evelyn Simpson. Berkeley: University of California Press, 1953–62.
Eliot, T. S. *On Poetry and Poets*. London: Faber & Faber, 1957.
Empson, William. *Seven Types of Ambiguity*. London: Chatto & Windus, 1949 [1930].
Erdman, David. *Blake: Prophet Against Empire*. Princeton, NJ: Princeton University Press, 1977.
Fiedler, Leslie. "A Review of *Leaves of Grass* and *Hiawatha* as of 1855." *American Poetry Review*, 2, no. 2 (March–April 1973): 45–46.
Fineman, Joel. *Shakespeare's Perjured Eye: The Invention of Poetic Subjectivity in the Sonnets*. Berkeley: University of California Press, 1986.
Fish, Stanley. *Doing What Comes Naturally*. Raleigh, NC: Duke University Press, 1989.
———. *Is There a Text in This Class?* Cambridge, MA: Harvard University Press, 1980.
———. *The Living Temple: George Herbert and Catechizing*. Berkeley: University of California Press, 1978.
———. *Self-Consuming Artifacts*. Berkeley: University of California Press, 1974.
Fletcher, Angus. *Colors of the Mind*. Cambridge, MA: Harvard University Press, 1991.
Frank, Isidor. *Der Sinn der Kanonbildung*. Freiburg: Herder, 1971.
Frank, Manfred, and Anselm Haverkamp, eds. *Individualität*. Munich: Fink, 1988.
Froula, Christine. *To Write Paradise: Style and Error in Pound's Cantos*. New Haven, CT: Yale University Press, 1984.
Gadamer, Hans-Georg. *Dialogue and Deconstruction: The Gadamer-Derrida En-*

counter. Ed. Diane P. Michelfelder and Richard E. Palmer. Albany: State University of New York Press, 1989.

———. "Die Universalität des hermeneutischen Problems." In *Kleine Schriften I*. Tübingen: Mohr, 1967.

Gill, Theodore. *Donne at Sermons*. New York: Meridian, 1958.

Goffman, Erving. *Forms of Talk*. Philadelphia: University of Pennsylvania Press, 1981.

Goldberg, Jonathan. *James I and the Politics of Literature*. Baltimore, MD: Johns Hopkins University Press, 1983.

Grenfell, Russell. *Unconditional Hatred*. Greenwich, CT: Devin-Adair, 1953.

Habermas, Jurgen. *Kultur und Kritik: Verstreute Aufsatze*. Frankfurt am Main: Suhrkamp, 1973.

Handwerk, Gary. *Irony & Ethics in Narrative*. New Haven, CT: Yale University Press, 1985.

Harman, Barbara Leah. *Costly Monuments*. Cambridge, MA: Harvard University Press, 1982.

Heidegger, Martin. *Erläuterungen zu Hölderlins Dichtung*. Frankfurt: Klostermann, 1971 [1944].

———. *Gesamtausgabe*. Vol. 39, *Hölderlin's Hymnen Germanien und Der Rhein*, 1980 [1934–35]; vol. 52, *Hölderlins Hymne Andenken*, 1982 [1941–42]; vol. 53, *Hölderlins Hymne Der Ister*, 1984 [1942]. Frankfurt: Klostermann, 1975–.

———. *Holzwege*. Frankfurt: Klostermann, 1950.

———. *An Introduction to Metaphysics*. New York: Anchor, 1961.

———. *Poetry, Language, Thought*. Trans. Albert Hofstadter. New York: Harper and Row, 1975.

———. *Der Ursprung des Kunstwerkes*. Stuttgart: Philipp Reclam Jun., 1977 [1960].

Hertz, Neil. *The End of the Line*. New York: Columbia University Press, 1985.

Hollander, John. *Vision and Resonance*. New Haven, CT: Yale University Press, 1985.

Holthusen, Hans Egon. "Uber den sauren Kitsch." In *Ja und Nein*. Munich: R. Piper, 1954.

Hutchinson, F. E., ed. *The Poetry of George Herbert*. Oxford: Clarendon Press, 1941.

Iser, Wolfgang. *The Act of Reading*. Baltimore, MD: Johns Hopkins University Press, 1978. Originally published as *Der Implizite Leser*. Munich: Fink, 1972.

Jauss, Hans Robert. *Literaturgeschichte als Provokation*. Frankfurt: Suhrkamp, 1970.

Kant, Immanuel. *Kritik der Urteilskraft*, I, 1. Trans. James Creed Meredith, as *The Critique of Judgement*. Oxford: Clarendon Press, 1952.

Kemal, Salim. *Kant and Fine Art*. Oxford: Clarendon Press, 1986.

Kenner, Hugh. *Historical Fictions*. San Francisco: North Point Press, 1990.

———. *The Pound Era*. Berkeley: University of California Press, 1971.

———. *Samuel Beckett*. New York: Grove Press, 1961.

Kincaid, James R. "What the Victorians Knew about Sex." Ed. Robert Viscusi. *Browning Institute Studies*, 16 (1988): 91–99.

Kirk, G. S., J. E. Raven, and M. Schofield. *The Pre-Socratic Philosophers*. Cambridge: Cambridge University Press, 1983.

Labov, William, and David Fanshel. *Therapeutic Discourse*. New York: Academic Press, 1977.

Lacan, Jacques. *Ecrits*. Paris: Seuil, 1966.
———. *Seminaire VII, L'Ethique de la psychanalyse*. Paris: Seuil, 1986.
Lakoff, George, and Mark Turner. *More Than Cool Reason: A Field Guide to Poetic Metaphor*. Chicago: University of Chicago Press, 1989.
Langer, Suzanne. *Mind: An Essay on Human Feeling*. Baltimore, MD: Johns Hopkins University Press, 1967.
Letwin, Shirley Robin. *The Gentleman in Trollope*. Cambridge, MA: Harvard University Press, 1982.
Levin, Samuel R. *Metaphoric Worlds: Conceptions of a Romantic Nature*. New Haven, CT: Yale University Press, 1988.
Lewalski, Barbara. *Donne's Anniversaries, and the Poetry of Praise*. Princeton, NJ: Princeton University Press, 1973.
Maritain, Jacques. *Creative Intuition in Art and Poetry*. New York: Bollingen, 1953.
Martz, Louis. *The Poetry of Meditation*. New Haven, CT: Yale University Press, 1954.
Massey, Irving. *Find You the Virtue: Ethics, Image, and Desire in Literature*. Fairfax, VA: George Mason University Press, 1987.
McFarland, Thomas. "Involute and Symbol in the Romantic Image." In *Coleridge, Keats, and the Imagination: Romanticism and Adam's Dream*, ed. J. Robert Barth, S.J., and John L. Maloney, 29–57. Columbia: University of Missouri Press, 1990.
———. *Shapes of Culture*. Iowa City: University of Iowa Press, 1987.
Meerbote, Ralf. "Reflection on Beauty." In *Essays in Kant's Aesthetics*, ed. Ted Cohen and Paul Guyer, 55–86. Chicago: University of Chicago Press, 1982.
Miller, J. Hillis. *The Ethics of Reading*. New York: Columbia University Press, 1987.
———. *Versions of Pygmalion*. Cambridge, MA: Harvard University Press, 1990.
Most, Glenn. "Alcman's Cosmogonic Fragment (Fgt 5 Page, 81 Calame)," *Classical Quarterly*, 37, no. 1 (1987): 1–9.
Nelson, Cary. *Repression and Recovery: Modern American Poetry and the Politics of Cultural Memory, 1910–1945*. Madison: University of Wisconsin Press, 1989.
Orgel, Stephen. *The Illusion of Power: Political Theatre in the English Renaissance*. Berkeley: University of California Press, 1975.
Palka, William H. *St. Augustine's Meter and George Herbert's Will*. Kent, OH: Kent State University Press, 1987.
Patterson, Annabel M. *Pastoral and Ideology: Virgil to Valéry*. Berkeley: University of California Press, 1987.
Rabate, Jean-Michel. *Language, Sexuality and Idealogy in Ezra Pound's Cantos*. Albany, NY: State University of New York Press, 1986.
Rapaport, Herman. *Derrida and Heidegger: Reflections on Time and Language*. Lincoln, NE: University of Nebraska Press, 1989.
Richard, Jean-Pierre. *L'Univers imaginaire de Mallarmé*. Paris: Seuil, 1961.
Ricks, Christopher. *The Force of Poetry*. Oxford: Oxford University Press, 1987.
Rilke, Rainer Maria. *Sämtliche Werke*. Munich: Insel, 1956.
Roberts, John R. *Essential Articles for the Study of George Herbert's Poetry*. Hamden, CT: Archon Books, 1979.
Rogers, William Elford. *The Three Genres and the Interpretation of Lyric*. Princeton, NJ: Princeton University Press, 1983.

Roussel, Roy. *The Conversation of the Sexes*. New York: Oxford University Press, 1986.
Sartre, Jean-Paul. *Saint Genet*. Paris: Gallimard, 1951.
Schafer, Roy. *The Analytic Attitude*. New York: Basic Books, 1983.
Schneiderman, Stuart. *An Angel Passes: How the Sexes Became Undivided*. New York: New York University Press, 1988.
Schoenfeldt, Mark C. *Prayer and Power: George Herbert and Renaissance Courtship*. Chicago: University of Chicago Press, 1991.
Scholes, Robert. *Protocols of Reading*. New Haven, CT: Yale University Press, 1989.
———. *Textual Power*. New Haven, CT: Yale University Press, 1985.
Scully, Vincent. *The Earth, the Temple, and the Gods*. New York: Praeger, 1969 [1962].
Singleton, Marion White. *God's Courtier: Configuring a Different Grace in George Herbert's Temple*. Cambridge: Cambridge University Press, 1987.
Skreb, Zdenko. *Das Epigram in Deutschen Musenalmanachen und Taschenbuchern um 1800*. Vienna: Verlag der Osterreichischen Akademie der Wissenschaften, 1977.
Smith, Barbara Herrnstein. *Contingencies of Value*. Cambridge, MA: Harvard University Press, 1988.
———. *On the Margins of Discourse*. Chicago: University of Chicago Press, 1978.
Stein, Arnold. *The House of Death: Messages from the English Renaissance*. Baltimore, MD: The Johns Hopkins University Press, 1986.
———. *John Donne's Lyrics*, Minneapolis, MN: University of Minnesota Press, 1962.
———. "Structures of Sound in Donne's Verse." *Kenyon Review*, 12 (1951): 21–36; 256–78.
Strier, Richard. *Love Known: Theology and Experience in Herbert's Poetry*. Chicago: University of Chicago Press, 1983.
Sypher, Wylie. *Four Stages of Renaissance Style*. New York: Doubleday, 1957.
Taylor, Mark C. *Altarity*. Chicago: University of Chicago Press, 1987.
Terrell, Carroll E. *A Companion to the Cantos of Ezra Pound*. Berkeley: University of California Press, [1980] 1984.
Todd, Richard. *The Opacity of Signs: Acts of Interpretation in George Herbert's* The Temple. Columbia, MO: University of Missouri Press, 1986.
Torrey, E. Fuller. *The Roots of Treason*. New York: McGraw-Hill, 1984.
Trakl, Georg. *Die Dichtungen*. Salzburg: Otto Müller Verlag, 1938.
Trilling, Lionel. *The Liberal Imagination*. New York: Anchor, 1953 [1950].
Van Doren, Mark. *American Poets, 1630–1930*. Boston: Little Brown, 1932.
Vendler, Helen. *The Poetry of George Herbert*. Cambridge, MA: Harvard University Press, 1975.
Vivante, Leone. *English Poetry and Its Contribution to the Knowledge of a Creative Principle*. London: Faber & Faber, 1950.
Walton, Izaak. "Life of Mr. George Herbert."
Warren, Austin. *Richard Crashaw: A Study in Baroque Sensibility*. Ann Arbor, MI: University of Michigan Press, 1957 [1939].
Weiskel, Thomas. *The Romantic Sublime: Studies in the Structure and Psychology of Transcendence*, Baltimore, MD: Johns Hopkins University Press, 1976.

Whigham, Frank. *Ambition and Privilege: The Social Tropes of Elizabethan Courtesy Theory*. Berkeley: University of California Press, 1984.
Wilhelm, James J. *The Later Cantos of Ezra Pound*. New York: Walker and Company, 1977.
Will, Frederic. "The Argument of Water." In *Thresholds & Testimonies*, 43–92. Detroit, MI: Wayne State University Press, 1988.
Wollheim, Richard. *On Art and the Mind*. Cambridge, MA: Harvard University Press, 1974.
Yeats, William Butler. *Essays and Introductions*. New York: Macmillan, 1961.

Index

Acker, Kathy, 136
Adorno, Theodor, 6, 7, 16, 17, 24, 86, 88, 156, 165–66, 169, 170, 172, 173, 182, 199
Aiken, Conrad, 171
Aiken, Henry David, 188
Alcaeus, 81, 166
Alcman, 64–66, 81, 182, 183
Allemann, Beda, 66, 183
Altieri, Charles, 164, 168, 170
Ānanda, 163
Andic, Martin, 197
Andrewes, Lancelot, 37, 127, 128
Apollonius the Sophist, 64, 66
Aquinas, Thomas, 23, 84
Arac, Jonathan, 195
Archer, Stanley, 193
Aristotle, 3, 56, 83, 135, 165, 190
Arnold, Matthew, 86, 87
Arvin, Newton, 170
Ashbery, John, 20
Austin, J. L., 79

Bachelard, Georges, 172
Bacon, Francis, 197
Baker, John, 186–88
Baker, Peter, 164, 198
Barnouw, Jeffrey, 196
Barth, J. Robert, S.J., 165
Barthes, Roland, 4, 132, 191
Baudelaire, Charles, 171
Beckett, Samuel, xiv, 55, 136, 142, 153–56, 158–61, 198, 199
Bellarmin, 59
Bellini, Giovanni, 148
Benét, William Rose, 171
Benjamin, Walter, 169
Bense, Max, 199
Béranger, Pierre-Jean, 4
Berger, Harry, 177
Bernstein, Michael André, 197, 198
Berryman, John, 15

Blackmur, R. P., 55, 136–38, 178, 196
Blake, William, 4, 5, 9, 12, 17, 166
Blanchot, Maurice, 55, 59, 60, 153, 156, 178, 183, 199
Bloch, Chana, 174
Bloom, Harold, 53, 178
Blumenberg, Hans, 2, 165
Bly, Robert, 20
Bollnow, Otto, 71, 185
Booth, Wayne, xv, 132, 134–35, 195
Bradford, Curtis, 94–95, 189
Bradley, F. H., 28, 174
Brecht, Bertolt, 7, 182
Brooke-Rose, Christine, 189
Brooks, Cleanth, 102, 189
Brown, Jane, 178
Brown, Marshall, 178
Bruns, Gerald L., 56, 68, 70, 178, 179, 185
Bryant, William Cullen, 171
Burckhardt, Jakob, 135
Burns, Robert, 20
Burroughs, William S., 136
Byron, George Gordon, Lord, 171

Carrithers, Gale, 127, 193
Catullus, 108
Cavalcanti, Guido, 97, 145
Celan, Paul, 56
Char, René, 24, 82
Chaucer, Geoffrey, 18, 178
Chekhov, Anton, 142
Cicero, 127, 135
Clements, A. L., 193
Cohen, Ted, 195
Cohn, Robert Greer, 3, 165
Coleridge, Samuel Taylor, 2
Colie, Rosalie, 192
Confucius, 149–51, 173, 198
Conrad, Joseph, 158
Coover, Robert, 142
Corneille, Pierre, 133

Index

Crashaw, Richard, 43, 107–8, 191
Creeley, Robert, 20
Crowther, Paul, 174
Curtius, Ernst Robert, 165

Daniel, Arnaut, 97, 188
Daniel, Samuel, 84–85
Dante Alighieri, 1, 3, 9, 18, 19, 27, 39, 40, 42, 51, 129, 145, 173, 178
Davie, Donald, 52, 177
Davis, Walter A., 179, 187, 188
Deleuze, Gilles, 25, 164
De Man, Paul, 56, 179, 183, 191, 197
De Neef, A. Leigh, 103–4, 189, 190, 191
De Quincey, Thomas, 165
Derrida, Jacques, 4, 25, 56, 79, 103, 105, 136, 144, 159, 163, 164, 169, 179, 181, 187, 190, 193
Dewey, John, 101
Dickinson, Emily, 14, 17, 18, 21, 50, 52, 89, 171
Didion, Joan, 134
Dilthey, Wilhelm, 8, 70, 172
Docherty, Thomas, 191
Donne, John xiv, 34, 41, 43, 45, 47, 50–52, 101–30, 190–92
Dryden, John, 15, 108
Du Bellay, Joachim, 173
Duccio di Buoninsegna, 148
Dylan, Bob, 21

Eliot, Thomas Stearns, xii, 2, 9, 16, 28, 88, 92, 123, 146, 164, 174, 178, 191
Emerson, Ralph Waldo, 22
Empson, William, 32, 174, 192
Erdman, David, 166

Fanshel, David, 16, 171
Farrer, Nicholas, 50, 175
Fiedler, Leslie, 171
Fineman, Joel, 54, 128, 178, 193
Fish, Stanley, 8, 29, 30, 33, 34, 37, 168, 169, 174, 191, 194
Flaubert, Gustave, 125, 142
Fletcher, Angus, 189
Fletcher, John Gould, 171
Fletcher, Phineas, 45, 130
Foucault, Michel, 25, 164
Frank, Isidor, 170
Frank, Manfred, 163
Freud, Sigmund, 28, 101, 121, 142, 159, 175
Frost, Robert, 14, 15, 18, 20
Froula, Christine, 189

Gadamer, Hans-Jacob, 8, 16, 22, 169, 172
Gandhi, Mahatma, xii
Gaskell, (Mrs.) Elizabeth Cleghorn, 4
Genet, Jean, 159, 196
George, Stefan, 17, 56
Gill, Theodore, 127, 193
Glass, Philip, xii
Goethe, Johann Wolfgang von, xiv, 18, 61, 62, 64–66, 143, 171, 182
Goffman, Erving, 16, 112, 171, 192
Goldberg, Jonathan, 191
Goodyer, Sir Henry, 193
Gosse, Edmund, 191, 193
Gower, John, xii
Gracian y Morales, Baltasar, 49, 125
Grenfell, Russell, 198
Guyer, Paul, 195

Habermas, Jürgen, 9, 22–24, 83, 164, 169, 170
Hamann, Henry Paul, 68, 79, 186
Handwerk, Gary, 158, 199
Harman, Barbara Leah, 37, 176
Hauser, Arnold, 24
Haverkamp, Anselm, 163
Hayes, Albert McHarg, 177
Hegel, Georg Wilhelm Friedrich, 7, 17, 25, 82, 159, 182
Heidegger, Martin, xiv, 9, 10, 15, 17, 55–80, 81, 83, 85, 86, 96, 103, 143, 155, 163–64, 168, 169, 170, 172, 178–81, 183, 186, 191, 197
Hemingway, Ernest, 143
Henley, William Ernest, 154
Heraclitus, 17, 23, 82, 91, 101
Heraclius, 92
Herbert, George, xiv, 27–54, 55, 85, 86, 88, 91, 96, 97, 102–4, 107, 129, 168, 174–78, 190
Herrick, Robert, 102, 188
Hertz, Neil, 23, 173
Hesiod, 17, 64, 81
Hesse, Eva, 189
Hirsch, E. D., 85
Hofstadter, Albert, 186
Hölderlin, Friedrich, xiv, 15, 17, 56, 57, 59, 62, 63, 66, 67, 71, 72, 77, 81, 82, 86, 160–61, 164, 179, 181, 183, 186
Hollander, John, 15, 192
Holmes, Oliver Wendell, 17
Holthusen, Hans Egon, 11, 171
Homer, xii, 15, 28, 64, 81
Hopkins, Gerard Manley, 52, 154–55
Horace, 108, 127, 166

Humboldt, Alexander von, 79
Husserl, Edmund, 10, 23, 79, 82, 164
Hutchinson, F. E., 174, 176

Ingalls, Daniel, 163
Isaiah, 97
Iser, Wolfgang, 8, 27, 159, 199

Jakobson, Roman, 66
James, Henry, 127
Jarrell, Randall, 15
Jauss, Robert, 8, 16, 27, 65, 183
Johnson, Samuel, 102
Jonson, Ben, 42, 109–13, 129
Joyce, James, 156
Jünger, Ernst, 197
Justinian, 92

Kafka, Franz, 132, 134, 136, 172, 193, 194
Kant, Immanuel, xii, xiii, 3, 4, 7–9, 16, 21, 23, 28, 29, 33, 52, 84, 85, 101, 131, 136–37, 165, 168, 174, 194, 195, 196
Keats, John, 59, 60, 86–89, 110
Kemal, Salim, 189
Kenner, Hugh, 19, 154, 172, 198, 199
Ker, Sir Robert, 191
Kincaid, James, 195
Kirk, G. S., 183
Kleist, Heinrich von, xiv, 138–42, 194
Kristeva, Julia, 164
Kundera, Milan, 186

Labov, William, 16, 171
Lacan, Jacques, 28, 103, 107–8, 121, 131, 164, 194
Lakoff, George, 83, 84, 93, 188
Landor, William Savage, 20
Langer, Suzanne, 28, 174
Latini, Brunetto, 1
Lawrence, David Herbert, 135
Layamon, 92
Leo the Wise, 92
Leopardi, Giacomo, 60
Letwin, Shirley Robin, 196
Lévi-Strauss, Claude, 173
Levin, Samuel, 23, 84, 93, 173, 186
Levinas, Emmanuel, 164
Lewalski, Barbara, 193
Logan, John, 21
Longfellow, Henry Wadsworth, 12, 14, 17, 170–71

Longinus, 23, 138, 163, 173
Lope de Vega, Félix, 19, 114, 192
Lowell, James Russell, 17
Lyotard, Jean-François, 164

Mailer, Norman, xiv, 134
Malatesta, 18, 23, 144–45
Mallarmé, Stéphane, 16, 71, 99
Maloney, John L., 165
Malory, Thomas, 144
Manfred, 19
Margoliouth, H. M., 189
Marinetti, Filippo Tommaso, 145
Maritain, Jacques, 55, 178
Markham, Edwin, 198
Marlowe, Christopher, 197
Martin, L. C., 191
Martz, Louis, 31, 123, 174, 193
Marvell, Andrew, 50, 51
Massey, Irving, 142, 194, 196, 197
McFarland, Thomas, 2, 164, 165
Meerbote, Ralf, 195
Melville, Herman, 14
Mensel, Bill, 176
Meredith, James Creed, 165
Merleau-Ponty, Maurice, 164
Merton, Thomas, 15
Michelfelder, Diane P., 172
Miller, J. Hillis, xiv, 4, 134, 136–42, 194–96
Miller, Henry, 135
Millet, Jean François, 198
Milton, John, 27, 50, 51, 92, 144, 168
Most, Glenn, 183
Murry, John Middleton, 39, 176

Nabokov, Vladimir, 158
Nelson, Cary, 4, 5, 6, 166
Niedecker, Lorine, 20
Nietzsche, Friedrich, 7, 62, 135, 186, 191

Oliphant, (Mrs.), Margaret, 4
Olson, Charles, 18, 24
Orgel, Stephen, 191

Palka, William H., 176
Palmer, Richard E., 172
Patterson, Annabel, 51, 175, 177, 178
Patterson, Lee, 178
Peirce, Charles S., 196
Percy, Bishop Thomas, 21
Petrarch, 16, 122, 127

Picasso, Pablo, 76
Pindar, 28, 97, 148
Plato, xv, 91, 101, 118, 131, 156
Plotinus, 98, 99
Poe, Edgar Allan, 171
Pollack, Felix, 194
Ponge, Francis, 4, 56
Pope, Alexander, 102, 109
Porphyry, 99
Porter, George, 190
Pound, Ezra, xiv, 2, 18–20, 22–24, 92–94, 97, 144–52, 164, 173, 197, 198
Propertius, 127
Proust, Marcel, 127, 138, 155, 156
Pushkin, Alexander, 102, 171
Putnam, Hilary, 132

Rabaté, Jean-Michel, 198
Racine, Jean, 133
Rapaport, Herman, 179, 181
Raven, J. E., 183
Rée, Paul, 135
Reznikoff, Charles, 5, 20
Richard, Jean-Pierre, 71
Ricks, Christopher, xii, 119, 163, 172, 192
Rilke, Rainer Maria, xiv, 17, 61, 71, 72, 74–79, 185, 186
Roberts, John R., 175
Roemer, Michael, 196
Rogers, William Elford, 85, 188
Rorty, James, 171
Rosenfeld, Alvin H., 188
Roussel, Roy, 120, 192
Russell, Bertrand, 54, 169

Sade, Marquis de, 131
Salome, Lou-Andreas, 135
Sappho, 21, 81, 102, 178
Sartre, Jean-Paul, 140, 196
Schafer, Roy, 124, 193
Schiller, Friedrich, 196
Schleiermacher, Friedrich, 70
Schneiderman, Stuart, 191
Schoenfeldt, Mark C., 177
Schofield, Malcolm, 183
Scholes, Robert, 168, 195
Schwartz, Delmore, 84
Scott, Sir Walter, 14
Scully, Vincent, 183
Searle, J. R., 79
Seneca, 197

Shakespeare, William, 18, 54, 110, 112, 114, 118, 122, 127, 128, 133, 142, 178
Shelley, Percy Bysshe, 13
Sidney, Sir Philip, 21, 41, 50, 112, 122
Simpson, Evelyn, 190
Simpson, Louis, 15
Singleton, Marion White, 51, 177
Sissman, L. E., 21
Skreb, Zdenko, 186
Smith, A. J., 191
Smith, Barbara Herrnstein, 4, 8, 52, 168, 178
Smith, Paul, 164
Sophocles, xii, 28, 61, 131
Spengler, Oswald, 143
Spenser, Edmund, 42, 43, 50, 51, 110, 112, 114, 122
Spinoza, Baruch, 71
Stafford, William, 20
Stein, Arnold, 38, 113, 119–20, 176, 177, 192
Stendhal (Marie Henri Beyle), 24
Stevens, Wallace, 9, 87, 88, 93, 171
Stickney, Trumbull, 21
Stoedten, Helmuth Freiherr Lucius von, 79
Strier, Richard, 174
Summers, Joseph, 37, 175
Sypher, Wylie, 191

Taylor, Edward, 18
Taylor, Mark C., 186
Tennyson, Alfred, Lord, 14, 92, 166
Terrell, Carroll E., 198
Theognis, 49
Thomson, James, 154
Tibullus, 84, 188
Todd, Richard, 176
Tolstoy, Count Leo, 142
Torrey, E. Fuller, 198
Traherne, Thomas, 102–5, 189, 190
Trakl, Georg, xiv, 17, 56, 61, 66, 68, 69, 71, 81, 82, 144, 181–82, 185, 186
Trilling, Lionel, 133, 195
Trollope, Anthony, 143
Turner, Mark, 83, 84, 93, 188
Tuve, Rosamund, 192
Twain, Mark, xiv, 132–33

Van Doren, Mark, 15, 171
Vaughan, Henry, 43, 53, 106–7
Vendler, Helen, 29, 45, 174
Vergil, 3, 18, 22, 51, 165
Vico, Giambattista, 22

Villon, François, 20, 144
Viscusi, Robert, 195
Vivante, Leone, 55, 178
Voltaire (François Marie Arouet de), 18

Wagner, Richard, 135
Wallace, Robert M., 165
Walton, Izaak, 41, 50
Warren, Austin, 191
Weber, Max, 24
Weil, Simone, 197
Weiskel, Thomas, 173
Wheelwright, John, 88–90, 93
Whigham, Frank, 191
Whitman, Walt, 12–15, 17, 18, 22, 23, 93, 97, 105, 171
Whittier, John G., 17

Wilbur, Richard, 20
Wilhelm, James J., 189
Will, Frederic, 172
Williams, Charles, 91
Williams, William Carlos, 94, 171, 182
Wittgenstein, Ludwig, 101, 168
Wollheim, Richard, 174
Wordsworth, William, 53, 60, 71, 72, 84–87, 89, 102
Wyatt, Thomas, 112

Yeats, William Butler, 2, 90–94, 96–97, 99–100, 164, 189

Zelter, Carl Friedrich, 62
Zukofsky, Louis, 5, 20

This book has been set in Linotron Galliard. Galliard was designed by Mergenthaler in 1978 by Matthew Carter. Galliard retains many of the features of a sixteenth-century typeface cut by Robert Granjon but has some modifications that give it a more contemporary look.

Printed on acid-free paper.